The MAILBOX® **Day-by-Day** Preschool **PLANS**

grade **PreK**

P9-BZJ-482

A Week's Worth of Ideas for Each of 52 Popular Themes

- Colors
- Farm animals
- Shapes
- Seasons
- Family
- Transportation

- Five senses
- Holidays
- Dinosaurs
- Nursery rhymes
- Baby animals
- Weather

- Garden
- Butterflies
- Ocean
- Zoo
- Bugs
- ...and many more!

Plans for the whole year!

Managing Editor: Kimberly Brugger-Murphy

Editorial Team: Nancy C. Allen, Becky S. Andrews, Diane Badden, Brenda Beuschel, Tricia Kylene Brown, Kimberley Bruck, Karen A. Brudnak, Kitty Campbell, Jenny Chapman, Patricia Conner, Pam Crane, Lynette Dickerson, Lynn Drolet, Laurie Espino, Sarah Foreman, Michelle Freed, Theresa Lewis Goode, Ada Goren, Tazmen Hansen, Marsha Heim, Lori Z. Henry, Lucia Kemp Henry, Amy Kirtley-Hill, Debra Liverman, Brenda Miner, Sharon Murphy, Jennifer Nunn, Tina Petersen, Mark Rainey, Greg D. Rieves, Hope Rodgers, Eliseo De Jesus Santos II, Donna K. Teal, Joshua Thomas, Zane Williard

www.themailbox.com

©2009 The Mailbox® Books
All rights reserved.
ISBN 978-156234-860-1

Printed in the United States
10 9 8 7 6 5 4

HPS 248490

Table of

52 Weekly Themes

Contents

What's Inside

Centers

Seasons
Centers for the Week

Art Center: Place a class supply of page 217 at the center along with tissue paper squares in orange, red, brown, pink, and green. A student colors the trees. Then she glues crumpled tissue paper squares to the trees to show the four seasons, leaving one tree bare for winter.

Literacy Center: Mount on a wall a tree cutout, minus foliage. Program pairs of colorful leaf cutouts with matching letters. Lightly attach one set of leaves to the tree. Spread the remaining leaves faceup on the floor. A student removes a leaf from the tree and places it with the matching leaf on the ground.

Sensory Table: Fill your sensory table with potting soil; then add plastic flowerpots, small plastic shovels, and artificial flowers. Also provide child-size watering cans, gardening gloves, and hats. A student uses the props to engage in pretend planting and flower arranging.

Math Center: Provide two construction paper sunflowers along with a supply of craft foam seed cutouts and a large die. Two students visit the center, and each child takes a sunflower. A student rolls the die and counts the number of dots; then she places the appropriate number of seeds on her sunflower. Her partner repeats the process. Then they compare the numbers of seeds.

Discovery Center: Place in the center items that correspond to each of the four seasons, such as fall leaves, a flowering plant, and photographs of snow. Also provide magnifying glasses and nonfiction seasonal books for investigating the items.

Each theme includes:

Day-by-Day Activities

Group Time	Literature	Art/Gross-Motor Skills	Songs and Such for the Week
Monday Program each of four seasonal cutouts with an appropriate sentence starter, such as, "In the summer, I like to..." Read aloud the sentence starters and invite students to finish each sentence as you write the words on the cutouts. *Oral language*	Read aloud *When Autumn Comes* by Robert Maass. This book shows real-life photographs that give youngsters a look at seasonal changes and what people do to prepare for these changes.	**Colorful Fall Leaf** (See directions on page 40.)	**Seasons Change** (tune: "Yankee Doodle") In wintertime the cold winds blow; There's lots of snow and ice. In springtime when the flowers bloom The weather gets real nice. Summertime is very warm; We splash in the pool. In autumn leaves change color, And we all go back to school!
Tuesday Announce several silly statements, such as, "I like to build snowmen in the summer" and "I wear a bathing suit to play in the snow." After each one, invite students to tell you what's wrong with the statement. *Listening skills, logical thinking*	After revisiting yesterday's story, have students draw a picture of something they like to do in the fall. Encourage each student to tell you about her picture; then record her dictation. Bind the pictures together to make a class book.	**Gross Motor:** Have students hold the edge of a parachute or bedsheet and walk in a circle as you lead them to the song below. When the song ends, have them lift up the parachute so the cutouts fall to the ground. (tune: "The Mulberry Bush") There are four seasons in a year. In a year, in a year, There are four seasons in a year: Winter, spring, summer, and fall!	**Four Seasons** The seasons bring changes; There are four seasons, you know. Winter brings cold winds and lots of snow. In spring flowers bloom in a garden plot. In summer the weather is very hot. In fall leaves change color everywhere; The crisp winds blow them here and there.
Wednesday Give a class supply of two different seasonal cutouts, such as a snowflake and a pumpkin. Seat students in a circle. Then have a child choose a cutout and lay it on the floor to begin a pattern. Continue around the circle until each student has had a chance to add a cutout to the pattern. Read the final pattern in two different ways: by repeating the names of the cutouts and by repeating the seasons they represent. *Copying a pattern*	Read aloud *The Seasons of Arnold's Apple Tree* by Gail Gibbons. This book shows a boy's love for an apple tree as it changes throughout the seasons.	**Pinecone Art** (See directions on page 40.)	
Thursday Color and cut out a copy of the cards on page 218 and then place them faceup on the floor. Invite students, in turn, to choose two cards that show items that go together and then to explain their reasoning. *Critical thinking, oral language*	Revisit yesterday's story, reminding students that Arnold enjoys going to the apple tree and spending time there. Ask students to share any special places where they like to spend their time.	**Gross Motor:** Make four seasonal stick puppets. Hold each puppet in the air at different times, prompting students to pretend to ice skate, swim, jump in a puddle, and move like a leaf in a gentle breeze.	**Seasons Song** (tune: "Do Your Ears Hang Low") When the summer ends, Then the season will be fall. Leaves drop off the trees, And we'll jump into them all. Winter brings the snow. In the spring the soft winds blow. Four seasons in all!
Friday Provide a supply of seasonal clothing and accessories along with an empty labeled box for each season. Invite volunteers to choose an item, name it, identify the season it is associated with, and then place the item in the corresponding box. *Vocabulary, categorizing, sorting*	Read aloud *How Do You Know It's Winter?* by Allan Fowler. Then serve warm cocoa and prompt students to discuss what they enjoy and don't enjoy about winter.	**A Snazzy Sunflower** (See directions on page 40.)	

Timesavers

Art Activities

Pinecone Art
Place a sheet of black construction paper in a box. Dip a pinecone in white paint and then place it on the paper. Next, manipulate the box so the pinecone rolls around on the paper, adding paint to the pinecone as needed. Sprinkle silver glitter over the paint.

Colorful Fall Leaf
Tint separate containers of white corn syrup red, yellow, and green. Place a leaf cutout on waxed paper. Then paint the leaf with the tinted syrup so it resembles a colorful fall leaf. Allow the project to dry for several days; then peel away the waxed paper.

A Snazzy Sunflower

To make a sunflower, glue a paper bowl upside down on a sheet of construction paper. Paint the bowl yellow. Then glue black seed cutouts to the bowl and yellow petal cutouts around the rim. Then glue a green construction paper stem and leaves to the project. Finally, fringe-cut a strip of green construction paper and glue it to the bottom of the paper so it resembles grass.

Seasonal Picture Cards
Use with the "Seasons" unit on pages 37–40.

Plus...

Online Extras at themailbox.com

- Patterns
- Full-color picture cards
...and more!

All About Me

Centers for the Week

Discovery Center: Personalize a hand cutout for each child and place the cutouts at a center along with a magnifying glass and an ink pad. A student finds her hand cutout and makes a fingerprint on each fingertip. Then she uses the magnifying glass to observe her fingerprints.

Play Dough Center: Place large name cards at the center with a supply of play dough. Each student covers the letters of his name with play dough.

Literacy Center: Label each student's photograph and place it in a class photo book. Place the book and a supply of paper, pencils, markers, and crayons at the center. A student looks in the book and chooses photos of one or two friends. On a sheet of paper, he creates drawings of his friends—using the photos to guide him—and labels the drawings with the appropriate names.

Math Center: Enlarge and cut out a copy of the cake pattern on page 213. Provide birthday candles, number cards, and a variety of craft foam cutouts. A child chooses the card that represents his age. He names the number and then places the corresponding number of candles on the cake. He uses the foam cutouts to decorate the cake as desired and then removes the items for the next child.

Block Center: Attach youngsters' photographs to blocks. Youngsters use these unique blocks during their block play.

Group Time	Literature
Monday Label the columns of a floor graph with different numbers. Each student looks at her nametag and counts the number of letters in her name. Then she places her nametag in the appropriate column on the graph. ***Graphing***	Read aloud *The Secret Birthday Message* by Eric Carle. In this story, a boy finds a secret message that helps him find his birthday present.
Tuesday Prior to this activity, have each student bring a baby picture to school. Place all the pictures in a basket. One at a time, choose a picture and share it with your little ones. Invite students to guess which classmate is in the picture. ***Visual discrimination***	Reread yesterday's book. Give each student a piece of wrapping paper folded in half. On the inside of the paper, the student draws a present he would like to receive for his birthday. After students share their drawings, attach a bow to the outside of each student's paper.
Wednesday Place the students' names in a basket. Choose two names and have those students stand. Choose another student to tell a way in which the two youngsters are alike and a way in which they are different. Continue in the same way with several student pairs. ***Comparing***	Read aloud *Today I Feel Silly & Other Moods That Make My Day* by Jamie Lee Curtis. The little girl in this story feels a lot of emotions and they change every day!
Thursday Seat youngsters in a circle. Have students pass a hand mirror around the circle as you play a recording of music. Stop the music and have the child holding the mirror state something that makes her special, such as, "I am special because I can jump really high." Play several rounds of this game. ***Oral language***	Revisit yesterday's story. Give each student a circle cutout that shows a happy face on one side and a mad face on the other. Name something that would cause one of these emotions. Then have each child hold up the appropriate face. Repeat this game with cutouts that show sad and scared faces.
Friday Show the students a picture of a skeleton and explain that everyone has a skeleton. Give each student a bone cutout. Point to a body part on the skeleton. Each student names that part of her body and touches it with her bone cutout. ***Gross motor***	Read aloud *Chester's Way* by Kevin Henkes. Chester and his best friend, Wilson, have a certain way of doing things. Then they meet Lilly, who also has her own way of doing things. After reading the story, enjoy a snack like Lilly's of sandwiches cut into various shapes with cookie cutters.

Art/Gross-Motor Skills

Names With Pizzazz
(See directions on page 8.)

Gross Motor: Have the students stand and then give them directions based on their likes and dislikes. For example, say, "If your favorite color is red, jump two times." Continue this activity for several rounds.

"Thumb-body" Special
(See directions on page 8.)

Braeden Is "Thumb-body" Special!

Gross Motor: Put students in groups of two. Name a body part, such as arms, knees, or elbows, and have the partners in each pair touch those parts together.

Mr. Bones
(See directions on page 8.)

All About Me
(tune: "If You're Happy and You Know It")

I'm a very special person, can't you see?
There is no one else who can be just like me.
I am different from you,
But you are special too.
I'm a very special person, can't you see?

This Is Me

Here are my fingers.
Here are my toes.
I have two ears
And a wiggly nose.
I have two eyes that help me see.
Now I have introduced all of me!

Here I Am
(tune: "This Old Man")

Here I am.
This is me.
I'm the best me there can be.
I am me from my head right down to my toes
And back up to my cute nose.

 # Art Activities

Mr. Bones

Glue simple skeleton head and body cutouts to a 9" x 12" sheet of construction paper. Then glue cotton swabs to the body to make arms and legs. (Bend or cut the cotton swabs as needed.) Add fingers and toes to the skeleton with a white crayon.

Names With Pizzazz

Write each child's name in large letters on a piece of tagboard. Have each student trace over each letter with glue and then cover the first letter with one of the following items: tissue paper, pom-poms, foam shapes, feathers, or colored noodles. Encourage her to do the same for the remaining letters to make a creative, colorful name!

"Thumb-body" Special

Write on a construction paper picture frame "[Child's name] Is 'Thumb-body' Special." Dip the child's thumb into washable tempera paint and help him make several thumbprints on the mat. When the paint is dry, use a permanent marker to add details to the thumbprints to make faces. Then attach a photograph of the child to the back of the mat.

Braeden Is "Thumb-body" Special!

Colors

Centers for the Week

Math Center: Make an even number of fried egg cutouts. Then color the yolks to make matching pairs. A child uses a spatula to place an egg in a frying pan. He finds the egg with the matching yolk and places it next to the original egg. He removes the eggs and continues in the same way with each remaining pair.

Literacy Center: Program a supply of adhesive labels with a color word and a corresponding color dot. A student chooses a label and attaches it to a sheet of paper; then he draws a picture using a corresponding color of marker or crayon.

Discovery Center: A student places a cup of milk on a double layer of paper towels. She places several drops of food coloring in the milk. Then she uses a straw to blow into the milk to create colorful bubbles that overflow onto the paper towels.

Dramatic Play: For this painters' workshop, provide items such as several button-down shirts, painter's caps, paintbrushes, sample paint cards, clean rags, paint-stirring sticks, and colorful containers (paint cans). Youngsters use the props for pretend play.

Art Center: Provide fingerpaint paper, washable markers, and spray bottles of water. A student uses the markers to draw a design on a sheet of paper. Then he sprays the design with a fine mist of water to blur and blend the colors.

	Group Time	Literature
Monday	Prepare a class supply of paper strips in red, yellow, and blue. Place corresponding colors of plastic hoops on the floor. Have each child pick a strip and identify its color. Then have her find an item of that color in the classroom and place it in the appropriate plastic hoop. ***Color identification, sorting***	Read aloud *A Color of His Own* by Leo Lionni. In this story, a chameleon wants to be one color, just like all the other animals. So he goes searching for a color of his own. Although he doesn't find what he's searching for, he does find a true friend along the way.
Tuesday	Label separate columns on a floor graph with different-colored circles. Then make a class supply of circle cutouts in corresponding colors and place them in a bag. Have each student pick a circle and place it on the graph. Then count the circles in each column and compare the results. ***Graphing, comparing***	Before students arrive, cut out a class supply of construction paper chameleons in a variety of colors and then use Sticky-Tac to mount them on objects in corresponding colors. After revisiting yesterday's story, have each youngster find a chameleon.
Wednesday	Place a dollop of red paint and a dollop of yellow paint in the opposite corners of a small resealable plastic bag. Fold the top of the bag over and secure it with packing tape. Play lively music and have youngsters pass the bag around the circle. Stop the music at short intervals and have students observe the paint and describe any changes. Continue passing the bag until the two dollops of paint have mixed together and changed color. ***Observation skills, oral language***	Read aloud *Little Blue and Little Yellow* by Leo Lionni. In this story, Little Blue and Little Yellow are so excited to see each other that they hug until they both turn green!
Thursday	Have each child wear a colorful paper wristband. (Be sure to prepare bands in a variety of colors.) Then give a direction such as "All reds, clap your hands" or "All pinks, stomp your feet." Next, hand a ball to a student and encourage the child to roll the ball to someone wearing a wristband of a specific color. Continue in the same manner until each child has had a chance to roll the ball. ***Color recognition, participating in a game, following directions***	Reread yesterday's story. Then give each student a sheet of waxed paper. Have each child use an eyedropper to put a drop of blue-tinted water and a drop of yellow-tinted water on the paper. Next, have her blow through a straw to mix the two colors. Ask her to experiment with the straw and the water to see if she can separate the two colors.
Friday	Display construction paper circles in different colors. Using coordinating colors, program several tagboard cards with different patterns. A student picks a pattern card and reads the pattern. Then he shines a flashlight on one of the displayed circles to indicate the next color in the pattern. ***Patterning***	Prepare three containers of paint: one red, one yellow, and one blue. Obtain three plastic mice and a large sheet of white construction paper. Read aloud *Mouse Paint* by Ellen Stoll Walsh. Then read the book again, this time using the toy mice and the paint to act out this color-mixing story.

Art/Gross-Motor Skills

Yarn Sculpture
(See directions on page 12.)

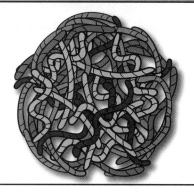

Gross Motor: Partially fill several clear plastic bottles with rice or sand; then screw the caps on tightly. Wrap colorful construction paper around each bottle and secure it in place with tape. In turn, have a child carry each bottle across the room and place it on a sheet of matching construction paper.

Sticky Collage
(See directions on page 12.)

Gross Motor: Provide a large box, a container of colorful beanbags, and a bag of pom-poms in colors that match the beanbags. In turn, have each child pick a pom-pom from the bag, identify its color, and place it back in the bag. Then instruct the child to hop, jump, or crawl to the container; take a corresponding-colored beanbag; and then throw the beanbag into the box.

Pail Painting
(See directions on page 12.)

Songs and Such for the Week

Color Song
(tune: "Twinkle, Twinkle, Little Star")

Red and yellow, orange too.
Purple, green, and also blue.
I see colors all around,
In the air and on the ground.
Lovely colors that I see.
Won't you come and look with me?

Color Mix

Mix blue paint with yellow
And you will get green—
The prettiest color
You've ever seen.
Mix red paint with yellow
For a new color too.
Now there's orange paint
For me and for you!

Colors of the Rainbow
(tune: "She'll Be Comin' Round the Mountain")

There's a rainbow in the sky—just look up there.
There are lots of colors floating everywhere:
Red, orange, yellow, green, and blue,
Indigo and purple too.
There's a rainbow in the sky—just look up there!

Art Activities

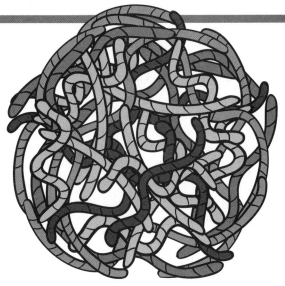

Yarn Sculpture

In advance, prepare shallow containers of diluted glue tinted in several colors and white yarn cut into varying lengths. Place a sheet of waxed paper on a table. To make a sculpture, use a craft stick to press a piece of yarn in a container of colored glue. Then pull the yarn out of the container and place it on the waxed paper. Repeat the process with the remaining colors, overlapping the strings until a desired effect is achieved. Allow the glue to dry completely; then peel the waxed paper away from the sculpture.

Sticky Collage

Provide an assortment of colorful collage materials, such as craft feathers, construction paper shapes, tissue paper scraps, ribbon, and craft foam shapes. Help a student peel the backing off of a piece of Con-Tact covering and place the covering sticky side up on a table. Then he presses materials on the Con-Tact covering to make a colorful collage.

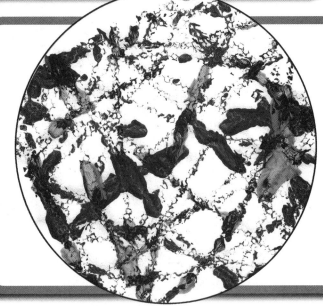

Pail Painting

Place a golf ball and spoon in each of several containers of paint. Cut out a white construction paper circle and place it in the bottom of a plastic pail. Use a spoon to place a paint-covered golf ball in the pail. Hold the pail and move it in a circular motion so the golf ball rolls around the bottom. Remove the golf ball from the pail and return it to its container. Continue in the same way with the remaining golf balls until a desired effect is achieved.

Apples

Centers for the Week

Water Table: Place two or three apples in the water. Students investigate what happens when they manipulate the apples, such as when they push down on the apples and release them or turn the apples upside down.

Play Dough Center: Set out a supply of red play dough (apples) and brown play dough (piecrust), a pie pan, a rolling pin, and plastic forks and knives. Students roll out crusts and cut up apples to make apple pies.

Math Center: Provide five of each of the following shapes cut from craft foam: red apples, brown stems, and green leaves. A student puts a stem on each apple and a leaf on each stem.

Art Center: Supply paper and red paint for fingerpainting. Later, cut a large apple shape from each child's painting. Have her glue a brown paper stem and a personalized green paper leaf to the cutout.

Dramatic Play: For this orchard stand, supply a toy cash register and nonbreakable cups and plates. Add items such as empty cider jugs; an apple box that holds red, yellow, and green yarn balls; and a doughnut box that contains cardboard doughnut shapes.

	Group Time	Literature
Monday	Seat students in a circle. Have individuals pass an apple cutout around the circle, counting as they go. When a student says, "Ten," have all students say, "Crunch! Munch!" Then begin a new round of counting with the next child in the circle. **Counting to ten**	Read aloud *Ten Apples Up on Top!* by Dr. Seuss. This apple-balancing competition between a dog, tiger, and lion invites lots of counting practice!
Tuesday	Prepare four of each of the following cards for a game of Concentration: red apples, green apples, yellow apples, and brown worms. Have students take turns turning over pairs of cards. Remove matches from the game. Continue play until all the cards have been matched. **Visual memory**	Reread yesterday's story; then give each child an apple cutout. Use the cutouts for counting practice. Also have students place the cutouts on different body parts, including the tops of their heads!
Wednesday	I like to play... Program apple cutouts with sentence starters, such as "I like to eat..." and "I feel happy when..." Put the apples in a basket. Invite several students to finish each sentence. **Oral language**	Read aloud *The Apple Pie Tree* by Zoe Hall. In this book, two sisters watch the seasonal changes of an apple tree and look forward to making apple pie.
Thursday	Put a tree cutout and ten colorful apple cutouts on the floor. Lead the group in counting the apples and naming their colors. Then have students take turns "picking" different combinations of apples. Return the apples to the tree after each child's turn. **Counting, color identification**	Revisit yesterday's story. Have students use the book's illustrations to retell the story. Then use apple cutouts to make a class graph that shows how many students like apple pie and how many do not.
Friday	Have each child pretend to hold an imaginary apple with both hands. Show students several pairs of picture cards, naming the pictures as you go. When the words rhyme, students say, "Crunch! Munch!" and take a bite from their pretend apples. **Identifying rhyming words**	Read aloud *Apple Farmer Annie* by Monica Wellington. Have students recall what Annie does with her apples. Then serve applesauce, cider, or another apple snack.

Art/Gross-Motor Skills

Apple Tree
(See directions on page 16.)

Gross Motor: Have students stand in a circle, join hands, and walk in the same direction as they sing. Have them stop and sway when the big breeze comes and then drop to the ground when the apples fall. Repeat several times.

(tune: "Ring Around the Rosie")

Ring around the apple tree,
Here comes a big breeze!
Apples, apples,
We all fall down!

Apple Ornament
(See directions on page 16.)

Gross Motor: Have students stamp their feet to lively music, pretending to mash apples into applesauce. Then stop the music and have students pretend to pick more apples for mashing. Start and stop the music several times.

Apple Print Transfer
(See directions on page 16.)

Songs and Such for the Week

Apples Up on Top
(tune: "Up on the Housetop")

Up in the treetop, way up high,
Three red apples for my pie.
How will I get them to the ground?
I'll shake that tree 'til they fall down!
Shake, shake, shake,
Watch them fall!
Shake, shake, shake,
Watch them fall
Into my basket,
One, two, three!
No more apples on the tree.

Tiny Apple Seed

I put a tiny apple seed
Underneath the ground.
I covered it with soft brown dirt
And patted all around.
The sun shone down; the rain fell too.
And what did my *eyes* see?
My tiny little apple seed
Is now a great big tree!

Apple Colors
(tune: "Three Blind Mice")

Red, yellow, green.
Red, yellow, green.
Growing on trees.
Growing on trees.
Sweet and crunchy
And good for you,
They grow on trees
In three colors; it's true!
Do you like apples?
Yes, I really do
In red, yellow, and green.

Art Activities

Apple Tree

Glue a tree cutout, minus foliage, on a sheet of construction paper. Paint green leaves on the tree. Then dip a pom-pom in red paint and press it on the tree several times to make apples.

Apple Ornament

Glue a white construction paper circle to the back of a plastic lid; then glue on several brown paper seeds. Turn the lid over. Glue small scraps of red tissue paper to the front of the lid. Then brush a layer of glue over the tissue paper. When the glue is dry, trim off any excess paper. Attach a torn paper stem and leaf to the apple. Then add a hanger to the ornament and hang it on a branch secured in a large pot.

Apple Print Transfer

Cut a large apple-shaped stencil from a sheet of poster board; then tape the stencil to a table. Put a few dollops of red, green, or yellow fingerpaint in the center of the stencil. Next, fingerpaint the tabletop inside the stencil; then remove the stencil from the table. Place a sheet of paper over the painted surface. Then gently smooth your hand back and forth across the paper. Finally, lift the paper from the table to reveal the transferred apple print.

Farm Animals

Centers for the Week

Sand Table: Fill your sand table (or a plastic tub) with potting soil. Add toy farm animals, people figurines, farm vehicles, and a small barn to the table. Students manipulate the toys to engage in pretend play.

Play Dough Center: Set out a supply of yellow and pink play dough and duck- and pig-shaped cookie cutters. Also provide laminated pond and mud puddle cutouts. A student uses the cookie cutters to make play dough ducks and pigs; then she places each animal on the appropriate cutout.

Math Center: Attach a length of green paper to a table; then draw two equal paths of game spaces on the paper. Place a large barn cutout at the end of the paths. To play this partner game, each child, in turn, rolls a large die, counts the dots, and moves a toy farm animal the corresponding number of spaces. Play continues until each animal reaches the barn.

Literacy Center: Label plastic egg halves with identical letters. Separate the eggs and then place them in a box filled with brown crinkle shreds so the box resembles a nest. A student puts each egg together by matching the letters and then places the eggs in a clean, sanitized egg carton.

Dramatic Play: For this dramatic-play farm, provide items such as flannel shirts, straw hats, stuffed farm animals, a stool, a bucket, sanitized egg cartons, plastic eggs, baskets, child-size shovels and rakes, and boxes covered with strips of yellow paper so they resemble bales of hay.

Group Time	Literature

Monday

Seat students in a circle. Play a recording of *Old MacDonald Had a Farm* while youngsters pass a small pail of toy farm animals around the circle. Each time you stop the music, ask the child who's holding the pail to show his classmates one animal. His classmates respond by making the animal's sound. Then the toy is returned to the pail and play continues in the same manner as time allows. ***Participating in a game***

Read aloud *Color Farm* by Lois Ehlert. Each page shows color and shape combinations that transform each farm animal into something different!

Tuesday

Give each child a simple red barn cutout and a die-cut farm animal. Instruct students to place their animals *on, beside, above, below,* and *under* their barns. For an added challenge, have volunteers tell their classmates where to place the animals. ***Positional words***

Revisit yesterday's story. Provide a supply of colorful shape cutouts. Have each child glue shapes to a sheet of paper to make his own farm animal.

Wednesday

Display several plastic farm animals and a toy barn. Have students identify each animal. Next, instruct youngsters to close their eyes; then hide one animal inside the barn. When students open their eyes, have them guess which animal is missing. For an added challenge, hide more than one animal in the barn. ***Visual memory***

Read aloud *Click, Clack, Quackity-Quack* by Doreen Cronin. After reading a note that the cows have typed, Duck takes the farm animals on an alphabetical adventure that leads them to a picnic surprise!

Thursday

Prepare an enlarged pink construction paper copy of the pig pattern on page 214. Also provide several items that begin with the /p/ sound and some that do not. Invite a student to choose an item and name it. Have her place the item on the pig if it begins with the /p/ sound. If it does not, have her place the item to the side. ***Beginning sounds***

Before students arrive, fill a basket with a special snack and hide it from view. Throughout the room, mount alphabet cards leading to the basket. Revisit yesterday's story, and then lead children along the alphabet trail to find the hidden surprise!

Friday

Make several farm animal stick puppets. Lead the class in singing *Old MacDonald Had a Farm,* prompting students to sing about a specific animal by holding up a different prop during each verse. ***Visual discrimination***

Read aloud *Rosie's Walk* by Pat Hutchins. Next, have one child pretend to be the fox and a second child pretend to be Rosie the hen. Then Rosie leads the fox through a prepared obstacle course in the classroom that takes them over, under, around, and through a variety of objects.

Muddy Pig
(See directions on page 20.)

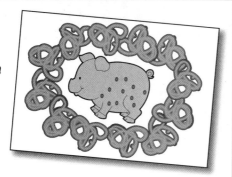

Gross Motor: Seat students in a circle. Ask a volunteer to pretend to be a farmer. The farmer walks around the outside of the circle and says "farm" as he taps each child. When the farmer names a farm animal, the child who was tapped stands, makes the sound of the named animal, and trades places with the farmer.

Fabulous Fowl
(See directions on page 20.)

Gross Motor: Arrange a class supply of chairs in a circle. Place a die-cut animal under each chair. During the activity, start and stop a recording of lively music. When the music plays, students hop around the inside of the circle. When the music stops, each child quickly sits in a chair and takes a turn making the animal sound that corresponds to the die-cut under her chair.

Grown on the Farm
(See directions on page 20.)

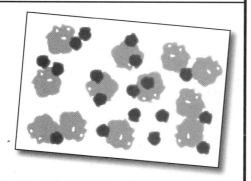

Down on the Farm
(tune: "Down by the Bay")

Down on the farm where the
    roosters crow,
There's a lot to see; I want to go.
And when I do, the farmer will say,
"Did you ever see a [goose drinking
    some juice]
Down on the farm?"

Continue with the following: *goat wearing a coat, sheep driving a jeep, duck driving a truck, pig wearing a wig, cow taking a bow*

Cock-a-Doodle-Doo
(tune: "Row, Row, Row Your Boat")

When the sun wakes up,
Farm animals do too.
They know it's morning when they hear
Cock-a-doodle-doo!

Animal Greetings
(tune: "Do Your Ears Hang Low?")

There are pigs that oink,
Gentle cows that say, "Moo, moo."
Woolly sheep say, "Baa,"
And the chickens cluck, cluck too.
All the animals we see
That live down on the farm
Say hello to you!

Fabulous Fowl

To make a chicken, glue a small white paper plate (head) and a large white paper plate (body) to a 12" x 18" sheet of construction paper. Glue white feathers to the body to make a wing and a tail. Then cut out facial features and other details from paper scraps and glue them in place. Make a handprint with red paint. When the paint is dry, cut out the print and glue it to the chicken's head to make a comb.

Muddy Pig

Mix potting soil and water to make a batch of mud. Cut out a pink construction paper copy of the pig pattern on page 214. Then glue the cutout to a sheet of fingerpaint paper. Next, dip your fingertips into the mud and pat them on and around the pig.

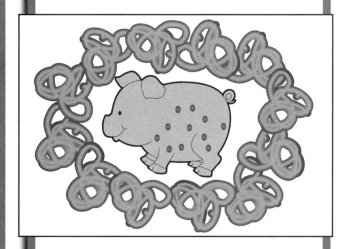

Grown on the Farm

Halve a variety of different vegetables. Put a thick layer of paint in each of several shallow containers. Then place a paper towel in each container and press down lightly. To make a print, press a vegetable on a paint-soaked towel and then press it on a sheet of paper. Repeat the process with each vegetable until a desired effect is achieved.

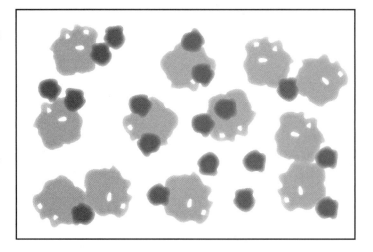

Leaves

Centers for the Week

Art Center: Attach several leaves to pieces of tagboard and then tape them to a table. Also supply a student with paper and crayons. She places a sheet of paper on a leaf and colors over it to create a leaf rubbing.

Math Center: Program each card in a supply of cards with a number and a corresponding number of dots. Place the cards and a basket of leaves or leaf cutouts at the center. A student chooses a card and counts out the corresponding number of leaves.

Game Center: Puzzle-cut large tagboard leaves and place the pieces of each in a separate resealable plastic bag. A student chooses a bag and puts the pieces together to create a whole leaf.

Discovery Center: Place at the center plastic magnifying glasses, transparent color paddles or colored cellophane, and a variety of leaves. A student uses the items to explore the features and colors of a leaf.

Literacy Center: Color and cut out a copy of the picture cards on page 215. Place the cards and a large leaf cutout at the center. A student looks at a picture and says its name. If the name of the picture begins with /l/, he places it on the leaf. He places the picture card beside the leaf if it begins with another sound.

	Group Time	Literature
Monday	Give each student a small brown paper bag. Go on a leaf hunt around the school and have each student collect a few fall leaves. After the leaves are collected, help youngsters sort them by color, size, or type. ***Sorting***	Read aloud *Fall Leaves Fall!* by Zoe Hall. This delightful story captures the excitement two siblings feel when leaves begin to fall from the trees.
Tuesday	Place on the floor a tree cutout minus foliage. Put a variety of leaf cutouts on the tree; then describe one of the leaves. Have a student find the leaf based on its description and then place it near the bottom of the tree. Continue until all the leaves have been removed. ***Listening***	Revisit yesterday's story. Draw a large leaf on the board. Have students tell things they like about fall and leaves as you write them inside the leaf.
Wednesday	Make leaf cutouts in different sizes and with different weights of paper. Choose two leaves and share them with the students. Tell the students you are going to drop both leaves at the same time. Have them make predictions about which leaf will reach the floor first. Drop the leaves to check the predictions. Continue the process with other pairs of leaf cutouts. ***Making predictions***	Read aloud *Fletcher and the Falling Leaves* by Julia Rawlinson. In this story, Fletcher, a little fox, becomes worried that his favorite tree is sick when the leaves change color and begin to fall.
Thursday	Place a supply of leaves around the room. Give each student a number card. Then have youngsters walk around the room and collect the appropriate number of leaves before returning to the group area. ***Counting***	Revisit yesterday's story. At the end of the story, Fletcher's tree loses all its leaves and is covered with frost and icicles. Throughout the next few days, have students remove leaf cutouts from a prepared tree cutout displayed on your wall. When the tree is bare, invite students to brush glue over the tree and sprinkle glitter on the glue.
Friday	Have students close their eyes while you place a leaf cutout in the room where it can be easily seen. After youngsters open their eyes, have them look for the leaf. Have each child give a thumbs-up when she sees the leaf. After several students indicate they see the leaf, choose one student to reveal the leaf's location using positional words. ***Positional words***	Read aloud *Leaf Man* by Lois Ehlert. Have each student pretend he is a leaf man being blown along by the wind. Prompt him to share a desired destination for his windy journey.

Art/Gross-Motor Skills

Leaf Headbands
(See directions on page 24.)

Gross Motor: Have students imagine they are fall leaves. Tell them it is a very windy day and prompt them to move about the room as if being blown by the wind. Repeat this activity with a lightly breezy day and a day without any wind at all.

Fall Trees
(See directions on page 24.)

Gross Motor: Label each of several leaf cutouts with a movement, such as "Jump three times." Place the leaves in a basket. Choose a leaf and read its label to the class. Then have students follow the directions on the leaf.

Leafy People
(See directions on page 24.)

Songs and Such for the Week

Leaves Are Falling
(tune: "Where Is Thumbkin?")

Leaves are falling.
Leaves are falling
All around,
To the ground.
They are such a nice sight
Dancing in the sunlight.
Floating down
To the ground.

Leafy Fun

Leaves around me
On the ground.
There is so much fun
To be found.
I rake them up
In a really big pile.
Then I jump right in
With a great big smile.

Changing Leaves
(tune: "London Bridge")

Leaves change color in the fall,
In the fall, in the fall.
Leaves change color in the fall.
They're so lovely!

Art Activities

Fall Trees

Tear a strip of brown paper to make a tree trunk and a few branches and then glue them to a sheet of paper. Tear scraps of yellow, red, and orange paper to make leaves. Then glue the leaves to the branches and the area under the tree.

Leafy People

Accordion-fold strips of paper and attach them to a large leaf cutout so they resemble arms and legs. Then attach leaf cutouts to the project to make a head, hands, and feet. Finally, use a permanent marker to add details to the head to make facial features.

Leaf Headbands

Sponge-paint each of several leaf cutouts with a mixture of tempera paint and glue. While the paint is still wet, sprinkle glitter on the leaves. Attach the dry leaves to a headband and then size the headband appropriately.

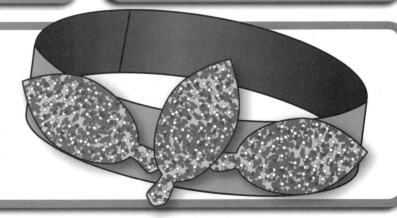

Fire Safety

Centers for the Week

Dramatic Play: For this fire station, provide items such as the following: child-size raincoats, boots, gloves, plastic fire helmets, a first aid kit, flashlights, pieces of rubber hose, a bell, a toy or disconnected telephone, pretend walkie-talkies, and fire safety posters.

Art Center: Place orange, red, and yellow construction paper scraps at the center. A child tears the paper to make flames and then glues them to a sheet of white paper until a desired effect is achieved.

Water Table: Float red craft foam flames in your water table. Provide water-filled squirt bottles. Students use the squirt bottles to spray water at the floating flames.

Literacy Center: Program a supply of orange paper flames with the sentence starter "To stay safe from fire I…" A student dictates or writes words to finish the sentence and then adds an illustration. Display the flames on a bulletin board.

Math Center: Program separate sheets of paper each with a simple ladder shape. Provide a firefighter figurine (or cutout) to each child and a large die. In turn, students roll the die, count the dots, and then move their firefighters up the ladder the corresponding number of rungs. Play continues until each firefighter is moved to the top and then back to the bottom of the ladder.

	Group Time	Literature

Monday

Program a large flame cutout as shown. Lead students in a discussion about different types of fire. Ask them to tell how they think fire can be good or bad, and record their responses on the chart. *Oral language, critical thinking*

Fire

Good ☺	Bad ☹
cooks food	burns houses
keeps us warm	trees burn down
birthday candles	people and animals get hurt
roast marshmallows	

Read aloud *Safety Around Fire* by Lucia Raatma. In this book, real-life photographs and simple text are used to show different sources of fire and help the reader learn how to stay safe around fires both indoors and outside.

Tuesday

Decorate a cardboard tube with red and orange tissue paper. Explain the importance of knowing how to stop, drop, and roll in case of fire. Then wave the makeshift flames over a volunteer's clothing and have her demonstrate the steps. *Listening for understanding, following directions*

Review yesterday's book with students and ask them to study the photographs. Have youngsters name the dangerous items in the appropriate photos and explain what they should do to remain safe around these items.

Wednesday

Display a card labeled "911." Explain that this is the number to call in case of an emergency, such as a fire. Using a toy or disconnected phone, have a volunteer dial 911. After he dials, lead the remaining students in asking, "What is your name?" and "What is your emergency?" as the child with the phone answers appropriately. *Speaking to give information*

Read aloud *Firefighters! Speeding! Spraying! Saving!* by Patricia Hubbell. In this book, colorful illustrations and rhyming text celebrate firefighters and the hard work they do when called to a fire.

Thursday

For additional practice dialing 911, have students pass a toy phone around the circle. When you give a signal, such as ringing a bell, the child holding the phone dials 911, gives her name, and tells the operator there is a fire. Then she hangs up and passes the phone around the circle again. Play continues as time allows. *Participating in a game*

Revisit yesterday's story. Talk with students about a fire safety plan for home and at school; then conduct a practice fire drill.

Friday

Give each student a picture of an item that might cause a fire or an item that would not. Place a red and a blue plastic hoop toy on the floor. In turn, each student identifies the item in his picture and tells whether he thinks it would or would not cause a fire and why. Then the child places the picture in the red hoop if it could cause a fire or the blue hoop if it would not. *Oral language, logical reasoning*

Read aloud *Fire Fighters* by Dee Ready. Then have students recall different types of protective gear firefighters wear and tools they use to help save people from fires.

Flamboyant Flames

(See directions on page 28.)

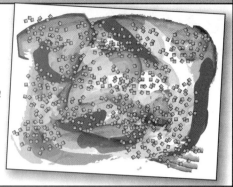

Gross Motor: Place a play tunnel or a long table in an open space. Designate an area on the other side of the tunnel as a safe area. In turn, students crawl through the tunnel (or under the table) to the safe area as the remaining students chant, "Stay low and go!"

Stuffed Fire Trucks

(See directions on page 28.)

Gross Motor: Separate your class into teams and give each team a container of water. Place a container decorated with a red craft foam flame several feet from each team. In turn, each student fills a cup with water, runs and dumps it into the container, and then runs back to the end of the line. Play continues until both containers are full.

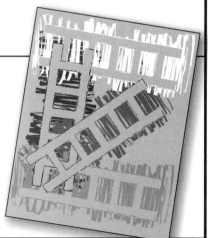

Ladder Rubbings

(See directions on page 28.)

Brave Firefighters

(tune: "The Itsy-Bitsy Spider")

The brave firefighters
Pack up a great big hose.
They hop on the fire truck
And then away they go.
They put out the fire
With a great big water spray.
Then they go home feeling proud
Of their very busy day.

Fire Safety Poem

Please don't play with matches,
A stove, or a lighter.
These things can start a fire;
Then you'll need a firefighter!

In an Emergency

(tune: "If You're Happy and You Know It")

If there's an emergency, what should
 you dial? 9-1-1!
If there's an emergency, what should
 you dial? 9-1-1!
If you need help in a hurry,
Please don't panic and don't worry.
If there's an emergency, what should
 you dial? 9-1-1!

 # Art Activities

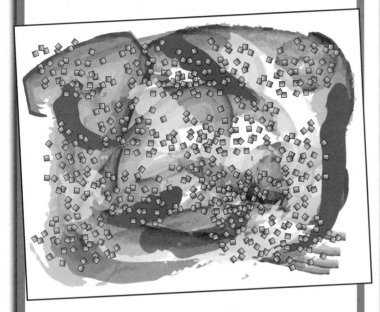

Flamboyant Flames

To make this flame-themed artwork, drizzle orange, red, and yellow paint on a sheet of construction paper. Then press a piece of waxed paper over the paint and smooth the surface of the waxed paper. Next, remove the waxed paper and sprinkle orange glitter on the paint.

Ladder Rubbings

Place tape on a tabletop so it resembles a firefighter's ladder. Then place a sheet of paper over the ladder and rub unwrapped crayons over the paper. Move the paper and repeat the process with different colors of crayons until a desired effect is achieved.

Stuffed Fire Trucks

Fold a sheet of red construction paper in half and staple it along the sides, leaving a small opening. Glue construction paper shapes to the project so they resemble windows, doors, and wheels. Then glue on a length of yarn so it resembles a hose. After the glue is dry, stuff the project with newspaper strips and staple the opening closed. If desired, use markers to add additional details to the resulting fire truck.

Shapes

Centers for the Week

Gross-Motor Area: Place several large tagboard shapes on the floor. A student tosses a beanbag onto a shape and then names the shape.

Block Center: Post pictures of shapes in your block center. Have students arrange the blocks to make the posted shapes.

Sensory Table: Place plastic or craft foam shapes in sand. Provide plastic pails for sorting. A student uses plastic scoops to dig for the shapes and puts each type of shape into a different pail.

Art Center: Attach magnetic strips to craft foam shapes and place them in the center along with metal cookie sheets. A student arranges the shapes on a cookie sheet to create a masterpiece.

Play Dough Center: Provide a variety of shape cookie cutters and laminated cards with the outlines of different shapes. A student rolls play dough and places it on the shape outlines to form the shape. He also uses the cookie cutters to make play dough shapes and then places the shapes on the corresponding cards.

	Group Time	Literature
Monday	Have students sit in a circle. Lay four plastic hoops in the middle of the circle and put a different shape inside each hoop. Place corresponding shape cutouts in a basket. Each student, in turn, takes a shape from the basket and places it in the appropriate hoop. **Sorting**	Read aloud *The Wing on a Flea* by Ed Emberley. This brightly colored book helps students identify shapes in their world.
Tuesday	Place shape cutouts in a basket and have a child choose a cutout. Then prompt the child to find an object in the room that is the same shape as his cutout. Continue in the same way with different youngsters. **Finding shapes in the environment**	Reread yesterday's book. Have students look around the classroom and point out different shapes they see. Write each shape on a sticky note and have each child attach his note to the object.
Wednesday	Puzzle-cut each of several large tagboard shapes into two pieces. Give each student a piece of a shape and have her find her shape partner. The pair sits down and put their pieces together to form the shape. Allow the partners to share the name of their shape. **Identifying shapes**	Read aloud *Mouse Shapes* by Ellen Stoll Walsh. Three little mice scare the cat by building three big mice out of shapes.
Thursday	Draw a different shape on several lunch-size paper bags. Place the corresponding shape cutout in each bag. Then place a variety of distracter shapes in the bags as well. Have a student look at the front of a bag. Then encourage him to reach into the bag and feel the shapes until he finds the one that corresponds to the drawing on the bag. **Tactile discrimination**	Revisit yesterday's story. Then give each child a handful of shape cutouts or plastic manipulatives. Encourage each child to arrange the shapes to make a house, a tree, and a wagon as the mice did in the book.
Friday	Give each student a blank card and access to paper shapes in a few colors. Instruct her to glue a different shape in each corner of the card. Announce a shape of a certain color, such as "blue circle." If a student has a blue circle, she draws an X on it. When she has an X on each shape, she stands and says, "Shapes." **Visual discrimination**	Read aloud *Circle Dogs* by Kevin Henkes. Give each child a partially open circle cutout similar to the circle the dogs form in the illustrations. Then have each child attach cutouts to the circle to make a nose, ears, legs, and a tail.

Art/Gross-Motor Skills

Rectangle Robots
(See directions on page 32.)

Gross Motor: For this circle game, have each student stand in a plastic hoop. Use a variety of movements and positional vocabulary to give students instructions, such as "Hop out of the circle," "Jump into the circle," or "Walk around the circle."

Shape Characters
(See directions on page 32.)

Gross Motor: Attach a class supply of shapes to the floor in a circle arrangement. While a recording of music plays, students walk around the circle of shapes. When the music stops, each student stands by a shape. Say, "Circles, please jump up and down!" and prompt the students standing by the circles to jump. Restart the music. Then continue in the same way with the remaining shapes and a variety of different movements.

Shapely Snakes
(See directions on page 32.)

Songs and Such for the Week

How Many Sides?
(tune: "My Bonnie Lies Over the Ocean")

A square has four equal sides.
A circle has no sides at all.
Rectangles have two little short sides;
The other sides are very tall.

Name Those Shapes

Here is a circle.
This is a square.
Let's draw a triangle
In the air.
You will see shapes
Wherever you go.
Stop when you see them
And name ones you know.

Shapes Everywhere
(tune: "Up on the Housetop")

Circles and squares, rectangles too.
Here is a triangle for you.
You can find shapes most anywhere.
Look! There's another one over there!
Shapes, shapes, shapes, can you see?
Shapes are all around me.
Oh, I can find shapes every day
As I go walking on my way.

Art Activities

Rectangle Robots

Put tempera paint in shallow containers and cut sponges into assorted sizes of rectangles. Sponge-paint a large rectangle in the middle of a 9" x 12" sheet of construction paper. Make smaller rectangle prints to create the head, arms, and legs. When the painting is dry, add details such as a face, antennae, and buttons.

Shape Characters

Draw a face on a large shape cutout. Then tape four pipe cleaners to the shape to make arms and legs. Tape smaller shapes to the ends of the pipe cleaners to make hands and feet. Consider making shape characters for a variety of different shapes.

Shapely Snakes

To make a snake, glue shape cutouts on a strip of construction paper, making a pattern if desired. Then use a marker to add an eye to the snake. Finally, glue a tongue cutout to the snake.

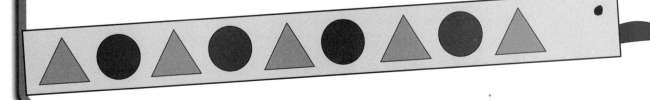

Pumpkins and More

Centers for the Week

Literacy Center: Gather two sets of identical letter cards. Also gather four blank cards and draw a piece of candy corn on each one. Place the cards facedown. A student turns over two cards at a time. If the cards match, she keeps them. If not, she turns them back over. If she picks a candy corn card, she keeps it and takes an extra turn.

Discovery Center: Obtain a variety of pumpkins in different shapes and sizes. Provide tape measures; nonstandard measurement tools, such as yarn or string; scales; and magnifying glasses for students to use to explore, measure, and compare the pumpkins.

Math Center: Glue strips of brown paper to the bottom of a large sheet of yellow paper so the brown strips resemble a fence. Use the pattern on page 216 to make several black cat cutouts in different sizes. Add a tail to each cat. A student places the cats in size order on the fence.

Art Center: Mix together two cups of flour, one cup of salt, orange tempera paint, and water to achieve a doughlike consistency. Mold some of the dough into a pumpkin shape and then insert a pipe cleaner stem and vine. After the dough hardens, paint on facial details.

Play Dough Center: Provide orange play dough, an empty pumpkin pie spice shaker, seasonal cookie cutters, rolling pins, plastic plates, and plastic forks and knives. Students roll out the dough and "sprinkle" on pumpkin pie spice to make cookies and pumpkin pies.

Group Time	Literature

Monday

Seat students in a circle. Play a recording of seasonal music and have youngsters pass a small pumpkin around the circle. Stop the music at short intervals and have the child holding the pumpkin say a word to describe it. Continue the game until each child has had a chance to describe the pumpkin. ***Using descriptive words, participating in a game***

Read aloud *The Biggest Pumpkin Ever* by Steven Kroll. In this story, two mice fall in love with the same pumpkin. They each care for the pumpkin without the other one's knowledge. The result of their combined love and caring is the biggest pumpkin anyone has ever seen!

Tuesday

Make a large poster board bat cutout. Gather a variety of items that begin with the /b/ sound, along with some that do not. Place the items in a box. Students take turns picking an item from the box. If the item begins with the /b/ sound, the student places it on the bat. If it does not, he puts the item aside. ***Beginning sounds***

Revisit yesterday's story; then ask students to think of other ways the mice could have moved the enormous pumpkin to the contest. Write down each student's response on chart paper.

Wednesday

In advance, decorate a large box to resemble a spooky house. Cut a door flap in the house. To play, have a child close her eyes while a classmate hides in the house. Direct the student to open her eyes and guess who's inside the house, providing clues as needed. After the name of the hidden child has been revealed, she becomes the guesser. ***Memory recall, participating in a game***

Read aloud *The Little Old Lady Who Was Not Afraid of Anything* by Linda Williams. The little old lady in this classic story is fearless. Then one evening when walking home through the forest, she gets the scare of her life!

Thursday

Gather a set of number cards from 1 to 10 and arrange them facedown. Give each child a pumpkin cutout and ten paper seeds. Choose a card and have students identify the number. Then have each child count the corresponding number of seeds and place them on her pumpkin. ***Number identification***

In advance, gather two shoes, a pair of pants, a shirt, two gloves, a hat, and a pumpkin with facial features. Then help students act out a rereading of *The Little Old Lady Who Was Not Afraid of Anything.*

Friday

Seat students in a circle. Tell them they are going to pretend to be monsters listening for rhyming words. Then say a pair of words. If the words rhyme, have youngsters give an enthusiastic monster roar. If the words do not rhyme, have students remain silent! ***Recognizing rhyming words, following directions***

Read aloud *Pumpkins* by Ken Robbins. Next, cut the top off your classroom pumpkin. Supervise students carefully as they explore and help clean out the inside of the pumpkin. Finally, have children observe as you carve the pumpkin into a jack-o'-lantern.

Art/Gross-Motor Skills

Friendly Black Cat

(See directions on page 36.)

Gross Motor: Place a spiderweb drawing on the floor. Have students move around the web as they act out the following song. Repeat the song several times, substituting other movements.

(tune: "The Mulberry Bush")

This is the way a spider [crawls],
A spider [crawls], a spider [crawls].
This is the way a spider [crawls]
All around its web.

Jazzy Jack-o'-Lantern

(See directions on page 36.)

Gross Motor: Obtain a variety of plastic or plush seasonal items, such as toy pumpkins, spiders, and mice. Place a plastic cauldron on your floor and attach a tape line several feet from the cauldron. A child chooses an item, stands on the tape line, and tosses the item into the cauldron. Then she stirs the spooky brew with a large mixing spoon. Repeat the process with other youngsters and ingredients.

Not-So-Spooky Spider!

(See directions on page 36.)

Songs and Such for the Week

Sing a Song of Pumpkins

(tune: "Sing a Song of Sixpence")

Can you see the pumpkins,
Orange, fat, and round?
Growing on a vine
All spread out on the ground.
Let's make jack-o'-lanterns
With smiles oh so bright!
Oh, won't it be a sight to see
On Halloween night?

The Owl Song

(tune: "I'm a Little Teapot")

Owls like to sit up in a tree,
Looking down at you and me.
Owls like to sleep in bright daylight.
Then they wake and fly at night.

Spidery Spiders

(tune: "Itsy Bitsy Spider")

Spiders have eight legs
That help them get around.
They crawl across the ceiling
And along the ground.
They spin their silky webs
To catch something to eat.
For insects and bugs are a
Spider's favorite treat!

Friendly Black Cat

Cut out a gray construction paper copy of the cat pattern on page 216. Label a gray circle cutout with spiral lines as shown. Then cut along the lines to make a tail and attach the tail to the back of the cat cutout. Glue craft foam eyes and a nose to the project. Then glue pieces of yarn near the nose so they resemble whiskers.

Jazzy Jack-o'-Lantern

Spoon a dollop each of red fingerpaint and yellow fingerpaint onto a sheet of fingerpaint paper. Paint the paper, mixing the two paints together to make orange. When the paint is dry, cut a large pumpkin shape from the paper. Then add a torn tissue paper stem and facial features to the project.

Not-So-Spooky Spider!

Tear eight construction paper strips and attach them to a small paper plate so they resemble spider legs. Crumple black tissue paper squares and glue them to the back of the plate. Then glue a large black pom-pom to the plate so it resembles the spider's head. Finally, glue hole-punch dot eyes to the head.

Seasons

Centers for the Week

Art Center: Place a class supply of page 217 at the center along with tissue paper squares in orange, red, brown, pink, and green. A student colors the trees. Then she glues crumpled tissue paper squares to the trees to show the four seasons, leaving one tree bare for winter.

Literacy Center: Mount on a wall a tree cutout, minus foliage. Program pairs of colorful leaf cutouts with matching letters. Lightly attach one set of leaves to the tree. Spread the remaining leaves faceup on the floor. A student removes a leaf from the tree and places it with the matching leaf on the ground.

Sensory Table: Fill your sensory table with potting soil; then add plastic flowerpots, small plastic shovels, and artificial flowers. Also provide child-size watering cans, gardening gloves, and hats. A student uses the props to engage in pretend planting and flower arranging.

Math Center: Provide two construction paper sunflowers along with a supply of craft foam seed cutouts and a large die. Two students visit the center, and each child takes a sunflower. A student rolls the die and counts the number of dots; then she places the appropriate number of seeds on her sunflower. Her partner repeats the process. Then they compare the numbers of seeds.

Discovery Center: Place in the center items that correspond to each of the four seasons, such as fall leaves, a flowering plant, and photographs of snow. Also provide magnifying glasses and nonfiction seasonal books for investigating the items.

	Group Time	Literature

Monday

Program each of four seasonal cutouts with an appropriate sentence starter, such as, "In the summer, I like to…." Read aloud the sentence starters and invite students to finish each sentence as you write their words on the cutouts. **Oral language**

In the summer, I like to…
…go swimming.—Jenny
…play outside.—Sam
…eat ice pops.—Aaron

Read aloud *When Autumn Comes* by Robert Maass. This book shows real-life photographs that give youngsters a look at seasonal changes and what people do to prepare for these changes.

Tuesday

Announce several silly statements, such as, "I like to build snowmen in the summer" and "I wear a bathing suit to play in the snow." After each one, invite students to tell you what's wrong with the statement. **Listening skills, logical thinking**

After revisiting yesterday's story, have students draw a picture of something they like to do in the fall. Encourage each student to tell you about her picture; then record her dictation. Bind the pictures together to make a class book.

Wednesday

Make a class supply of two different seasonal cutouts, such as a snowflake and a pumpkin. Seat students in a circle. Then have a child choose a cutout and lay it on the floor to begin a pattern. Continue around the circle until each student has had a chance to add a cutout to the pattern. Read the final pattern in two different ways: by repeating the names of the cutouts and by repeating the seasons they represent. **Copying a pattern**

Read aloud *The Seasons of Arnold's Apple Tree* by Gail Gibbons. This book shows a boy's love for an apple tree as it changes throughout the seasons.

Thursday

Color and cut out a copy of the cards on page 218 and then place them faceup on the floor. Invite students, in turn, to choose two cards that show items that go together and then to explain their reasoning. **Critical thinking, oral language**

Revisit yesterday's story, reminding students that Arnold enjoys going to the apple tree and spending time there. Ask students to share any special places where they like to spend their time.

Friday

Provide a supply of seasonal clothing and accessories along with an empty labeled box for each season. Invite volunteers to choose an item, name it, identify the season it is associated with, and then place the item in the corresponding box. **Vocabulary, categorizing, sorting**

Read aloud *How Do You Know It's Winter?* by Allan Fowler. Then serve warm cocoa and prompt students to discuss what they enjoy and don't enjoy about winter.

Art/Gross-Motor Skills

Colorful Fall Leaf
(See directions on page 40.)

Gross Motor: Have students hold the *edge* of a parachute or bedsheet with seasonal cutouts placed on top; then walk in a circle as you lead them in the song below. When the song ends, have them lift up the parachute so the cutouts fall to the ground.

(tune: "The Mulberry Bush")

There are four seasons in a year,
In a year, in a year.
There are four seasons in a year:
Winter, spring, summer, and fall!

Pinecone Art
(See directions on page 40.)

Gross Motor: Make four seasonal stick puppets. Hold each puppet in the air at different times, prompting students to pretend to ice skate, swim, jump in a puddle, and move like a leaf in a gentle breeze.

A Snazzy Sunflower
(See directions on page 40.)

Songs and Such for the Week

Seasons Change
(tune: "Yankee Doodle")

In wintertime the cold winds blow;
There's lots of snow and ice.
In springtime when the flowers bloom
The weather gets real nice.
Summertime is very warm;
We splash in the pool.
In autumn leaves change color,
And we all go back to school!

Four Seasons

The seasons bring changes;
There are four seasons, you know.
Winter brings cold winds and lots of snow.
In spring flowers bloom in a garden plot.
In summer the weather is very hot.
In fall leaves change color everywhere;
The crisp winds blow them here and
    there.

Seasons Song
(tune: "Do Your Ears Hang Low?")

When the summer ends,
Then the season will be fall.
Leaves drop off the trees,
And we'll jump into them all.
Winter brings the snow,
In the spring the soft winds blow.
Four seasons in all!

Art Activities

Colorful Fall Leaf

Tint separate containers of white corn syrup red, yellow, and green. Place a leaf cutout on waxed paper. Then paint the leaf with the tinted syrup so it resembles a colorful fall leaf. Allow the project to dry for several days; then peel away the waxed paper.

Pinecone Art

Place a sheet of black construction paper in a box. Dip a pinecone in white paint and then place it on the paper. Next, manipulate the box so the pinecone rolls around on the paper, adding paint to the pinecone as needed. Sprinkle silver glitter over the paint.

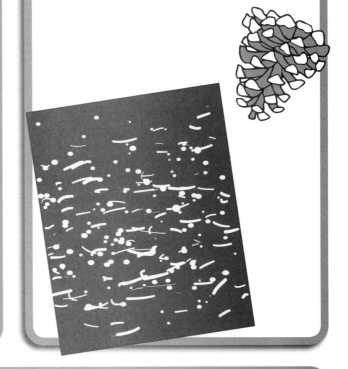

A Snazzy Sunflower

To make a sunflower, glue a paper bowl upside down on a sheet of construction paper. Paint the bowl yellow. Next, glue black seed cutouts to the bowl and yellow petal cutouts around the rim. Then glue a green construction paper stem and leaves to the project. Finally, fringe-cut a strip of green construction paper and glue it to the bottom of the paper so it resembles grass.

Fall Harvest

Centers for the Week

Dramatic Play: For this farmers' market, provide items such as baskets, small bales of straw, a variety of real or plastic fruits and vegetables, a scale, a cash register, play money, grocery bags, straw hats, bandanas, and flannel shirts. Students use the props to engage in pretend market play.

Discovery Center: Provide resealable plastic bags, paper towels, and pumpkin seeds. A student puts pumpkin seeds on a folded wet paper towel placed in a plastic bag; then he seals the bag and tapes it to a window. Once the roots begin to grow, he transfers the seeds to a cup of soil and continues to care for them.

Fine-Motor Area: Provide several ears of fresh corn and an empty plastic container. Students pull the husks off the corn and put them in the container. Cook the corn and serve it as a healthy snack!

Math Center: Obtain a pumpkin. Label each of three trays with the words "too short," "just right," or "too long." Then cut lengths of string that match these categories when placed around the middle of the pumpkin. Place all the items in the center. Students use the strings to measure the pumpkin and then sort the strings onto the trays.

Sensory Table: Place several pumpkins, potatoes, sweet potatoes, and carrots in the water, along with several vegetable scrubbing brushes. Students use the brushes to wash the vegetables.

	Group Time	Literature
Monday	Display several fruits and vegetables and have students identify them. Then place the produce out of sight. Secretly put a fruit or vegetable in a sock. Invite several students to feel the produce and try to guess what it is; then remove it from the sock to reveal its identity. Continue in the same manner with the remaining produce. **Tactile discrimination**	Read aloud *The Carrot Seed* by Ruth Krauss. This is the story of a little boy who plants a carrot seed and waits patiently for it to grow while everyone around him insists that it won't. Despite what everyone says, he continues to care for his seed until something wonderful happens!
Tuesday	After discussing that crows like to eat corn, have a volunteer (the scarecrow) sit on a chair with an ear of corn underneath. Have her close her eyes while another child (the crow) quietly removes the corn and places it out of sight. Have the scarecrow open her eyes; then provide clues to help her guess the identity of the crow. **Participating in a game**	Reread yesterday's book; then provide the necessary props and have volunteers act out the story.
Wednesday	Program a sheet of bulletin board paper with five corn stalks labeled with numbers from 1 to 5. Also program each cutout in a class supply of corn cutouts with one of the same numbers. In turn, each student picks an ear of corn, identifies the number, and then places it on the corresponding corn stalk. **Number identification, number matching**	Read aloud *The Little Scarecrow Boy* by Margaret Wise Brown. In this story, a little scarecrow longs to go with his father to scare the crows, but is not allowed. Then one day, he sneaks off to the cornfield to test all the things he has learned from his father, with very encouraging results!
Thursday	Prepare a class supply of scarecrow and crow cutouts from page 219. Give positional directions, such as "Put the crow *beside* the scarecrow." Then have each child position her crow appropriately. For an added challenge, give two positional directions, such as "Put the crow *on* the scarecrow's head and then *beside* its foot." **Positional words, following directions**	Revisit yesterday's story. Then, in turn, invite each student to pretend to be a scarecrow. Have her tell what she would do to scare the crows away and then make her scariest scarecrow face.
Friday	Place several vegetables in a bag and place a soup pot and ladle on the floor. Play a recording of lively music and have students pass a potato around the circle. When the music stops, the child with the potato removes a vegetable from the bag, names it, puts it in the pot, and uses the ladle to stir the soup. After all the vegetables are in the pot, everyone pretends to eat some of the delicious soup! **Vocabulary, following directions**	Read aloud *I Am a Seed* by Jean Marzollo. Have students describe the similarities and differences between the marigold and the pumpkin in the story.

Corn Rolling
(See directions on page 44.)

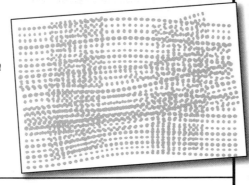

Gross Motor: Students stand still, pretending to be scarecrows in a field. Then recite the chant below, having youngsters perform the actions when indicated. Repeat the chant several times, substituting different actions each time.

> Silly little scarecrows
> Guard the field all day.
> They [wave their arms]
> And [stamp their feet]
> To scare the crows away!

Apple Basket
(See directions on page 44.)

Gross Motor: Divide the group into teams, and have each team stand in a line. Mark a finish line about six to eight feet away from the first student in each line. In turn, each student slides a small pumpkin with his foot to the finish line; then he runs back and gives the pumpkin to the next child in line. Play continues until each child has had a turn to slide the pumpkin across the finish line.

Harvest Soup
(See directions on page 44.)

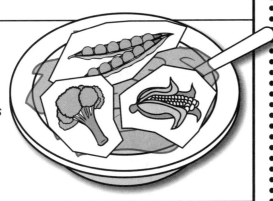

Fall Harvest
(tune: "My Bonnie Lies Over the Ocean")

Oh, fall is the time that we harvest
The veggies we worked hard to grow.
We use them to cook yummy dinners.
Fall harvest is great, don't you know!

Harvest Poem

At harvest time we pick the foods
From our garden plot,
Like tasty big potatoes
That we mash up in a pot.
We add some gravy, salt, and pepper.
Now they're almost done.
We top them with some butter.
Harvest time is so much fun!

Harvest Soup
(tune: "Row, Row, Row Your Boat")

Chop, chop, chop the [carrots].
Add them to the pot.
Stir the soup nice and slow;
Then serve it while it's hot!

Art Activities

Apple Basket

Cut a basket shape from a brown paper grocery bag. Then glue the basket to a sheet of light-colored construction paper. Dip a circular sponge in a shallow container of red tempera paint and then press the sponge on the paper above the basket several times. Glue a green yarn stem and construction paper leaves to each resulting apple.

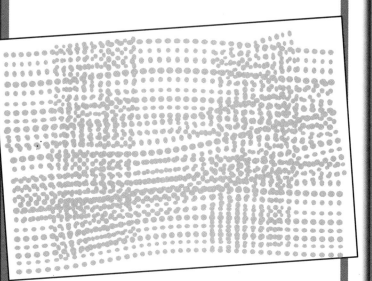

Corn Rolling

Prepare a shallow container with yellow paint. Place a sheet of white paper in a box. Dip an ear of corn (husks removed) in the paint; then place the corn on the paper. Manipulate the box so the corn rolls back and forth across the paper. Add more paint as needed. Remove the paper from the box and set it aside to dry.

Harvest Soup

Glue slightly crumpled wads of brown tissue paper in a disposable bowl so it resembles soup broth. Cut from magazines or grocery store circulars pictures of a variety of vegetables and then glue the pictures to the tissue paper. Finally, glue a plastic spoon to the resulting soup.

Family

Centers for the Week

Literacy Center: Make several copies of the family member patterns on page 220 and cut them out. Write uppercase letters on the parents' shirts and corresponding lowercase letters on the children's shirts. A student matches each parent to the correct child.

Dramatic Play: Set up a dramatic-play area that resembles a nursery. Along with a baby doll, add supplies such as empty baby powder containers, blankets, bibs, bottles, diapers, plastic baby food containers, spoons, and a recording of lullabies.

Math Center: Place several house cutouts at the center along with a supply of adult and child cutouts (see patterns on page 220). A student identifies how many people live in his home. Then he glues the appropriate number of people to a house, making sure he has the correct number of adults and children.

Block Center: Place pictures of several types of houses in the block center along with toy people. Then encourage youngsters to use the blocks to build homes for several different families.

Fine-Motor Area: Have each child bring a family photograph to school; then enlarge and copy each photo. Laminate and puzzle-cut the copied photos. Place each photo in a resealable plastic bag and then place the bags in the center. A youngster chooses a bag and puts together the photo to reveal a classmate's family.

	Group Time	Literature
Monday	Have each student bring a family picture to school. Place four plastic hoops on the floor and then label each hoop "2," "3," "4," or "5 or more." In turn, each student counts the number of people in his family and places his picture in the correct hoop. When all the pictures are in the hoops, have students compare the results. ***Counting, sorting***	Read aloud *Lucky Pennies and Hot Chocolate* by Carol Diggory Shields. This sweet story tells of all the fun things a boy does with his grandfather. After reading the story, enjoy a treat of hot chocolate with marshmallows.
Tuesday	Program heart cutouts with names of relatives, such as "grandma," "uncle," and "brother." Place the hearts in a basket. Invite each student to choose a heart and tell something about the relative named on the heart. If a student does not have the relative named on his heart, he chooses another heart. ***Oral language***	Reread yesterday's story. Place a large mug cutout on the board. Invite students to share the things they like to do with a special relative while you write their words on the mug.
Wednesday	Invite students to name different activities they enjoy doing with their families, such as swinging at the park or baking cookies. Then prompt students to stand and pantomime each activity. ***Prior knowledge***	Read aloud *Families* by Ann Morris. Families work together, play together, and take care of each other. This is the message of this nonfiction book, which shows delightful photographs of families around the world.
Thursday	Collect a few pairs of shoes in a variety of sizes and styles. Share the shoes with students. A student selects a pair of shoes and names a relative in her family who might wear those shoes. Write the name on a card and place it in front of the corresponding shoes. ***Classifying***	Revisit yesterday's story. As you review the book, ask youngsters what the people in the photographs might be thinking or saying. Write students' words on sticky notes and attach them to the appropriate photos. Then reread the book, adding youngsters' text to the read-aloud.
Friday	Invite a few grandparents to visit your class. Have the students sit in small groups with these special visitors and listen and ask questions while the visitors share stories about when they were young. At the end, have the students share a special snack with the grandparents. ***Listening***	Read aloud *Julius, the Baby of the World* by Kevin Henkes. Prompt youngsters to notice how Lilly does not include a picture of her brother Julius in her family drawing. Then invite students to draw pictures of their families, including all the members.

Art/Gross-Motor Skills

A Family Bouquet
(See directions on page 48.)

Gross Motor: Demonstrate a chore that a family member might complete, such as sweeping the floor or cooking dinner. Invite students to share who completes this chore in their families. Then have students stand and pantomime the chore.

Family Pets
(See directions on page 48.)

Gross Motor: Instead of playing Simon Says, play Mommy Says. Instruct students to do various movements, such as hopping or running in place, after listening to be sure Mommy said to do it. Play several rounds of this game, using a different relative's name for each round.

Helping Hands
(See directions on page 48.)

Songs and Such for the Week

Families Are Nice
(tune: "Jingle Bells")

Families, families
Are the best you see!
Our families take care of us;
I'm sure that you'll agree.
Families care for us
In the nicest way.
Our families all love us
Each and every single day.

Families Are Special

Families are special.
Each of us has one.
No matter who they're made up of,
Families are fun.

All Kinds of Families
(tune: "Do Your Ears Hang Low?")

There are families
Everywhere that you may go:
From the sunny south
To the north in ice and snow.
And no matter where our families might be,
They love you and me!

Art Activities

A Family Bouquet

Glue a vase cutout to a sheet of paper and then glue a flower and stem above the vase for each family member. Draw each family member on a separate white circle cutout and then attach each one to a different flower. Finally, attach leaf cutouts to each stem.

Family Pets

Pets are part of families too! Draw a picture of a family pet or a desired pet. Then, depending on the type of pet, glue hole-punch dots (scales), craft feathers, or felt squares (fur) to the pet.

Helping Hands

Have a youngster make several handprints with paint on a sheet of paper. When the paint is dry, encourage him to dictate different ways he helps his family as you write his words on different handprints.

I help my mother dry the dishes.

I clean up my toys.

I help feed my little sister.

I help Dad in the garden.

Thanksgiving

Centers for the Week

Math Center: Make several turkey cutouts without tail feathers. Place the turkeys at a center along with a container of colorful plastic clothespins (feathers). A child attaches feathers to a turkey to make a simple pattern. Then he counts the number of clothespins on his turkey.

Play Dough Center: Set out a supply of play dough, plastic flatware, and plastic plates. A student uses the materials to "cook" and "eat" a fabulous Thanksgiving meal.

Literacy Center: Make a sample Thanksgiving card labeled "Happy Thanksgiving Day!" Place the card at a center, along with card-making supplies and small word cards, each labeled "Happy," "Thanksgiving," or "Day!" A child attaches word cards to his card, using the sample as a guide. Then he decorates his card as desired.

Dramatic Play: Place various articles of clothing and accessories in the center. A student pretends to be a turkey who wants to disguise herself on Thanksgiving. She uses the props to create the perfect disguise.

Sensory Table: Cut from craft foam orange circles (carrots), white squares (potatoes), and green strips (beans). Place the pieces in a container near your water table along with craft foam turkey cutouts, a strainer, and a spoon. A child tosses desired craft foam pieces into the water table, stirs the resulting soup, strains the water from the pieces, and returns the pieces to the container.

Group Time	Literature

Monday

Attach a large turkey cutout with no feathers to a display. Place feather cutouts and a marker in your group-time area. Tell students they are going to help the turkey get his feathers back. Invite each student to tell something for which he is thankful. Write his words on a feather and then attach the feather to the turkey. *Oral language*

Read aloud *The Perfect Thanksgiving* by Eileen Spinelli. In this story, two different families have very different Thanksgiving traditions. One family is chaotic and unorganized, while the other is serene and detail oriented.

Tuesday

Before the students arrive, place several Pilgrim cutouts around the room. Invite a student to find a cutout and then tell another student its location using positional vocabulary. The second student listens to the directions and retrieves the cutout. *Positional words, listening*

After reading the story, discuss traditions with the class. Place a house cutout on the board and have a student tell about her family's Thanksgiving traditions as you write her words on the cutout.

Wednesday

Write the word *turkey* on a magnetic whiteboard. Place the magnetic letters for the word *turkey* in a small paper bag along with a few other letters. A student chooses a letter from the bag. If the letter is found in the word, he places it on the board above the corresponding letter. He continues in this manner until the word is complete. *Visual discrimination*

Read aloud *'Twas the Night Before Thanksgiving* by Dav Pilkey. A group of youngsters takes a field trip to a turkey farm in this twist on the traditional Christmas poem.

Thursday

Decorate a tissue box to look like a turkey. Place in a bag some pictures of objects that begin with /t/ and some pictures of objects that do not. Have a child choose a picture. If the picture's name begins with /t/, the students say, "Gobble, gobble," and the child "feeds" the picture to the turkey. *Letter sounds*

After a brief review of yesterday's story, read aloud a picture book version of the rhyme *The Night Before Christmas*. Then help students compare the two books.

Friday

Place a supply of fruit and vegetable cutouts around the room. Tell the students that they will be gathering food for the Thanksgiving feast. Give each pair of students a basket and a simple list that shows one or two fruits and vegetables. The pair walks around the room collecting the items on its list and then returns to the group-time area. *Counting, following directions*

Read aloud *A Plump and Perky Turkey* by Teresa Bateman. Then give each student a scoop of oatmeal cookie dough and a piece of aluminum foil. Have her mold the dough into a turkey just like the oatmeal turkey in the book. Bake the cookies as directed.

Art/Gross-Motor Skills

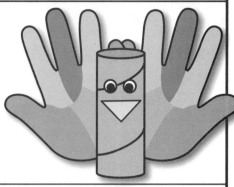

Tubular Turkey
(See directions on page 52.)

Gross Motor: Partially fill six soda bottles with sand and then replace the caps. Decorate the bottles to look like turkeys. Set the turkeys on the ground so they resemble bowling pins. In turn, each student rolls a large beach ball toward the turkeys and tries to knock down as many as possible.

Cornucopia
(See directions on page 52.)

Gross Motor: Place colorful construction paper circles (nests) on the floor. Play a recording of "Turkey in the Straw" as youngsters strut around the room pretending to be turkeys. Then stop the music and say, "Turkeys, turkeys, find a nest!" After each child quickly sits on a nest, have her name the color of her nest.

Pilgrim Hat
(See directions on page 52.)

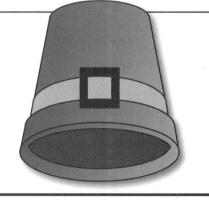

Songs and Such for the Week

Thanksgiving Is Here
(tune: "Up on the Housetop")

Thanksgiving Day is almost here.
It's a special time of year.
It's when we give thanks for all things
And for the love our family brings.
Thanksgiving's the time to share.
Thanksgiving's the time to care.
Thanksgiving Day is almost here.
It is a special time of year!

Thanksgiving Day

Thanksgiving Day is coming
With lots of good things to eat.
Like cranberry sauce and potatoes,
And pie—what a treat!

Giving Thanks
(tune: "This Old Man")

Thanksgiving Day is here.
It's our favorite time of year.
We give thanks for friends, food, and
family.
Won't you please give thanks with me?

Art Activities

Tubular Turkey

Have each child paint a small cardboard tube brown to make a turkey body. Next, paint his hands with fall colors and have him make a print with each hand. When the paint is dry, have him cut out the handprints and glue them to the turkey body. Then encourage him to glue beak, wattle, and eye cutouts to the turkey.

Cornucopia

Glue a cornucopia cutout to the middle of a sheet of paper. Then tear paper scraps in a variety of colors and glue them to the paper so they resemble fruits and vegetables coming out of the cornucopia.

Pilgrim Hat

Paint a small clay pot black so it resembles a Pilgrim hat. Then carefully paint a brown stripe on the hat. Glue a buckle cutout to the stripe as shown. When the paint is dry, use this clever craft as a Thanksgiving Day table centerpiece.

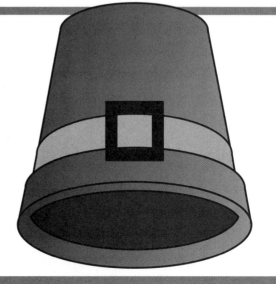

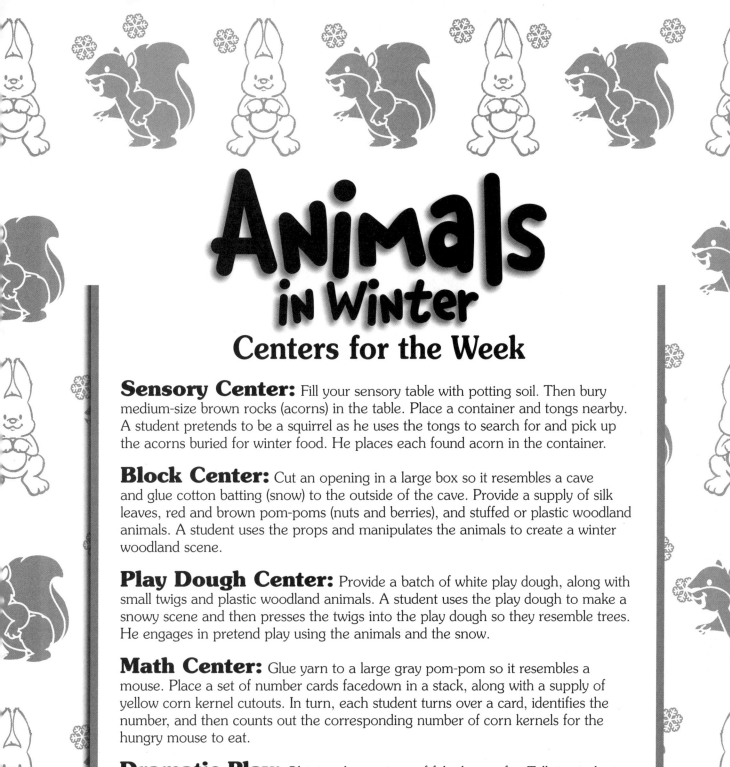

Animals in Winter

Centers for the Week

Sensory Center: Fill your sensory table with potting soil. Then bury medium-size brown rocks (acorns) in the table. Place a container and tongs nearby. A student pretends to be a squirrel as he uses the tongs to search for and pick up the acorns buried for winter food. He places each found acorn in the container.

Block Center: Cut an opening in a large box so it resembles a cave and glue cotton batting (snow) to the outside of the cave. Provide a supply of silk leaves, red and brown pom-poms (nuts and berries), and stuffed or plastic woodland animals. A student uses the props and manipulates the animals to create a winter woodland scene.

Play Dough Center: Provide a batch of white play dough, along with small twigs and plastic woodland animals. A student uses the play dough to make a snowy scene and then presses the twigs into the play dough so they resemble trees. He engages in pretend play using the animals and the snow.

Math Center: Glue yarn to a large gray pom-pom so it resembles a mouse. Place a set of number cards facedown in a stack, along with a supply of yellow corn kernel cutouts. In turn, each student turns over a card, identifies the number, and then counts out the corresponding number of corn kernels for the hungry mouse to eat.

Dramatic Play: Obtain a large piece of fake brown fur. Talk to students about what it would be like to be a bear that sleeps most of the winter. Then encourage youngsters to cover themselves with the fur and pretend to be a sleeping bear that wakes up, goes out looking for food, and then goes back to sleep.

	Group Time	Literature
Monday	Gather a clipboard, paper, and a pencil and take your group for a walk outdoors. Look for animals that may be eating or gathering food. Observe the ground around trees and bushes for nuts, acorns, and berries that look like they may have been nibbled on. Write down student observations for later discussion. *Observation*	Read aloud *The Happy Day* by Ruth Krauss. In this story, all the animals are fast asleep as the snow falls down. They are suddenly awakened by a lovely smell! They run around sniffing the air until they come upon a sweet-smelling flower growing in the snow.
Tuesday	Introduce the concept of hibernation to students; then hide a stuffed bear in the classroom. On separate index cards, write directions to locate the bear, such as "Turn left at the sand table." Tell youngsters they are going to search for a hibernating bear. Then read aloud each card and have students follow the directions to find the hibernating bear. ***Following directions, participating in a group task***	Assign children the roles of bears, squirrels, snails, mice, and groundhogs. Then have children reenact yesterday's story as you read it aloud. At the end of the story have everyone call out, "Oh! There's a flower growing in the snow."
Wednesday	Explain to students that bears get ready to hibernate by eating lots of food and putting leaves and grass in their dens. Then ask students to name ways that they get ready to go to sleep. Write each student's words on a separate pillow cutout. Then display the pillows in the classroom. ***Dictating information*** *I brush my teeth. Lee*	Read aloud *Time to Sleep* by Denise Fleming. In this story, Bear smells winter in the air and heads off to tell Snail it's time for a winter nap. Then Snail tells Skunk, who tells Turtle, and so on, until Ladybug rushes off to tell Bear, who is already fast asleep in her cave.
Thursday	Hide a supply of small, medium, and large acorn cutouts in the room and place one of each size on the floor in your group-time area. Students search for acorns, pretending to be squirrels gathering nuts for the winter. Then they sort their acorns by placing each one near the appropriate cutout in your group-time area. ***Size discrimination***	Ready the patterns on page 221 for flannelboard use. Then reread yesterday's story and invite several students to place the animals on the board in the order in which they appear in the story. Leave the book and the cutouts in a center for independent use.
Friday	Transform a large box into a cave. Face the cave entrance away from your students. Have a child leave the area and close her eyes. Choose another child to be the bear and go inside the cave. Bring the first child back to the group and have her classmates chant, "Who's the bear inside the cave?" Have the child guess who the bear is, providing clues as needed. The child who was the bear then becomes the guesser. ***Visual memory, participating in a game***	Read aloud *Brown Bear, Brown Bear, What Do You See?* by Bill Martin Jr. Encourage students to chant the text with you as you read the story aloud. Then have each child illustrate a page for a class book titled "Children, Children, What Do You See?"

Art/Gross-Motor Skills

Snow Shower
(See directions on page 56.)

Gross Motor: Students pretend to be little rabbits hopping around in the snow. When they hear you say, "The fox is coming!" they quickly lie down and stay very still and quiet, blending in with the surrounding snow. When they hear you say, "The fox is gone!" they get up and begin hopping again. Repeat several times.

A Winter Den
(See directions on page 56.)

Gross Motor: Set up chairs front-to-back in a meandering row. Students crawl under the chairs, pretending to be woodchucks crawling through a tunnel to their burrow. Then they curl up and take a winter nap. When they hear you say, "It's springtime!" they crawl back through the tunnel and pretend to scamper around outside.

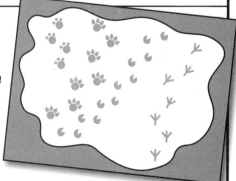

Animal Trails
(See directions on page 56.)

Songs and Such for the Week

Sleeping Time
(tune: "The Farmer in the Dell")

The [squirrels] like to sleep.
The [squirrels] like to sleep.
Sleep, sleep; it's wintertime.
The [squirrels] like to sleep.

Continue with the following:
turtles, frogs, bears, bats, snakes

A Bear's Den

Bears prepare a den
For a winter's rest.
They use leaves and twigs
Like birds do for a nest.
They eat nuts and berries,
Then they curl up in a ball.
They sleep during the winter
With little food at all.

Ready for Winter
(tune: "Skip to My Lou")

The hare gets ready; what does it do?
Does it wear boots and mittens too?
That's not something a hare would do.
It grows white fur for the winter.

Art Activities

Snow Shower

Prepare a spray bottle with diluted white tempera paint. Make construction paper cutouts of desired animals from the patterns on page 221. Glue the animals to a large sheet of black construction paper. Then use the spray bottle to mist the paper with white paint so the scene resembles animals in the falling snow.

A Winter Den

Paint the inside of a paper bowl half with gray tempera paint; then glue the bowl half to a construction paper base to make a cave. Next, slightly crumple orange, red, and brown tissue paper and glue it to the construction paper inside the cave so it resembles leaves. Glue brown pom-poms to the tissue paper to create a bear. Finally, glue cotton batting snow to the outside of the cave.

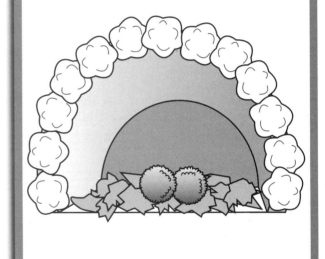

Animal Trails

Mix equal amounts of white paint and shaving cream in a medium-size bowl. Then paint a thick layer of the mixture on a sheet of brown construction paper. To make animal trails, a student moves a plastic woodland animal over the mixture on the painted paper. He continues in the same manner until a desired effect is achieved. After several days of drying, the youngster takes his project home.

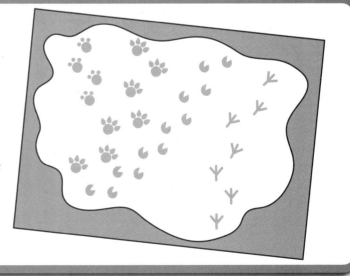

Transportation

Centers for the Week

Math Center: Attach transportation cards (see page 222) to strips of tagboard to make several pattern strips. Place the patterns at the center along with a supply of loose vehicle cards. A student uses the cards to copy and extend the sample patterns, or he creates a pattern of his own.

Literacy Center: Label each of four shoeboxes (airplane hangars) with a different letter. Place the hangars at the end of a sheet of bulletin board paper; then draw lines on the paper so the lines resemble airplane runways. Label each of several toy airplanes with a letter that matches a labeled hangar. A student moves each airplane down the runway to its corresponding hangar.

Sensory Table: Press a ball of clay onto the center of each of several small foam meat trays (cleaned and sanitized). Hot-glue a craft foam triangle to a craft stick for each tray; then push the sticks into the clay. Place the resulting boats in your water table. Students investigate what happens when they each blow through a straw to sail a boat around in the water.

Block Center: Use masking tape to create train tracks on the floor near your block center. Cut arches on opposite sides of several boxes to create tunnels. Provide toy trains, people figurines, and train-related books. Students use the blocks to build houses, train stations, and other buildings along the tracks.

Dramatic Play: For this travel agency center, provide items such as the following: a telephone; a cash register; play money; a calendar; road maps; paper tickets; used airplane, train, or boat tickets; travel magazines; brochures; and posters.

	Group Time	Literature
Monday	Cut out from copies of page 222 cards that show the modes of transportation used by students to get to school. Then label each column of a large floor graph to correspond to one of the modes of transportation. Have each child tell how he gets to school and then attach a corresponding card in the appropriate column on the chart. ***Graphing***	Read aloud *Freight Train* by Donald Crews. The brightly colored train cars that travel past cities, through tunnels, and across trestles in this book give youngsters plenty of color-recognition practice!
Tuesday	Arrange a class supply of chairs so they resemble the seats on a train. Give each student a paper ticket labeled with a shape. Have youngsters stand together as if waiting to board a train. Call out the name of a shape. Each child holding a ticket with the matching shape boards the train. Continue in the same way until everyone is on board. Then lead little ones in chanting, "Choo! Choo!" as they pretend to take a ride. ***Shape recognition***	Give each of eight children a train car cutout that corresponds to one in *Freight Train*. Reread the story and have the youngsters line up in the same order as the train cars in the book. Then have them chug around the room together at the end of the story.
Wednesday	Place in a basket a variety of transportation cards (see page 222). Have a child choose a card and name the mode of transportation. Then invite students to move about the room pretending to be that type of transportation. Repeat the process several times. ***Following directions***	Read aloud *Red Light, Green Light* by Anastasia Suen. In this book, a little boy sets up his toy vehicles to show just how busy a highway can be! The colorful pictures and rhyming text show why it's important to know that red means stop and green means go!
Thursday	Make one red, one blue, one green, and one yellow bus card (see page 222). Give each card to a different child. Then have each child pretend he is a bus driver driving up to the school. Say, "The blue bus arrives first," and prompt the corresponding child to get in line. Repeat the process to line up the second, third, and fourth buses. Then have the buses "drive" away from the school. ***Ordinal positions***	Revisit yesterday's story; then have students use a variety of construction paper vehicles, markers, and collage materials to make a class mural of a busy highway.
Friday	Gather youngsters around a large toy vehicle. Give a student a beanbag and have her place the beanbag *on* the vehicle. Then encourage the child to give the beanbag to a classmate. Repeat the process, having the next child place the beanbag *under* the vehicle and then pass it to a classmate. Continue in the same way for several rounds. ***Positional words***	Read Aloud *What James Likes Best* by Amy Schwartz. Have students tell what they think James liked best from the choices given at the end of each visit. Then ask youngsters what they would have liked best.

Art/Gross-Motor Skills

Little Yellow School Bus
(See directions on page 60.)

Gross Motor: Arrange a class supply of chairs in a circle. Tape a numbered car cutout to each chair. Give each child a paper plate to use as a steering wheel. During the activity, alternately start and stop a recording of lively music. When the music plays, students "drive" around the inside of the circle. When the music stops, each child quickly sits in a chair. In turn, each youngster identifies the number on the car taped to her chair.

Toot! Toot!
(See directions on page 60.)

Gross Motor: Cover openings cut in black construction paper with red, yellow, and green cellophane so the paper resembles a traffic light. Have students stand at one end of the room. Shine a flashlight through the green cellophane and prompt students to quickly move toward you. Repeat the process with the yellow cellophane (walk slowly) and the red cellophane (stop). Continue alternating the colors until students reach you. Then play another round.

Fancy Big Rigs
(See directions on page 60.)

Songs and Such for the Week

Transportation Song
(tune: "Row, Row, Row Your Boat")

Airplanes fly around
Way up in the sky.
Boats float in the water as
Cars and trucks drive by.

Getting Around
(tune: "I've Been Working on the Railroad")

We all need some transportation
To get us around.
We all need some transportation
In the air and on the ground.
There are trains and planes and buses
That can take us anywhere.
We all need some transportation
To take us here and there!

Transportation Poem

Transportation means a way to move
From one place to another.
You can take a car or a train,
Ride a bus or fly on a plane,
Ride a bike right down the lane—
The choice is up to you!

Art Activities

Little Yellow School Bus

Draw a simple outline of a school bus on a large sheet of yellow construction paper; then cut it out. Glue white construction paper windows to the bus. Then glue black craft foam wheels to the bus. Add white and red sticky dots, as shown, to make headlights and red warning lights. After the glue is dry, use markers to draw a child's face in each window.

Toot! Toot!

Cut out several colorful construction paper rectangles, squares, and triangles. Put a thin layer of black paint on a paper plate. To make railroad tracks, roll a toy vehicle's wheels through the paint and then roll the vehicle across a sheet of white paper. Dip a cotton swab in the paint and then draw lines on the tracks to make railroad ties. Glue shape cutouts to the paper above the tracks. Then dip the end of an empty spool in paint and press it on the paper beneath the cutouts to make wheels. Finally, dip a cotton ball in gray paint and pat it on the paper above the train engine so it resembles smoke.

Fancy Big Rigs

Use craft glue to attach a cube-shaped box to one end of a shoebox so it resembles the cab of a truck. Paint the boxes a desired color using tempera paint. Then glue a variety of craft materials to the truck to make wheels, headlights, doors, and windows.

December Holidays

Centers for the Week

Math Center: Place red, black, and green paper strips (Kwanzaa candles) at the center along with flame cutouts. A child arranges the candles in a row to make a simple pattern and then places a flame above each candle.

Art Center: A child glues squares of brown tissue paper to a small paper plate to make a latke. She glues the latke to a large blue paper plate and then drizzles white paint (sour cream) over the latke.

Fine-Motor Area: Set out several dreidels of different sizes. Encourage youngsters to practice spinning the dreidels.

Literacy Center: Weight down several lunch-size white paper bags with blocks. Arrange them around your reading area to resemble luminarias. Place a variety of books about Hanukkah, Kwanzaa, Las Posadas, and Christmas in the center. If desired, place a glow stick in each luminaria. Then invite youngsters to the center to look at the books.

Gross-Motor Area: Place a large frying pan on the floor. Then place brown cardboard circles (latkes) near a tape line several feet from the pan. A child stands on the tape line and attempts to toss the latkes into the pan.

	Group Time	Literature

Monday

Make five large candle cutouts with flames. Cut out a copy of the rhyming word cards from page 233. Attach one card from each rhyming pair to a different candle flame; then attach the candles to a wall. Place the remaining cards in a bag. Have a child choose a card from the bag. Then have youngsters name the picture and attach it to the candle with the rhyming picture on its flame. **Rhyming**

Read aloud *My First Kwanzaa* by Karen Katz. During the seven days of Kwanzaa, a little girl learns the importance of family, friends, and community.

Tuesday

In advance, collect a variety of candles and then give each student a candle. Help youngsters sort the candles into groups by height, color, width, and scent. **Sorting**

Revisit yesterday's story. During Kwanzaa, handmade gifts are given. Ask a student to draw a picture of a gift he would make for someone. Then invite him to display his picture, name the gift, and tell whom he would give it to.

Wednesday

Place a class treat in a box wrapped like a present. Have the students sit in a circle and pass the box around. Invite each student to guess what is inside the box. Then open the box and reveal the special gift. **Oral language, critical thinking**

Read aloud *Little Porcupine's Christmas* by Joseph Slate. All the animals have a part in the play except for Little Porcupine. But it is Little Porcupine's quick thinking that saves the play.

Thursday

Label pairs of dreidel cutouts (see patterns on page 223) with matching uppercase and lowercase letters. Attach a sticker to the back of some of the uppercase dreidels and place the uppercase dreidels faceup on the floor. Place the lowercase dreidels on a table nearby and have a child choose one. The child finds the matching dreidel on the floor. If the matching dreidel has a sticker on the back, the class sings a round of the traditional song "Dreidel, Dreidel, Dreidel." Then the child sets the pair aside. **Matching uppercase and lowercase letters**

Revisit yesterday's story. The other animals are mean to Little Porcupine. Allow youngsters time to discuss how unkind words make them feel. Invite students to think of nice things they could say to one another. Record their thoughts on chart paper.

Friday

Place in a small bag several clip art pictures that represent aspects of Hanukkah, Kwanzaa, and Christmas. Create three columns on a pocket chart labeled "Hanukkah," "Kwanzaa," and "Christmas." Have each student choose a card from the bag and place it in the correct column. **Classifying**

Read aloud *The Runaway Latkes* by Leslie Kimmelman. In this story, Rebecca is preparing latkes for a Hanukkah celebration when they jump out of the pan! People chase the latkes through the town in a story reminiscent of the gingerbread man. After the read-aloud, serve youngsters a snack of latkes and applesauce.

Adorable Angels
(See directions on page 64.)

Gross Motor: Give each student a candle. Have her manipulate the candle to perform various actions. For example, have youngsters place their candles on the floor and step over them, raise the candles above their heads, and wave them from side to side. Use a variety of actions and positional words.

Corn for Kwanzaa
(See directions on page 64.)

Gross Motor: Have the students pantomime the making of latkes. They pretend to shred potatoes, crack eggs, add salt and pepper, and mix everything together. They pretend to put oil in a pan, drop some of the mixture into the pan, and cook the latke. Youngsters say, "Sizzle, sizzle, sizzle" several times as they dance around while their pretend latkes cook.

Marvelous Menorahs
(See directions on page 64.)

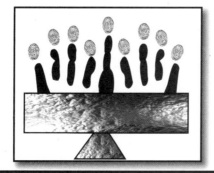

The Kinara
(tune: "I'm a Little Teapot")

I am a kinara,
Shining bright!
Look and see my candlelight.
I have candles red
And black and green—
The loveliest you've ever seen!

Gifts

I give a gift to you.
You give a gift to me.
December is a time
We show our love, you see!

Hanukkah Time
(tune: "My Bonnie Lies Over the Ocean")

It's Hanukkah time in December.
The menorah is glowing so bright.
The children are spinning the dreidel.
The fun lasts for eight happy nights!
Eight nights, eight nights.
The fun lasts for eight happy nights,
    eight nights!
Eight nights, eight nights.
The fun lasts for eight happy nights!

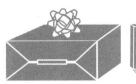 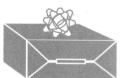

Adorable Angels

Trim a headshot photograph into a circle and attach it to the top of a yellow triangle. Cut a doily in half and glue the halves to the triangle to make wings. Twist a pipe cleaner to make a halo and tape it to the back of the project. Add dots of glue to the triangle and sprinkle glitter over the glue.

Corn for Kwanzaa

Tape a length of bubble wrap to the top of a table and use a paint roller to spread yellow tempera paint on the bubble wrap. To make a print, press a sheet of paper onto the bubble wrap. When the print is dry, cut a corn shape from the paper. Then glue green construction paper husks to the corn.

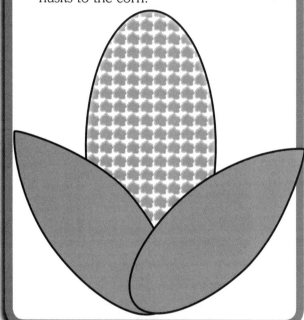

Marvelous Menorahs

Glue a simple aluminum foil menorah to a sheet of white paper. Then press four fingers of each hand in a shallow pan of light blue tempera paint. Press the fingers above the menorah so they resemble candles. Then use the edge of a hand to make a longer candle in the middle of the menorah. Add yellow fingerprint flames to the candles.

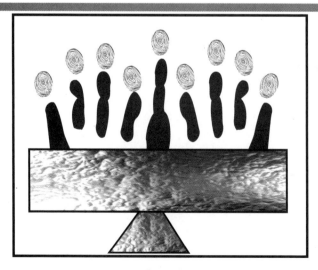

Five Senses

Centers for the Week

Math Center: Place in separate film canisters strong-smelling items, such as coffee, cinnamon, or cotton balls soaked with cooking extracts. Place a lid on each container and then poke holes in each lid. Place the containers and two circle cutouts labeled "Like" and "Don't Like" at the center. A student smells each container and places it on a circle according to his opinion.

Sensory Table: Bury a variety of different-colored items in the sand table. A student digs in the sand to find all the items of a designated color.

Art Center: Collect materials with a variety of textures, such as wallpaper, Bubble Wrap cushioning material, and corrugated cardboard. Place these items and a supply of paper and unwrapped crayons at the center. A student makes a texture rubbing by placing his paper on top of a selected material and coloring over it.

Discovery Center: Partially fill pairs of film canisters with different objects, such as rice, beans, pennies, beads, and popcorn. Tape each lid securely closed. A student shakes each container and determines which containers are filled with matching items.

Literacy Center: Place different food samples on trays and place the trays at a center along with some sticky notes. A student samples a food and then draws on a sticky note a smiley face if he liked the food or a sad face if he didn't. He sticks his note in front of the appropriate tray. Then he repeats the process for each remaining type of food.

	Group Time	Literature
Monday	Have students sit in a circle. Describe a student to the class. Then have students guess who the classmate is based on the description. **Listening**	Read aloud *My Five Senses* by Aliki. A little boy tells about his five senses and how he uses them.
Tuesday	After sharing a variety of objects with your students, place them in a sensory box made as shown. Instruct a student to stick his hand in the box and find a certain item. **Using the sense of touch**	Revisit yesterday's story. Make picture cards that show a mouth, an ear, a nose, an eye, and a hand. Show youngsters the ear card and have several volunteers name something they have heard. Repeat the process with each remaining card.
Wednesday	Give each child a small cup of crisp rice cereal. Have students describe what the cereal looks like and feels like as you write their words on a simple chart. Pour a little milk on each child's cereal and have them describe what they hear. Add the words to the chart. Then continue in the same way as the children eat their cereal. **Speaking to describe**	Read aloud *Lunch* by Denise Fleming. A mouse eats a variety of colorful foods for his lunch! This brilliant book focuses on both the senses of sight and taste.
Thursday	To show students that smell and taste are related, have each student gently pinch his nose and eat an animal cracker. Then have him eat an animal cracker without pinching his nose. Ask youngsters which cracker had more flavor, leading them to conclude that smell enhances taste. **Comparing**	Reread yesterday's story. Then have little ones help to make and eat a fruit salad.
Friday	Set a timer so it will ring in two minutes. Tell students to cover their eyes as you hide the timer. When the timer rings, invite students to speculate about the timer's location. After a short discussion, show the class where the timer is hidden. **Listening, oral language**	Read aloud *Five for a Little One* by Chris Raschka. Then revisit the book and have little ones name other things they can see, hear, taste, smell, and feel. Write their thoughts on sticky notes and stick them to the appropriate pages. During a rereading of the book, read aloud youngsters' contributions as well.

Art/Gross-Motor Skills

Totally Touchable

(See directions on page 68.)

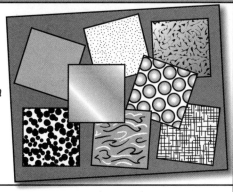

Gross Motor: Show the class a few musical instruments and assign a movement to each one. Make a sound using a chosen instrument and prompt children to move in the designated way. Continue this activity using the other instruments.

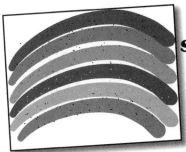

Scented Rainbows

(See directions on page 68.)

Gross Motor: Instruct students to dance while you play a recording of lively music. Occasionally stop the music. When you do, each student sits down as quickly as possible. When the music resumes, he gets up and begins dancing again.

Beautiful Drum

(See directions on page 68.)

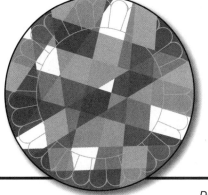

Songs and Such for the Week

Five Great Senses

(tune: "Ten Little Indians")

You can see
And you can hear.
You can smell
And you can taste things.
You can touch things with your fingers.
You have five great senses!

Use Your Senses

Touch with your hands.
Smell with your nose.
Hear with your ears—
That's how it goes.
Taste with your tongue.
See with your eyes.
Use your five senses;
You're so wise!

Five Senses Every Day

(tune: "She'll Be Comin' Round the Mountain")

You can use your five senses every day.
You can use your five senses every day.
When you learn and when you play,
They will help in a big way!
You can use all five senses every day!

Art Activities

Totally Touchable

Cut into small pieces a variety of textured items, such as felt, fake fur, cellophane, corrugated cardboard, Bubble Wrap cushioning material, and wallpaper. Glue a variety of the items onto a sheet of tagboard to make a textured collage.

Scented Rainbows

Mix water, glue, and food coloring to make paints in the following colors: red, orange, yellow, green, blue, and purple. Place the paints at a table along with six flavors of sugar-free powdered gelatin in corresponding colors. Paint a purple arc near the bottom of your paper and then sprinkle a small amount of purple gelatin powder on the arc. Continue the same process, painting each arc above the previous one, until all six colors are used.

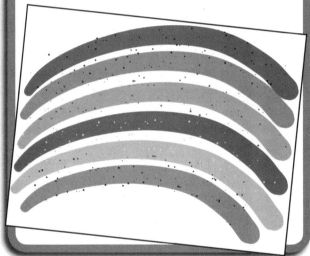

Beautiful Drum

Brush glue over a sturdy paper plate and then place tissue paper squares over the glue. Brush another layer of glue over the tissue paper. When the resulting hand drum is dry, sing a song and tap this handmade instrument with your fingers.

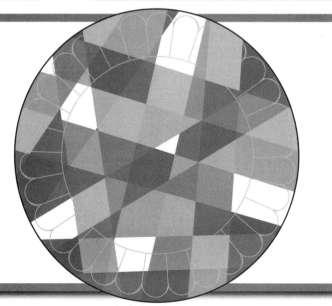

Merry Christmas

Centers for the Week

Math Center: Attach holiday light cutouts to tagboard strips to make pattern starters. Place the starters and more light cutouts at the center. A student chooses a starter and then copies and continues the pattern.

Sensory Table: Place wrapped candy canes (large and small) in a tub filled with red and white rice. A student digs for the candy canes and sorts them into two piles based on size.

Game Center: Collect holiday cards and cut the picture from the front of each card. Puzzle-cut each picture into a few large pieces and put each set of pieces in separate resealable plastic bags. A student chooses a bag and puts the pieces together to form the picture.

Literacy Center: Collect a supply of holiday cards and cut out the messages from the inside of the cards. Place these at the center along with paper, glue, holiday stamps, ink pads, and crayons. A student uses the materials to create a holiday card of his own.

Dramatic Play: Set out age-appropriate tools—such as plastic hammers, screwdrivers, and wrenches—along with various types of toys. Also provide work aprons, if desired. A student pretends she is one of Santa's elves getting the toys ready for Christmas Eve.

	Group Time	Literature
Monday	Make a supply of holiday cookie cutouts and glue one of each type to a separate paper plate. Place the plates on the floor. Give each student a cookie cutout and have him place his cutout on the matching plate. When all the cookies have been sorted, count the cookies on each plate. **Sorting, counting**	Read aloud *The Little Reindeer* by Michael Foreman. In this story, a boy accidentally receives a very special present from Santa.
Tuesday	Place in a stocking a familiar object that someone might receive for Christmas. Have the students sit in a circle and pass the stocking around. Invite each child to shake the stocking and feel the object. Next, ask students to guess what is in the stocking. Finally, reveal the object. **Oral language, using the sense of touch**	Revisit yesterday's story. Give each student a sheet of paper and have her draw a picture to show how she would take care of a reindeer. Write her dictated sentence describing her picture on her paper. Bind all the finished pages together to make a class book.
Wednesday	Obtain a class supply of candy canes in different colors. Designate an area of the room for each color of candy cane. Give each student a wrapped candy cane and play holiday music as each child dances toward the correct area of the room holding her candy cane. Finally, have each child take home her candy cane. **Color matching**	Read aloud *Bear Stays Up for Christmas* by Karma Wilson. In this story, Bear manages to stay awake for Christmas, and he learns that giving is the best present of all.
Thursday	Display three large Christmas tree cutouts, each labeled with a different uppercase letter. Give each child a circle cutout (ornament) labeled with a corresponding lowercase letter. Have each child attach his ornament to the appropriate tree. **Matching uppercase and lowercase letters**	Revisit yesterday's story. Attach a supersize present cutout to the board. Invite each student to share a time when he gave someone a present and how it made him feel. Record youngsters' thoughts on the cutout.
Friday	Display two different pictures of Santa Claus. Have each student examine the pictures and state how they are alike and how they are different. Record these ideas on the board using a T chart. **Comparing/oral language**	Read aloud *Snowmen at Christmas* by Caralyn Buehner. Have little ones make snowy sweets like the snowmen eat. Have each child stir vanilla pudding and holiday sprinkles in a cup. Help her place foil over the cup and then insert a craft stick in the foil. Pop the sweets in the freezer until they harden. Then have little ones enjoy them!

Art/Gross-Motor Skills

Trimming the Tree
(See directions on page 72.)

Gross Motor: Have the students stand in a circle. Then have them pass a stocking around the circle while they move to a recording of Christmas music. When the music stops, students stand still, and the youngster holding the stocking names something he would like to receive in his stocking. The music resumes and play continues.

Nosy Reindeer
(See directions on page 72.)

Gross Motor: Tie a bow to the top of a green plastic hoop to make a holiday wreath. Prop the wreath against a chair. Then give each student a beanbag and allow him to toss the beanbag through the wreath. After everyone has had a turn, repeat the activity, this time increasing the distance between the wreath and the student.

Heartfelt Santa
(See directions on page 72.)

Songs and Such for the Week

Candy Cane
(tune: "Clementine")

Candy cane, oh, candy cane, oh—
You are such a pretty sight
With your stripes all wound around you,
Looking good in red and white!
You are straight and you are curvy.
You are oh so good to eat!
Candy cane, oh, candy cane, oh—
You're my favorite Christmas treat!

Christmas Sounds

I love the Christmas sounds I hear
Playing in my little ear!
I hear sleigh bells—ring, ring, ring!
I hear carols—sing, sing, sing!
I hear Santa—"Ho, ho, ho!"
I hear "No peeking"—no, no, no!
I hear the fire—pop, pop, pop!
I wish those sounds would never stop!

We Are Santa's Elves
(tune: "Bingo")

[We all live up at the North Pole.]
We work hard every day, oh!
We are Santa's elves; we are Santa's elves; we are Santa's elves.
We work hard every day, oh!

Continue with the following: we all make toys for girls and boys, we care for Rudolph and his friends, we look for naughty and for nice

Art Activities

Trimming the Tree

Paint a cone-shaped disposable drinking cup green so it resembles a tree. After the cup is dry, decorate your tree by gluing pom-poms and sequins to the cup. Then wind sparkly pipe cleaners around the tree. Glue a star cutout to the top of the tree. Finally, display the tree on a piece of cotton batting (snow).

Nosy Reindeer

In the middle of a sheet of construction paper, glue a brown triangle to make a reindeer head. Then glue hand cutout tracings to the top of the reindeer head to make antlers. Glue a pom-pom nose and construction paper eyes to the reindeer. Finally, name the reindeer and write its name on the paper.

Polly, the Purple-Nosed Reindeer

Heartfelt Santa

Turn a flesh-colored heart cutout upside down and glue a red triangle (hat) to the top. Glue a cotton ball to the top of the hat. Then pull apart cotton balls and glue them to the edge of the hat to make fluffy trim and around the edge of the heart to make a beard. Finally, draw eyes and a nose below the hat.

Opposites

Centers for the Week

Play Dough Center: Place half a batch of play dough in the freezer for about 30 minutes. Just before removing it, heat the remaining half of the play dough in the microwave for a few seconds. (Knead the play dough before using it!) Provide cookie cutters and rolling pins. Students explore and manipulate the cold and warm play dough.

Art Center: Provide fingerpaint paper and several different colors of fingerpaint. Add a small amount of sand to some of the containers. A student fingerpaints with the different paints and identifies which ones feel smooth and which ones feel rough.

Discovery Center: Each day, place in the center items that are opposite textures, sounds, sizes, and colors (remove the items at the end of each day). Provide two labeled trays. Students sort the items onto a corresponding tray. Some suggested opposites are soft and hard, smooth and rough, quiet and noisy, big and little, and black and white.

Literacy Center: Cut out and mount the cards from pages 224 and 225 on separate pieces of tagboard. Puzzle-cut each card differently to make two-piece puzzles. Store the puzzle pieces in a resealable plastic bag. A student removes the puzzle pieces from the bag; then he puts the puzzles together and looks for opposite pairs.

Fine-Motor Area: Provide several small and large laminated tagboard lacing cards with attached laces. A student chants "in and out" as he moves the laces in and out through the holes.

Group Time	Literature

Monday

Give each student a small toy and a disposable cup. Give directions such as "Put your toy in the cup" and "Put your toy behind the cup." Students place their toys in the location opposite of each direction given. *Opposite positions*

Read aloud *Olivia's Opposites* by Ian Falconer. Throughout this book, a little piglet named Olivia humorously demonstrates a variety of opposites!

Tuesday

For each child, prepare a shaker, such as a film canister filled with rice. Allow students time to explore the shakers. Then have students shake their shakers as you call out commands such as stop and go, up and down, fast and slow, quiet and loud, in front of and behind, and left and right. *Following directions*

Revisit yesterday's book. Have students pretend to be Olivia and demonstrate the opposite actions on each page. Provide articles of dress-up clothing and jewelry for youngsters to demonstrate the word *fancy*.

Wednesday

Make a class supply of the opposite pairs on pages 224 and 225. Keep one card from each pair and give each remaining card to a different child. Hold a card in the air and read the card. Each child holding the corresponding opposite card stands up and, in turn, names his card. *Identifying opposites*

Read aloud *What's Opposite?* by Stephen R. Swinburne. This book explores the concept of opposites through simple text and bright, colorful photographs that clearly show why two things are considered opposites.

Thursday

Prepare a set of cards from pages 224 and 225 and place them facedown on the floor. Students take turns flipping over pairs of cards to find opposites. Remove matches from the game when they are found. Play continues until all the opposite cards have been matched. *Recognizing opposites, participating in a game*

full empty

Reread yesterday's book, pausing to allow students to answer the "What is the opposite of…" questions before revealing each answer on the following page.

Friday

Write on separate index cards statements that incorrectly use opposite words. For example, you might say, "We play inside on the playground" or "When I eat a lot of food, my stomach feels empty." Students listen to each statement and then repeat it using the appropriate opposite. *Listening skills, oral language*

Read aloud *Looking at Opposites: Hot, Cold, Shy, Bold* by Pamela Harris. Take photographs of youngsters demonstrating some of the opposites in the book.

Art/Gross-Motor Skills

Over-and-Under Art
(See directions on page 76.)

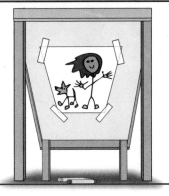

Gross Motor: Glue a sign labeled "Stop" and a sign labeled "Go" to craft sticks. To begin, have students stand side-by-side, facing you from several feet away. Call out a movement, such as hop, run, gallop, crawl, march, or skip. Hold up each sign at different times to signal students when to stop and when to begin moving again.

Double Opposites
(See directions on page 76.)

Gross Motor: Give each student a scarf or a streamer. In turn, play two recordings of music: one fast and one slow. Students move the scarves as they dance to the tempo of each recording.

Left-and-Right Art
(See directions on page 76.)

Songs and Such for the Week

The Opposite Shout
(tune: "Shoo Fly")

Shout out the opposite!
Shout out the opposite!
Shout out the opposite,
The opposite of [up]!

Repeat the verse, substituting additional opposites in the last line.

Say It With Me

Opposites are a pair
Of two things that do not share
Anything alike, you see.
Say these opposites with me:
Up, down;
In, out;
Front, back;
Whisper, shout;
On, off;
High, low;
Open, shut;
Stop and go!

Things That Are Different
(tune: "The Wheels on the Bus")

Things that are different are opposites,
Opposites, opposites.
Things that are different are opposites.
Can you name some for me?

[Up and down] are opposites,
Opposites, opposites.
[Up and down] are opposites.
They are not alike!

Repeat the verse, substituting additional opposites where indicated.

Art Activities

Over-and-Under Art

Provide paper, markers or crayons, and tape. To begin, a student places a piece of paper on a tabletop and draws a picture. Before the picture is complete, he removes it from the tabletop and tapes it to the underside of the table. He lies down or sits under the table to finish his picture.

Double Opposites

Press the rim of a large plastic container in white paint and then press the rim on a sheet of black paper. Repeat the process with the rim of a small plastic container. Continue making prints until a desired effect is achieved.

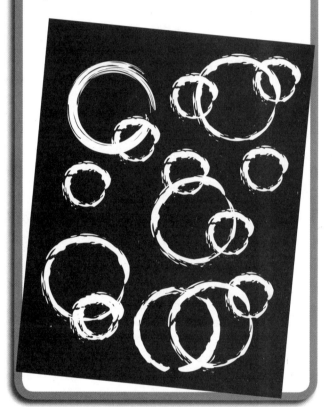

Left-and-Right Art

Gather a variety of painting tools, such as paintbrushes, sponges, and rollers. Place paint in shallow containers. Draw a vertical line down the center of a large sheet of paper; then label the appropriate sides "Left" and "Right." A student holds a paint tool with her right hand to paint the right side of the paper and then with her left hand to paint the left side of the paper. She changes tools as desired.

Left

Right

Snow and Mittens

Centers for the Week

Literacy Center: Pour a shallow layer of salt (snow) in a large plastic tray. Label each of several snowball cutouts with a different simple seasonal word—such as *snow, cold, hat, coat,* and *ice*—and place them near the tray. A student uses his finger to copy the words in the salt.

Math Center: Program the upper portion of several mitten cutouts with a number and the lower portion with a corresponding set of stamped snowflakes; then puzzle-cut each mitten, separating the information. A student matches each number to its corresponding set.

Discovery Center: Fill several containers with water. Place a small object, such as a plastic animal or toy car, in each container and then put the containers in a freezer. When the water is frozen, remove the blocks of ice and put them in separate bowls. A student uses a sponge to squeeze warm water on the ice so it will melt and he can remove the toy.

Art Center: A student uses a white crayon to draw a winter scene on a sheet of dark paper. Then she paints a piece of Bubble Wrap cushioning material with white paint and presses it onto her picture. She slowly removes the Bubble Wrap cushioning material from the paper to reveal a scene with falling snow.

Dramatic Play: For this winter clothing shop, provide a cash register, play money, and paper shopping bags. Add items such as spare coats, snow pants, scarves, hats, mittens, gloves, and boots for students to try on and "purchase."

	Group Time	Literature
Monday	Have each student don a pair of mittens. Play a recording of lively music and have youngsters pass an ice cube around the circle. Stop the music at short intervals and allow students to observe and describe the ice cube. Then have students remove their mittens. Continue as before until the ice cube melts. Encourage children to share what it's like holding the ice with and without mittens. ***Observation skills, critical thinking, cause and effect***	Read aloud *The Mitten* by Jan Brett. In this story, a lost mitten becomes shelter to a host of woodland animals. The last to squeeze in is a tiny mouse that makes the bear sneeze, scattering the animals everywhere!
Tuesday	Display a variety of small items. Review the items with students; then secretly place each item in a separate large mitten. Give each mitten to a different child. Have each child try to figure out the object's identity by feeling the outside of the mitten. After all of the guesses are announced, reveal each object. ***Tactile awareness***	Have each student lace together two mitten cutouts, leaving an opening at the cuff. Then encourage each child to cut out a copy of the cards on page 226. Reread yesterday's story and have youngsters place each animal card in the mitten at the appropriate time.
Wednesday	Prepare a class supply of mitten cutouts using four different colors. Gather a sheet of paper to match each mitten and mount each paper in a different corner of your classroom. Give each child a pair of matching mittens and have her identify the color. Then call out directions such as, "Red mittens go to the yellow corner." Continue in the same way, moving groups of children from one corner to another. ***Identifying colors, following directions, participating in a game***	Read aloud *The Snowy Day* by Ezra Jack Keats. This is a story about a little boy who spends an adventurous day in the snow and then ends his adventure by putting a snowball in his pocket to bring home as a souvenir!
Thursday	Give each student a sheet of blue construction paper and a supply of cotton balls (snowballs). Draw a square on your board. Ask each student to arrange her snowballs on her paper to re-create the shape. Repeat the activity several times, drawing a different shape each time. ***Reproducing shapes***	Revisit yesterday's story. Help students use the pictures to retell the story; then have students make marks in the snow as Peter did. To do this, students dip a twig in a container of white paint. Then they drag the twig along a sheet of dark paper and observe the marks.
Friday	Cut from magazines pictures of people and animals in the snow. Show students a picture and encourage them to tell what is happening in the picture. Then encourage students to share what they think might happen next. ***Oral language, creative thinking***	Read aloud *Snowballs* by Lois Ehlert. Then have students collect random items in or outside the classroom. Have them place the items on a snowman cutout. Take a photograph of each snowman and display the photos in the classroom.

Art/Gross-Motor Skills

A Snowy Tree
(See directions on page 80.)

Gross Motor: Divide your class in half and have students face each other. Then give each youngster a large white pom-pom (snowball) and call out, "Ready, aim, throw!" and let the fun begin! When it's time to clean up, have each student toss his snowball into a container.

Glistening Winter Scene
(See directions on page 80.)

Gross Motor: Set up a winter-themed obstacle course. Have students crawl under tables draped with white sheets (snowdrifts), carry white trash bags stuffed with newspaper (snowballs), and jump over tape lines (cracks in the ice).

Pretty Pasta Snowflakes
(See directions on page 80.)

Songs and Such for the Week

Oh, My Mittens
(tune: "Clementine")

Oh, my mittens! Oh, my mittens!
So soft and warm and snug.
All the fleece that's on the inside
Gives my hands a winter hug!

Glistening Snow

Cold white snow
Gently falls down.
Flakes stick together
Covering the ground.
A glistening blanket
Oh, so white.
Such a beautiful scene
On a winter's night.

Snowflakes A-fallin'
(tune: "She'll Be Comin' Round the Mountain")

Oh, the snowflakes are a-fallin' from the sky!
Oh, the snowflakes are a-fallin' from the sky!
With this frosty little flurry
It'll be white in a hurry!
Oh, the snowflakes are a-fallin' from the sky!

Art Activities

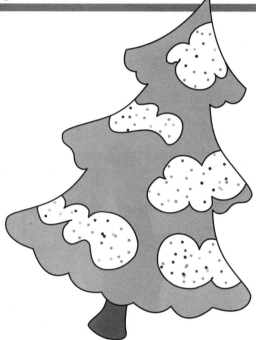

A Snowy Tree

Draw a simple outline of an evergreen tree on a sheet of tagboard. Whip equal amounts of Ivory Snow powder laundry detergent and water in a bowl until stiff peaks form. Scoop some of the mixture and place it in the tree outline; then use it as fingerpaint. Add more of the mixture as needed. When finished, sprinkle the tree with clear glitter. If desired, cut around the tree when the project is dry.

Glistening Winter Scene

Paint a snowy scene on a sheet of black construction paper, sprinkling salt over each element of the scene while the paint is still wet. Use a cotton swab to dab white paint on the paper to make snowflakes. Then sprinkle salt over the snowflakes as well. If desired, add construction paper details to the picture.

Pretty Pasta Snowflakes

Make a base for the snowflake by gluing three craft sticks together so it creates six different points; then set it aside to dry. Next, glue an assortment of pasta shapes to the base and allow the glue to dry. Then paint the project with white tempera paint and sprinkle the resulting snowflake with glitter or salt. Finally, attach a white satin ribbon to the project for hanging.

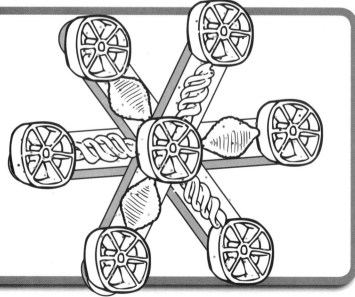

Getting Along
With Others
Centers for the Week

Literacy Center: Program heart-shaped cutouts with the sentence starter "I can be kind by…" Students dictate or write words to complete the sentence and then draw a picture to illustrate their thoughts.

Math Center: Prepare a supply of different-colored hand shapes. Make a sample pattern with the hands on a sheet of tagboard. Using the sample as a guide, students take turns adding a hand shape to copy and extend the pattern. For an added challenge, have students work together to create a pattern.

Art Center: Provide markers, crayons, collage materials, glue, and sheets of light-colored paper. Students draw a self-portrait, decorate the paper as desired, and then dictate or write how they can be a friend. To create a class quilt, attach the papers to bulletin board paper to create a grid; then attach bulletin board border around the grid.

Block Center: Provide a large die. Students take turns rolling the die and then gathering the corresponding number of blocks to add to a cooperative structure.

Play Dough Center: Prepare separate laminated mats with words such as *peace, love, friend,* and *kind.* Provide a large supply of play dough. Students roll the play dough into ropelike shapes and then place it along each letter on a mat to form the word.

Group Time	Literature

Monday

Prepare a punch bowl with fruit juice. After discussing Dr. King's dreams of peace and friendship, tell students they are going to make friendship punch. In turn, have each child say, "I'm adding [love] to our friendship punch." Then have him stir the punch with a ladle. Then invite everyone to drink a cup of friendship punch! *Oral language*

Read aloud *Happy Birthday, Martin Luther King* by Jean Marzollo. This book contains simple, informative text that describes the life of Martin Luther King Jr. and the important ideas he believed in.

Tuesday

Lead a discussion about problems children may face, such as having their toys taken or being pushed. Invite students to offer solutions on how to solve the problems; write their responses on chart paper. Then ask volunteers to role-play problem situations and demonstrate choices they can make to solve each problem. *Role-playing, problem solving*

Revisit yesterday's story. Begin a discussion by talking about your classroom rules. Ask students what they think it would be like if there were no rules.

Wednesday

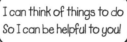

I can think of things to do
So I can be helpful to you!

To make a helping hand, stuff a garden glove with cotton batting and then hot-glue the glove closed. Give a glove to a youngster. Have students pass the glove around the circle as you lead them in reciting the chant shown. Then have the child with the glove tell a way she can be helpful. *Critical thinking*

Read aloud the story *The Little Red Hen* by Paul Galdone. In this story, the little red hen asks which of her housemates will help with the tasks necessary to make bread. But none are willing to help, so the little red hen does all the work. When the bread is finally baked, her housemates come running, but they are in for a big surprise!

Thursday

Have each student remove one shoe and place it in a basket. Place each shoe somewhere in the classroom. Have students search the room to find one shoe that does not belong to them and bring it back to the circle. Then have each child, in turn, walk around the circle to find the owner of the shoe and return it. *Cooperative play, matching*

Reread yesterday's story; then provide props for students to act out the story. Ask students whether they think it's fair that the cat, the dog, and the mouse didn't get to eat the bread. Then talk about how helpful it is when everyone does their share of work.

Friday

Cut several large rectangles from bulletin board paper to serve as picnic blankets; then have small groups of students sit around the blankets. Provide each group with a plate with twice as many snacks as there are children in the group. In turn, each student removes one snack from the plate until all the snacks are gone. Then children count the snacks to determine whether the food was divided equally. *Counting, recognizing equal amounts*

Read aloud *The Crayon Box That Talked* by Shane DeRolf. Have students talk about ways they are similar and different from their classmates. Then have students use crayons to make a collaborative mural.

Art/Gross-Motor Skills

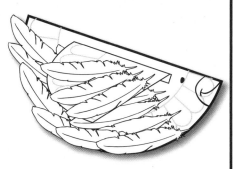

Wings of Peace
(See directions on page 84.)

Gross Motor: Have students stand in line side by side and link their arms with their neighbors. Stand about ten feet in front of the group. Give directions such as, "Take two giant steps" or "Take four baby steps." Youngsters keep their arms linked together until they reach you.

Circle of Harmony
(See directions on page 84.)

Gross Motor: Place several plastic hoops (rocks) on your floor. Have students walk, hop, or jump around the hoops. When they hear a signal, such as a bell, encourage youngsters to stand on a rock. Remove one rock and continue in the same manner. Each time the bell rings, students work together to fit as many classmates as they can on the rocks.

Helping Hands Headband
(See directions on page 84.)

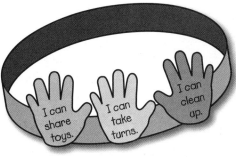

Songs and Such for the Week

Be Kind
(tune: "Shoo Fly")

Be kind to everyone.
Be kind to everyone.
Be kind to everyone,
And they will be kind to you too!

Getting Along

A smile and a few kind words
Will go a long, long way
In helping you to get along
With others every day!

Friendly Style
(tune: "Jingle Bells")

Use nice words.
Share your toys.
Give a great big smile.
Treat the people that you meet
With a friendly style.
Use nice words.
Share your toys.
Give a great big smile.
Treat all people that you meet
With a friendly style.

Circle of Harmony

Shake green powdered paint onto a circle cutout and then spray it with a mist of water. Repeat the process with blue powdered paint. After the paint is dry, glue people cutouts in a variety of skin tones to the project and add the title shown.

Circle of Harmony

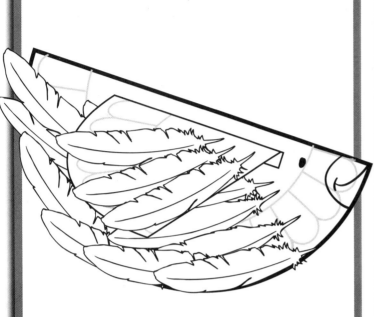

Wings of Peace

To make a dove, cut a white paper plate in half. Set one half aside (body) and then cut the other half into two equal pieces (wings). Fold a tab on each wing and then attach the wings to the body. Use a marker to draw a beak and an eye on the dove. Finally, glue white craft feathers to the project.

Helping Hands Headband

Make colorful handprints on a sheet of paper. When the paint is dry, use a permanent marker to write on each hand a way to be helpful, thoughtful, or kind. Cut out the hands and attach them to a headband. Then size the headband appropriately.

I can share toys.

I can take turns.

I can clean up.

Polar Animals

Centers for the Week

Game Center: Make five tagboard copies of the penguin pattern on page 227 in graduated sizes. Attach a piece of cardboard tube to the back of each penguin to make it self-standing. Youngsters order the penguins from shortest to tallest.

Sensory Table: Attach numbered penguin cutouts (see page 227 for a penguin pattern) to plastic containers. Label fish cutouts with matching numbers and nestle them in your sand table with a supply of packing peanuts (ice). Youngsters "dig" in the ice for fish and then "feed" each fish to a penguin by placing it in the appropriate container.

Block Center: Provide a supply of white or transparent plastic cups in a variety of sizes. Children use the cups to build ice structures.

Literacy Center: Place white fingerpaint (snow) in a resealable plastic bag. Seal the bag and tape the top for added security. Little ones use their fingers to trace letters in the snow.

Math Center: Make several white construction paper copies of the polar bear pattern on page 227. Cut out the bears and then cut pieces of white bulletin board paper to look like ice. Make black dots at opposite ends of each piece of ice. A youngster measures a piece of ice by placing polar bears side by side from one dot to the other dot. Then she counts the bears.

Group Time	Literature
Monday Have a student don a headband similar to the one shown. The child covers her eyes while a classmate sits on a fish cutout. Then youngsters chant, "Penguin, penguin, where's your fish?" Then the penguin uncovers her eyes and guesses who has the hidden fish. ***Following directions***	Read aloud *Splash! A Penguin Counting Book* by Jonathan Chester. Youngsters practice counting as they explore a day in the life of a group of penguins.
Tuesday Label iceberg cutouts with different letters and attach them to the floor in a circle. Play music and have little ones waddle like penguins around the icebergs. When the music stops, each child stops behind an iceberg. Choose two or three students to identify the letters or letter sounds on their icebergs. Continue until all youngsters have had a turn. ***Letter/sound identification***	Revisit yesterday's story. Cut out ten enlarged copies of the penguin pattern on page 227. Read aloud the first page of the book and have a child attach a penguin cutout to a sheet of chart paper. Continue reading, having a student add a new penguin to the chart paper after each page to reflect the growing number of penguins.
Wednesday Cut out enlarged white construction paper copies of the animal patterns on page 227, omitting the penguin pattern. Demonstrate how the animals' fur or feathers camouflages them by placing the animal cutouts on a brown background and asking little ones to spot the animals. Then move the cutouts to a white background and point out how much harder it is to see each animal. ***Investigating living things***	Read aloud *The Lonesome Polar Bear* by Jane Cabrera. In this story, a lonely bear cub meets several snowy friends, but he wants a real friend that won't melt.
Thursday Cut out a copy of the animals on page 227. Make a graph by placing each animal at the bottom of a pocket chart and cards labeled with numbers along the side. Invite each student to choose his favorite polar animal by placing a sticky note above the appropriate animal. Then discuss the results of the graph. ***Graphing*** 	Reread yesterday's story. Have students use the book's illustrations to retell the story. Then invite little ones to fingerpaint the snow animal of her choice on blue construction paper.
Friday Program pairs of polar bear cutouts (pattern on page 227) with rhyming pictures. Place the cards facedown in a pocket chart. Have a child turn over the first bear and identify the picture. Have a second child turn over the next bear. Help students decide if the pictures on the bears rhyme. If they do, move the bears to another row of the chart. If not, turn the second card over and have a volunteer turn over the third card. ***Rhyming pictures***	Read *Mama, Do You Love Me?* by Barbara M. Joose. Assist youngsters in recalling the different polar animals in the story. Discuss the animals shown and their movements. As you point to an animal, invite children to move the way each animal might move.

Art/Gross-Motor Skills

Perky Penguins
*(See directions on
page 88.)*

Gross Motor: Tape two iceberg cutouts on the
floor several yards apart. Remind students how a father
penguin takes care of his egg by balancing it on top of
his feet. Place a beanbag on top of a youngster's feet.
Have him waddle slowly like a penguin from one iceberg
to the other while balancing the beanbag.

Fuzzy Fur
*(See directions on
page 88.)*

Gross Motor: Encourage youngsters to pretend to be
polar bears as you lead them in pantomiming the poem
shown.

> Polar bear, polar bear, walk on the snow.
> Polar bear, polar bear, run to and fro.
> Polar bear, polar bear, dive deep down.
> Polar bear, polar bear, swim around.

Polar Painting
*(See directions on
page 88.)*

Songs and Such for the Week

Penguin Parts
(tune: "Head and Shoulders")

Beak and belly, flippers, feet; flippers,
feet.
Beak and belly, flippers, feet; flippers,
feet.
I'm a penguin, black and white and
neat!
Beak and belly, flippers, feet; flippers,
feet.

What Is It?

What waddles by in its black-and-white
suit
Or slides on the ice looking very, very
cute?
What dives in cold water with a splashy
splash
And catches lots of fish in a flashy flash?
Can you guess what it might be?
It's a penguin, yes sirree!

I'm a Polar Bear
(tune: "I'm a Little Teapot")

I'm a polar bear, so big and tall.
My paws are huge; my tail is small.
I live way up on the Arctic ice.
Yum! I think that fish taste nice!

# Art Activities

Perky Penguins

Paint a small paper plate black and set it aside to dry. Round one end of a 9" x 12" sheet of black construction paper and then paint the center of the paper white. Glue beak and feet cutouts to the resulting penguin body. Then use a marker to draw eyes above the beak. Cut the prepared plate in half and staple the halves to opposite sides of the penguin to make flippers.

Fuzzy Fur

To make a furry polar bear, make an enlarged copy of the polar bear pattern on page 227. Cut out the bear and then glue white cotton balls on the cutout to make fur.

Polar Painting

Tape a polar animal cutout (see page 227 for patterns) to a sheet of white construction paper. Dip a damp sponge into blue tempera paint and paint all around the pattern, being sure to cover the white paper. Then carefully remove the pattern to reveal the animal shape underneath. Finally, make white fingerprint snowflakes around the animal and use a crayon to add details as desired.

Fairy Tales

Centers for the Week

Play Dough Center: Mix nutmeg, cinnamon, and ginger into a batch of brown play dough. Place the play dough at a center along with craft foam cutouts, mixing bowls, cookie sheets, and gingerbread man–shaped cookie cutters. Encourage youngsters to visit the center and make gingerbread men that look like they could get up and run away!

Dramatic Play: Place three different sizes of bowls and spoons in your housekeeping center along with a mixing spoon and a cooking pot full of yellow paper shreds. If desired, provide teddy bears in different sizes as well. Encourage youngsters to whip up batches of porridge for the bears.

Art Center: Set out a supply of red construction paper rectangles (bricks) and sheets of construction paper. Also provide three pig cutouts for each child. A child glues the pigs to a sheet of paper. Then he glues bricks to the paper to build a house around the pigs to keep them safe.

Literacy Center: Enlarge the wolf pattern on page 228 and then make a gray construction paper copy. Cut out the wolf and attach it to a table. Provide magazines, scissors, and glue sticks. Encourage students to cut examples of the letter *W* from the magazines and then glue them to the wolf.

Block Center: Place plastic goat toys in your block center along with a supply of blue tissue paper (water). Have each youngster construct a bridge that spans over the water as in the tale *The Three Billy Goats Gruff*. Then have him test the strength of his bridge by marching the goats across the bridge.

	Group Time	Literature
Monday	After a reading of *The Three Billy Goats Gruff,* place student name cards in a bag. Lead youngsters in chanting, "Trip, trap, trip, trap! Who's that crossing over my bridge?" Then, with great fanfare, reveal a name card and have youngsters identify the name. ***Name recognition***	Read aloud *The Little Red Hen* by Byron Barton. This simple version of the well-known tale maintains the same strong message of the benefits of hard work.
Tuesday	Read aloud your favorite version of *The Three Little Pigs.* Then have youngsters use raffia (straw), sticks, and blocks (bricks) to act out a simple retelling of the story. ***Dramatizing a story***	Reread yesterday's story. Then ask youngsters whether they think the Little Red Hen was right to keep the bread to herself. If desired, have youngsters attach red hen cutouts to a graph to share their opinions.
Wednesday	Discuss with youngsters some unique fairy-tale character names, such as *Rumpelstiltskin* and *Cinderella.* Then lead the group in replacing the initial sound of each name with different letter sounds to create sillier names, such as Minderella, Finderella, and Binderella instead of Cinderella! ***Phonological awareness***	Read aloud *Wolf's Coming!* by Joe Kulka. In this story, the adult animals shoo the little ones inside because the wolf is on the way—but not because it is dangerous!
Thursday	Following a retelling of the *Jack and the Beanstalk* tale, discuss with youngsters how the magic beans grew into a beanstalk that reached up to the sky. Have youngsters help you plant beans in a large pot. Then invite each child to share what they would hope to find in the castle at the top of the beanstalk. ***Speaking to share an opinion***	Revisit yesterday's story. Have youngsters look at the illustrations and help them point out signs of the party preparations. Then have youngsters compare this book to stories, such as *Little Red Riding Hood,* in which the wolf is a dangerous creature.
Friday	Place two gold and several white egg cutouts in a bag. Seat youngsters in a circle. Have a youngster remove an egg. If the egg is white, he places it back in the bag. If the egg is gold, he says, "Honk, honk, honk, I'm the golden goose!" and sits in the middle of the circle with his egg. Play continues. When another child becomes the golden goose, she displaces the first goose, who puts his egg back in the bag and returns to the circle. ***Following rules to a game***	Read aloud *Gingerbread Baby* by Jan Brett. Have each youngster stuff, staple, and decorate a lunch-size paper bag so it resembles a gingerbread house for the gingerbread baby.

Art/Gross-Motor Skills

A Little Red Hen
(See directions on page 92.)

Gross Motor: Have youngsters pretend to plant magic beans, climb a beanstalk, and walk on fluffy clouds. Then prompt each student to run in place as if being chased by a giant, climb down the beanstalk, and chop the beanstalk down.

Wishing Wand
(See directions on page 92.)

Gross Motor: Have students move around the room using big Papa Bear steps, medium-size Mama Bear steps, and tiny Baby Bear steps.

The Magic Beanstalk
(See directions on page 92.)

Songs and Such for the Week

Three Pigs' Houses
(tune: "Short'nin' Bread")

The [first] little pig built a [straw] house,
[straw] house.
The [first] little pig built a house of
[straw].
(Repeat two times.)
Wolf came a-huffin'! Wolf came
a-puffin'!
Wolf tried to blow down that house of
[straw].

Continue with the following: *sticks, bricks*

Fairy-Tale Features

Bears and pigs and castles grand,
Boys with magic beans in hand,
Princesses, wolves so mean,
Candy houses, wicked queens.
They're in fairy tales, it's true.
Which tale can I tell to you?

A Girl Named Goldilocks
(tune: "The Itsy-Bitsy Spider")

A girl named Goldilocks
Was walking through the woods.
She saw the Three Bears' house
And thought it looked quite good!
She tasted all their porridge
And sat in all their chairs.
But Goldilocks was frightened
When she saw those three bears!

Art Activities

A Little Red Hen

Paint a paper plate red. Glue a red construction paper circle and two star cutouts to the plate to make a head and feet. Glue beak and eye cutouts to the hen. Then glue red craft feathers to the head and body as shown.

Wishing Wand

Drizzle glue over a star cutout and sprinkle glitter over the glue. When the glue is dry, attach the star to a paint stick. Then attach curling ribbon to the stick as shown.

The Magic Beanstalk

Have a child roll and crumple a long sheet of green tissue paper to create a stalk. Then encourage him to glue the stalk to a light blue sheet of construction paper. Have him paint large green leaves along each side of the stalk. Then invite him to stretch a few cotton balls so they resemble clouds and glue the clouds at the top of the stalk. Finally, have him trim a photograph of himself and glue it next to the stalk.

Groundhogs and Shadows

Centers for the Week

Discovery Center: Cover a table with white cloth or paper. Provide a supply of small blocks and a flashlight. A student builds a structure with the blocks and then shines the flashlight around the structure to change the size and shape of the shadow.

Math Center: Cut out a copy of the shapes on page 229. Make a black construction paper cutout of each shape. A student matches each silhouette to its corresponding shape.

Literacy Center: Provide white paper, stencils, and black crayons. A student traces a different shape onto several separate sheets of paper and then colors each shape black. She dictates or writes the name of each object on the paper. Then she binds the pages together and adds a title to create a book full of shadows.

Dramatic Play: Hang a white cloth or bedsheet in the room. Place an overhead projector on a table behind the sheet. A student stands between the projector and the sheet. Then he performs actions and the remaining youngsters observe his shadow on the sheet.

Play Dough Center: Provide a supply of brown play dough and washable markers. A student molds play dough into a mound (groundhog's burrow); then he uses a marker to draw a simple face on his index finger (groundhog). He pushes his finger up through the burrow so the groundhog can take a look around.

	Group Time	Literature
Monday	Take students outside to look for shadows. Help them discover that a shadow is made when an object blocks the sun's light. Then invite each child to have a little shadow fun, such as trying to run from her own shadow, hopping on a classmate's shadow when she is running, and shaking hands with a classmate's shadow without touching hands. ***Exploration, observation***	Read aloud *Guess Whose Shadow?* by Stephen R. Swinburne. In this book, a world full of shadows is portrayed with simple text and stunning photographs.
Tuesday	Help students understand that shadows can also be made with artificial light. Have several students stand between an overhead projector and a wall. Have each child move around and experiment with his shadow to make it bigger and smaller. Then turn the projector off. Have him describe what happened when you turned the light off and explain why. ***Experimentation, oral language, critical thinking***	Revisit yesterday's book. In turn, have students cover their eyes while a classmate sits between an overhead projector and a white sheet. Then have youngsters guess to whom the shadow belongs.
Wednesday	Obtain a flashlight, along with opaque objects (such as a book or piece of tagboard), translucent objects (waxed paper or a tissue), and transparent objects (plastic wrap or a scrap of used laminating film). Have students predict which objects they think will cast a shadow. Record their predictions on chart paper. Shine the flashlight on each object and then record the results. ***Making predictions, vocabulary***	Share with students *Shadows and Reflections* by Tana Hoban. This is a wordless picture book that contains an array of beautiful photographs depicting the shadows and reflections of everyday objects, people, and animals.
Thursday	Gather several familiar objects, such as a pair of scissors, a key, and a paper clip; then store them out of sight. One at a time, secretly place the objects on the screen of an overhead projector. Then have students try to guess the identity of each object by the shadow it makes on the wall. Provide clues if needed. ***Observation, activating prior knowledge***	Revisit yesterday's book and invite students to add words to the photos. Write youngsters' words on sticky notes and attach them to the pages of the book. Then flip through the pages and read aloud youngsters' additions.
Friday	Have a student leave the group and close his eyes. Have another child (the groundhog) get inside a box. Have the first child return to the group and try to guess the identity of the groundhog. When the groundhog is named, have him pop out of the box and shout, "Happy Groundhog Day!" ***Visual memory***	Read aloud *Go to Sleep, Groundhog!* by Judy Cox. Then gather a cutout for each holiday mentioned in the book. Use a calendar to help youngsters arrange the cutouts in order to represent the holidays throughout the year.

Art/Gross-Motor Skills

Groundhog Puppet
(See directions on page 96.)

Gross Motor: Take students outside on a sunny day and have them follow directions such as the following: *make your shadow jump up and down, hop on one foot, squat down low, stretch up high, run, gallop, skip,* and *twist.*

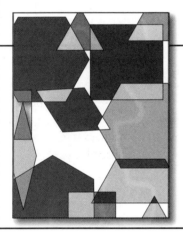

Geometric Shadows
(See directions on page 96.)

Gross Motor: Seat students in a circle. Invite a volunteer to be the shadow. The shadow walks around the outside of the circle and says, "Shadow," each time she taps a different classmate. When the shadow says, "Groundhog," the child who was tapped pops up and says, "My shadow looks like [shadow's name]!" Then the groundhog trades places with the shadow.

Portrait Shadow
(See directions on page 96.)

Songs and Such for the Week

My Shadow
(tune: "My Bonnie Lies Over the Ocean")

My shadow does everything I do.
My shadow always copies me.
My shadow does everything I do.
Just look at my shadow and see!

When the Sun's Out

When the sun's out,
Someone comes out
To play all day with me.
Always near me,
But can't hear me.
It's my shadow, yes sirree!

On This Groundhog Day
(tune: "Did You Ever See a Lassie?")

Will the groundhog see its shadow,
Its shadow, its shadow?
Will the groundhog see its shadow
On this Groundhog Day?

Art Activities

Groundhog Puppet

Glue brown tissue paper squares to the outside of a disposable cup and set it aside to dry. To make a groundhog, glue a medium-size brown pom-pom and a large brown pom-pom to one end of a jumbo craft stick. Embellish the groundhog with features as desired. After the glue is dry, push the end of the craft stick through a slit in the cup and pull the groundhog inside. To use the puppet, push up the craft stick so the groundhog pops out of its burrow.

Geometric Shadows

Using an overhead projector, project a shadow of an object onto a sheet of paper and trace the shadow. Then move the object and trace the shadow again, or trace a different object, so the tracing overlaps. Continue tracing shadows in the same way until a desired effect is achieved. Then use markers or crayons to color the different shapes created by the overlapping tracings.

Portrait Shadow

Trace a shape—such as a teddy bear, a car, or a fish—using a stencil. Make a second tracing near the first tracing. Use markers or crayons to decorate one of the tracings. Then color the remaining tracing black so it resembles the decorated object's shadow. Decorate the remainder of the page as desired.

Valentine's Day

Centers for the Week

Math Center: Label each of five plastic cups with a number from 1 to 5. Label a supply of heart stick puppets with corresponding numbers. A student matches the numbers by placing each heart puppet in the corresponding cup.

Art Center: Cut different sizes of heart shapes from sponges. Soak the sponges and squeeze out the excess water. A student colors the surface of a sponge with chalk pastels and then presses the heart onto a white paper bag. He embellishes the bag with glitter, sequins, or ribbon. The bags may be used as valentine mailboxes.

Play Dough Center: Provide red and pink play dough and a supply of lace. A child flattens a lump of play dough, places lace over the play dough, and then rolls over the lace with a rolling pin. Then she removes the lace to look at the impression left behind.

Gross-Motor Area: Laminate large construction paper heart cutouts and tape them to the floor to make a heart-shaped path. Youngsters first hop around the heart with two feet; then they hop around the heart on one foot.

Literacy Center: Program pairs of cupid and arrow cutouts (see patterns on page 230) with corresponding uppercase and lowercase letters. Students pair the cutouts by matching the letters.

Group Time	Literature

Monday

Have students sing the song shown as they pass a basket of personalized heart cutouts around the circle. When the song ends, the youngster holding the basket pulls out a heart and reads the name (with help). Then she identifies the classmate. **Name identification**

(tune: "This Old Man")
Valentine, you're so fine.
I'm so glad that you are mine.
With a heart for me and a heart just for you,
You can be my valentine too!

Read aloud *Mouse's First Valentine* by Lauren Thompson. There are many positional words in this story about a little mouse who follows his big sister as she makes a surprise valentine just for him!

Tuesday

Cut out a reduced copy of the cupid pattern on page 230. Place letter cards in a pocket chart. While youngsters cover their eyes, hide Cupid behind a card. Then have students uncover their eyes. A child guesses where Cupid is hiding by naming a letter and then checking behind the letter for the cutout. **Letter identification**

Reread yesterday's story. Give each student a heart-shaped cutout to use in a game of Simon Says. Use positional words from the story throughout the game. For example, say, "Simon says put your heart *over* your head."

Wednesday

Prepare several paper hearts in different sizes. Have volunteers stand in front of the class holding the hearts. Select a student to put her classmates in order from the smallest heart to the largest. Repeat the activity several times. **Ordering by size**

Read aloud *If You'll Be My Valentine* by Cynthia Rylant. In this book, a boy makes valentine cards with cheerful rhymes for his pets, his family members, his friends, and even his stuffed bear!

Thursday

Make pairs of cupid and arrow cutouts (see patterns on page 230), each pair a matching color. Have each child close his eyes and hold his hands behind his back. Walk behind students and place either a cupid or an arrow in each child's hands. On your signal, have little ones open their eyes and find the classmate with the matching-colored cutout. Once all matches have been made, invite each pair of partners to identify their color. **Color identification**

Reread yesterday's story. Give each child a card with the sentence starter "If you'll be my valentine, I'll…" Have each student name the recipient of her card and then complete the sentence as you write her words on the card. Encourage her to decorate the card as desired.

Friday

Lead students in singing the song shown as you post ten valentines. After singing, invite little ones to count the valentines with you. Then sing the song again, this time beginning with the number 10 and removing the cards appropriately. **Counting**

(tune: "Ten Little Indians")
One little, two little, three little valentines.
Four little, five little, six little valentines.
Seven little, eight little, nine little valentines.
Ten valentines to share!

Read *Valentine Mice!* by Bethany Roberts. To make his own valentine mouse, a youngster draws eyes and a nose on an upside-down heart cutout. Then he glues crinkled paper shreds to either side of the nose to make whiskers.

Art/Gross-Motor Skills

A Heart Full of Love
(See directions on page 100.)

I wanted to give you a valentine gift;
Something to give you a smile and a lift.
What should I give you?
I thought and I thought.
Something homemade
Or something store-bought?
A bouquet of flowers would really be sweet.
A box full of candy would be a nice treat.
I looked everywhere, below and above.
Your valentine gift is...

...a heart full of love!

Jenny

Gross Motor: Have students stand in a circle with one child in the center. Lead little ones in the song shown as they join hands and walk in a circle. During the third line, the child in the center points to a classmate. They switch places and repeat the song as time allows.

(tune: "The Farmer in the Dell")

Today is Valentine's Day!
Today is Valentine's Day!
Oh, won't you be my valentine?
Today is Valentine's Day!

Heart Art
(See directions on page 100.)

Gross Motor: Lead students in performing the song shown. Repeat the song using different actions.

(tune: "If You're Happy and You Know It")

If you'll be my valentine, [clap your hands].
If you'll be my valentine, [clap your hands].
If you'll be my valentine, then my smile will really shine.
If you'll be my valentine, [clap your hands].

Stuck on You
(See directions on page 100.)

Songs and Such for the Week

My Secret Valentine
(tune: "The Bear Went Over the Mountain")

I have a secret valentine.
I have a secret valentine.
I have a secret valentine.
I bet you don't know who.

My valentine is special.
My valentine is special.
My valentine is special.
My valentine is you!

Just for You

Valentine red,
Valentine sweet,
Valentine lacy,
Valentine neat,
Valentine pretty,
Valentine true,
Valentine special,
Just for you!

Lovely Little Valentines
(tune: "Twinkle, Twinkle, Little Star")

Lovely little valentines,
Sending wishes oh-so-fine.
To my family, to my friends,
Sending love that never ends!
Lovely little valentines,
Sending wishes oh-so-fine.

Art Activities

I wanted to give you a valentine gift:
Something to give you a smile and a lift.
What should I give you?
I thought and I thought.
Something homemade
Or something store-bought?
A bouquet of flowers would really be sweet.
A box full of candy would be a nice treat.
I looked everywhere, below and above.
Your valentine gift is...

...a heart full of love!

Jenny

A Heart Full of Love

Program the outside of a card with the poem shown, writing the final line inside the card. Also on the inside, make two handprints to form a heart. Once the paint is dry, add any desired decorations to the card.

Heart Art

Remove the backing from a 9" x 12" sheet of Con-Tact covering and place it on a table sticky side up. Place red, pink, and white tissue paper scraps over the Con-Tact covering, leaving an empty border. Place a second piece of Con-Tact covering over the first, sealing the edges. Fold a 9" x 12" sheet of construction paper in half and cut a half-heart shape on the fold. Discard the heart cutout. Unfold the paper and attach the heart-shaped frame to the tissue collage.

Stuck on You

To make this colorful window cling, attach a heart-shaped pattern to a table. Tape a transparency over the pattern. Trace the outline of the heart with tinted glue and then fill in the tracing completely. Place sequins, glitter, or other decorations on top of the glue. When the glue is dry, peel the heart from the transparency and attach it to a window.

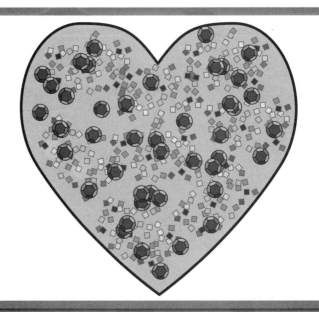

Terrific Teeth

Centers for the Week

Dramatic Play: Provide items such as white shirts (dentists' coats), surgical masks, a small flashlight, disposable gloves, paper-towel bibs, tongue depressors, empty dental floss containers, and a hand mirror. Display posters of the parts of a tooth and provide models of teeth if possible. Also provide stuffed animals to be patients.

Game Center: Take a close-up photograph of each child's face as he smiles broadly. Then laminate the photos and cut each photo in half between the student's nose and mouth. Place the photo pieces at a center. A child puts the pieces together to complete the picture of each smiling classmate.

Discovery Center: Laminate several tooth cutouts. Place the teeth at the center along with dry-erase markers and unused toothbrushes. A student makes marks on a tooth to represent plaque and tartar. Then she uses a toothbrush to brush away the stains.

Math Center: Draw a happy face or a sad face on each of several tooth cutouts. Make several dark marks on the unhappy teeth to represent cavities. A youngster sorts the teeth and then uses the teeth to make a simple pattern.

Art Center: Place large yellow tooth cutouts at the center. A youngster "cleans" a tooth by brushing white paint over the cutout. Then she sprinkles white glitter over the wet paint.

Group Time	Literature

Monday

Label a class supply of tooth cutouts with shapes; then place the teeth on the floor in a circle and have each student stand behind a tooth. Have youngsters march around the circle as you play music. When the music stops, call out the name of a shape. Students who are standing behind a tooth with that shape bring it to you (the dentist) for a checkup. Check for the correct shapes and then have little ones return the teeth to the circle. **Shape recognition**

Read aloud *Little Bear Brushes His Teeth* by Jutta Langreuter. In this book, Little Bear refuses to brush his teeth until Mama Bear finds a clever way to convince him.

Tuesday

Display three tooth cutouts in a row on a pocket chart. Recite the rhyme shown, removing one tooth after each appropriate line. **Subtraction**

Three little teeth were lined up in a row. Others were on top, but these were below.
One little tooth had some brushing to do. He fell out and then there were two.
One little tooth wanted tooth fairy fun. He fell out and then there was one.
One little tooth bit an apple core. Now there are no more!

Review yesterday's story and discuss the importance of brushing one's teeth. Invite youngsters to add motions as you recite the following rhyme.

Brush up and down; brush up and down. Then you brush them all around. Swish with water; then you spit. Now you've got the hang of it!

Wednesday

Label each column of a floor graph with a different color. Cut out a copy of the toothbrush card from page 231 for each child. Have each student color her toothbrush to match the one she has at home. Invite each youngster to identify the color of her toothbrush and place it in the correct column of the graph. Assist youngsters in comparing the columns. **Color identification, graphing**

Read aloud *Food for Healthy Teeth* by Helen Frost. The colorful photographs in this book encourage little ones to eat foods that help keep teeth healthy and strong.

Thursday

Cut from magazines and grocery store circulars pictures of things that are good or bad for teeth. Display happy and sad tooth cutouts. Then hold up the magazine pictures one at a time and have volunteers tape each picture on the appropriate tooth. **Sorting**

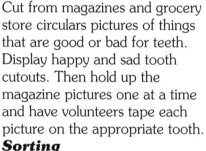

Revisit yesterday's book. Help students cut out pictures of healthy foods from grocery store circulars and glue the pictures on paper plates.

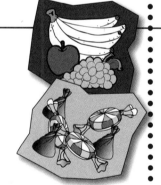

Friday

Pair students and give each pair a length of yarn. Have one partner hold up his hand with his palm facing his partner and his fingers together. Help the other child use the yarn to "floss" gently between the fingers of his partner. Point out that flossing between fingers is similar to flossing between teeth, and it is important to clean carefully between each tooth in our mouths. **Cooperation**

Read *The Mixed-Up Tooth Fairy* by Keith Faulkner. Assist little ones in decorating cardboard tubes with craft supplies to make tooth fairy puppets. Invite youngsters to move their puppets appropriately during a rereading of the book.

Art/Gross-Motor Skills

Healthy Tooth Mobile
(See directions on page 104.)

Gross Motor: Laminate a supersize toothbrush shape and attach it to your floor. Invite youngsters to carefully walk from one end of the brush to the other as if they were on a balance beam.

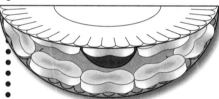

Cheery Chompers
(See directions on page 104.)

Gross Motor: Lead students in singing the song shown as they walk in a circle. Repeat the song using other types of movement.

(tune: "The Bear Went Over the Mountain")

We're [walking] to the dentist.
We're [walking] to the dentist.
We're [walking] to the dentist
So she can check our teeth!

Dental Design
(See directions on page 104.)

Songs and Such for the Week

Do Your Teeth Shine Bright?
(tune: "Do Your Ears Hang Low?")

Do your teeth shine bright?
Do you brush them every night?
Do you brush them in the morning?
Do you brush them all just right?
Do you brush them up and down?
Do you brush them all around?
Do your teeth shine bright?

Tooth Care

Taking good care of your teeth
Is oh so easy to do.
Brush them each day
Keep sugar away,
And visit your dentist too!

Brush Your Teeth
(tune: "Three Blind Mice")

Brush your teeth. Brush your teeth
Every day, every day.
Brush all your teeth both morning and night.
Brush them to make them all shiny and bright.
Brush them and they will be clean and so white.
Just brush your teeth.

Art Activities

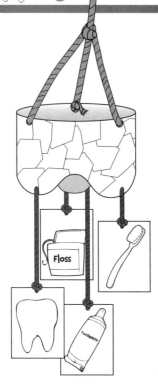

Healthy Tooth Mobile

Trim the top half from a two-liter soda bottle so the remaining portion resembles a tooth. Brush glue on the outside of the tooth and then press white tissue paper squares on the glue. Then use yarn to suspend dental health cards (see page 231) from the tooth. Finally, attach a yarn hanger to the mobile.

Cheery Chompers

To make this oversize mouth model, paint the front of a paper plate pink. Fold the plate in half so the painted side is inside and then glue a tongue cutout to the project as shown. Glue packing peanuts around the edge of the plate so they resemble teeth.

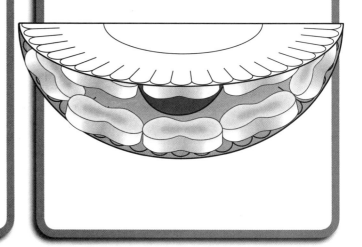

Dental Design

Dip an unused toothbrush into a pan of tempera paint. While holding the brush bristle-side down over a sheet of construction paper, gently pull your thumb across the bristles, spattering paint onto the paper. Repeat the process with different brushes and colors of paint until a desired effect is achieved.

Community Helpers

Centers for the Week

Block Center: Place several toy tools in the center. Youngsters pretend to be construction workers as they use the tools and blocks to create buildings.

Dramatic Play: For this grocery store–themed dramatic play, supply baskets, plastic fruits and vegetables, empty food boxes and bottles, and a toy cash register.

Literacy Center: Supply white paper, flesh-colored crayons, and adhesive bandages for this activity. A student traces her hand and arm on the paper. Then she colors the tracing. After putting a bandage on the tracing, she dictates or writes a story about a time she went to the doctor.

Discovery Center: Set out a variety of child-safe tools that are used by different community helpers. A student explores how the tools work and why the helpers need them.

Math Center: Glue fruit and vegetable cutouts to paper strips and place them at a center along with additional cutouts and strips, glue, and a grocery bag. A student copies a pattern or creates one of his own by gluing cutouts to a strip. Then he pretends to be a grocery store–cashier as he places his finished strip in the bag.

	Group Time	Literature
Monday	Glue a picture of a community helper to the front of a paper bag. (See the cards on page 232.) Inside the bag, place objects or pictures of objects that are used by the community helper along with some items that are not. Share with the students who the community helper pictured on the bag is and then show the objects inside the bag. Have the students determine which objects do not belong. ***Categorizing***	Read aloud *Guess Who?* by Margaret Miller. This fun book helps youngsters identify community helpers by asking questions such as "Who cuts your hair?" The silly options will make youngsters giggle before the book gives the reader the logical answer.
Tuesday	Give each child a community helper card attached to a hand cutout. (See the cards on page 232.) Describe a way a particular community helper gives a helping hand. For example, you might say, "I go to this person when my tooth hurts." Then have the youngsters with corresponding community helper cards hold their cutouts in the air. ***Listening*** 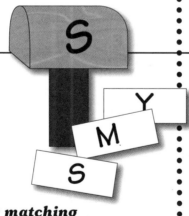	Revisit yesterday's book. Then have students name other community helpers as you write the names on a sheet of chart paper. Ask youngsters a question relating to one of the helpers, such as, "Who puts out fires?" Give students silly options, such as a dog, a tiger, or a teacher. Then prompt youngsters to give the correct answer.
Wednesday	Pretend to be a reporter wanting to get the scoop about your students' future ambitions. Hold a plastic microphone and invite each student to answer the question, "What would you like to be when you grow up?" ***Oral language***	Read aloud *Officer Buckle and Gloria* by Peggy Rathmann. Officer Buckle teaches students many important safety tips, and his dog, Gloria, adds her own entertaining demonstrations to the presentation.
Thursday	Create five mailbox cutouts and label each one with a different letter. Program a class supply of envelopes with the same letters and give one to each student. Have each child "deliver" his envelope by placing it on the appropriate mailbox. ***Letter matching***	Revisit yesterday's story. Write each student's dictated safety tip on a star cutout. Then have him glue the star to a sheet of paper and illustrate his tip. When everyone has finished their illustrations, bind the pages together to make a book.
Friday	Draw a supersize telephone keypad on a sheet of bulletin board paper and place it on your floor. Invite students to share times when it is necessary to call a community helper. Make a list of the responses on the board. Then have youngsters practice dialing 911 by jumping on the appropriate numbers on your supersize keypad. ***Number recognition***	Read aloud *Sally Goes to the Vet* by Stephen Huneck. Draw two circles on your board and label one "doctor" and the other "vet." Invite students to compare a trip they have taken to the doctor to Sally's trip to the vet. Write their thoughts in the appropriate circles.

Art/Gross-Motor Skills

Future Community Helpers
(See directions on page 108.)

Gross Motor: Place crumpled newspaper in several trash bags and tie each bag closed. Arrange chairs to make a rectangle (garbage truck) and place the bags nearby. Youngsters pretend they are garbage collectors as they enthusiastically toss the bags into the truck.

Cake Decorator
(See directions on page 108.)

Gross Motor: Place the hand cutouts from Tuesday's group-time activity in a basket. Choose a cutout from the basket and share it with the students. When given the signal, the students pretend to be doing the job of the chosen community helper.

Health Care Collage
(See directions on page 108.)

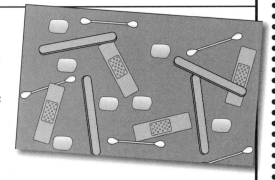

Songs and Such for the Week

Which Helper?
(tune: "The Farmer in the Dell")

Which helper in your town,
Which helper in your town
Will [put a fire out]?
Which helper in your town?

Continue with the following:
bring you all your mail, help you when you're sick, take care of your pet, keep you nice and safe, bake a nice big cake

We Need Helpers

A doctor helps when you are sick.
A firefighter comes oh so quick.
A postal worker brings your mail.
A police officer helps you without fail.
A vet takes care of every pet.
A pilot takes you in a jet.
We need these helpers, every one,
To keep our town both safe and fun!

In Our Community
(tune: "She'll Be Comin' Round the Mountain")

Oh, they always help in our community.
Oh, they always help in our community.
Firefighters, teachers too,
Police, and dentists all help you.
Oh, they always help in our community.

Art Activities

Future Community Helpers

Think of a community helper you would like to be. On a large body tracing, draw the clothes you would wear as that helper. Draw and cut out construction paper tools you would need and glue them to your tracing. Glue yarn (hair) to the tracing and draw any desired facial features. Display the finished project with a sign naming the community helper.

Cake Decorator

Cover a cereal box with white bulletin board paper so it resembles a cake. Write a message in the middle of the cake with a brightly colored marker. Use assorted materials—such as paper scraps, garland, ribbon, pom-poms, and confetti—to decorate the rest of the cake.

Happy Birthday

Health Care Collage

Spotlight workers in health care with this simple collage. Gather a variety of health care collage items, such as cotton balls, tongue depressors, cotton swabs, bandages, and gauze. Glue items to a sheet of brightly colored construction paper until a desired effect is achieved.

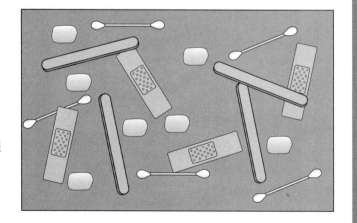

Dr. Seuss

Centers for the Week

Literacy Center: For each child, provide two squares of paper stapled at the top. Label the front square "Fun-in-a-Box," referring to the game in *The Cat in the Hat*. Place these minibooklets at the center. A child draws inside her minibooklet a picture of something she thinks is fun. Then she tells about her picture as an adult writes her words under her drawing.

Math Center: Make a supply of white, green, red, and blue fish in a variety of sizes so they resemble the fish from the story *One Fish, Two Fish, Red Fish, Blue Fish*. Place the fish at the center. Encourage youngsters to sort and arrange the fish in patterns as desired.

Play Dough Center: Laminate several white top hat cutouts and place them at the center along with red play dough. Students roll the play dough between their hands into ropelike shapes. Then they place the play dough on a hat so it resembles the stripes on the cat's hat in *The Cat in the Hat*.

Literacy Center: Prepare five green egg-shaped and five green ham-shaped cutouts. Attach to each egg cutout a card from each rhyming pair on a copy of page 233. Then attach to each ham cutout the rhyming cards from each pair. Place the shapes facedown. In turn, each student flips over a ham and an egg. She removes the shapes if the pictures rhyme. If they do not, she turns the shapes back over.

Block Center: Attach a turtle cutout to each of several blocks and place them in the center along with the story "Yertle the Turtle" from *Yertle the Turtle and Other Stories*. Encourage youngsters to stack the turtle blocks so they resemble the stack of turtles in the story. Then prompt students to knock down the stack.

Group Time	Literature

Monday

Place an object in a red box and then place a lid on the box. Tell students you are going to play a game similar to Fun-in-the-Box in *The Cat in the Hat*. Then give clues about the object and encourage students to guess what it might be. Continue until a youngster names the object. Then reveal the item with great fanfare. ***Listening for information, critical thinking***

Read aloud *The Cat in the Hat*. This is the story of a brother and sister who are stuck in the house on a cold rainy day with nothing to do until the Cat in the Hat bursts through the door and turns the day into a chaotic adventure!

Tuesday

Collect pairs of rhyming objects. Place one object from each pair in the red box from yesterday's activity. Have her choose an object and then find the rhyming object in the box. Then lead students in reciting the chant shown, substituting the appropriate words where indicated. ***Rhyming, vocabulary***

Yes, [sock] rhymes with [rock];
I am quite sure of that!
It's fun to find rhymes,
My dear Cat in the Hat!

Revisit yesterday's story. Have students draw a picture of something fun they could do on a rainy day; then have them dictate or write about their pictures.

Wednesday

Draw on a large sheet of paper two intersecting fishbowls. Provide red and blue fish cutouts along with some cutouts that include both colors. Have students place the fish on the matching bowl or in the center as appropriate. ***Organizing data***

Red   Blue

Read aloud *One Fish, Two Fish, Red Fish, Blue Fish*. This zany adventure starts out with a few simple fish and then becomes filled with silly creatures, rhyming words, and opposites.

Thursday

Program chart paper with the phrase "I do not like…" Invite students to name foods they do not like as you write their words on the paper. Lead a discussion to find out if youngsters have *ever* refused to eat something because of how it looked or smelled. Then find out if they tasted the food and what they thought. ***Oral language, print awareness***

Revisit yesterday's story. Have students point out rhyming words and opposites on selected pages as you read. Record the words on separate sheets of chart paper.

Friday

Make a ballot box and display it in your large-group area along with the Dr. Seuss books you have read aloud in class. Prepare cutouts—such as a hat, a fish, and an egg—to represent each book. Briefly review the books with your youngsters and then prompt each child to choose a cutout that represents his favorite book. After each child has voted, count the cutouts and have youngsters compare the final numbers. ***Counting, comparing amounts***

Read aloud *Green Eggs and Ham*. Have students sample plain eggs and eggs tinted with green food coloring. Then ask each child if the eggs taste different.

Art/Gross-Motor Skills

The Cat's Hat
(See directions on page 112.)

Gross Motor: Mark a starting line and a finish line in an open area. Place a variety of soft objects near the starting line. Encourage a youngster to balance an object on his head, much like the Cat in the Hat does, and then walk to the finish line.

One Fish, Two Fish
(See directions on page 112.)

Gross Motor: Put a twist on the game Duck, Duck, Goose. Ask a volunteer to wear a top hat (see "The Cat's Hat" on page 112) and pretend to be the Cat in the Hat. The cat walks around the outside of a circle of classmates and says "Thing 1" each time he taps a different classmate. When the cat says "Thing 2," the child who was tapped chases the cat around the circle to try to catch him. Then "Thing 2" becomes the Cat in the Hat.

Green Eggs and Ham
(See directions on page 112.)

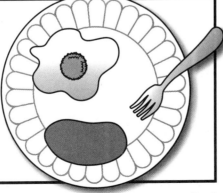

Songs and Such for the Week

Do You Know a Cat?
(tune: "Do Your Ears Hang Low?")

Do you know a cat
In a very tall striped hat?
An umbrella on his arm,
He is always full of charm!
He is silly as can be.
If you meet him, you will see.
Do you know this cat?

Seuss at Storytime

A book by Dr. Seuss, you say?
Dr. Seuss? Hooray! Hooray!
His books are full of silly rhymes.
Let's read one for storytime!

Green Eggs and Ham
(tune: "Old MacDonald Had a Farm")

Have you tried green eggs and ham?
Yum, yum, yum, yum, yum!
The favorite food of Sam-I-Am.
Yum, yum, yum, yum, yum!
With a mouse in a house
And a fox in a box,
Eat them here.
Eat them there.
Eat them, eat them anywhere!
Have you tried green eggs and ham?
Yum, yum, yum, yum, yum!

Art Activities

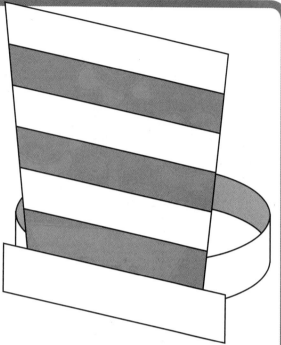

The Cat's Hat

Cut a hat shape from white poster board so it resembles the hat of the Cat in the Hat. Cut a supply of red construction paper strips. Glue the strips to form horizontal stripes on the hat cutout. After the glue is dry, trim any paper extending beyond the edge of the cutout; then staple the cutout to a poster board headband. Size the headband appropriately, and staple it in place.

One Fish, Two Fish

Lightly tint a container of white corn syrup with blue food coloring. Cut out a white construction paper fishbowl along with a red and a blue construction paper fish. Place the fishbowl on a sheet of waxed paper; then paint the fishbowl with the corn syrup. Place the fish in the wet syrup. Allow several days for the project to dry; then remove the fish bowl from the waxed paper.

Green Eggs and Ham

Mix together equal amounts of shaving cream and glue. Place dollops of the mixture on a paper plate so it resembles an egg white. Then place a large green pom-pom in the center of the mixture so it resembles a green yolk. Glue a plastic fork and a ham shape cut from green craft foam to the plate. Then allow the project to dry for several days.

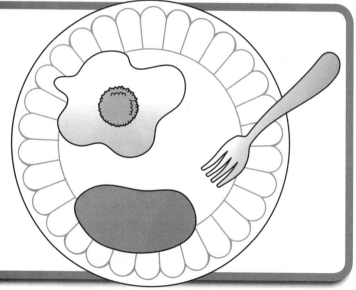

Dinosaurs

Centers for the Week

Play Dough Center: Post dinosaur pictures in your play dough center. Set out various colors of play dough along with plastic cutting and molding tools. A student creates dinosaur sculptures.

Math Center: Cut out ten construction paper copies of the dinosaur patterns on page 234. Sort the dinosaurs by type, and number each set from 1 to 10. Then scramble the dinosaurs and place them at a center. A child sorts the dinosaurs and arranges each set in a row from 1 to 10.

Block Center: Place a supply of plastic dinosaurs in the block center. A student uses the blocks to build a landscape for the dinosaurs.

Sensory Table: Laminate and puzzle-cut enlarged copies of the dinosaur patterns on page 234. Then nestle the pieces in your sand table. Provide brushes, tweezers, and other tools. A child pretends to be a paleontologist as he uses the tools to uncover the pieces. When he finds all the pieces, he reassembles each dinosaur.

Art Center: Enlarge and cut out copies of the dinosaur patterns on page 234. Attach several textured materials to a tabletop and give students access to the patterns and crayons. A student chooses a dinosaur and places it on a textured material. Then she colors over the dinosaur to create the appearance of textured skin.

Group Time	Literature
Monday Display a large dinosaur cutout divided into three sections. Invite students to share things they know about dinosaurs while you record their ideas in the first section. In the second section, record things the students would like to learn about dinosaurs. At the end of the dinosaur unit, record in the remaining section things your little ones learned about dinosaurs. **Prior knowledge, print awareness**	Read aloud *If the Dinosaurs Came Back* by Bernard Most. A boy imagines all the things dinosaurs might do if they came back. Best of all, he imagines dinosaurs would make great pets!
Tuesday Hide a class supply of plastic eggs around the room. Have each child search for an egg and, when he finds one, bring it back to your large-group area. Place the eggs in a container lined with crinkle paper so they resemble eggs in a nest. Then explain to students that dinosaurs hatched from eggs as chickens do. Display the nest in your room during your dinosaur unit. **Investigating living things**	Revisit yesterday's story. Ask students if they think dinosaurs would make good pets or bad pets, encouraging them to give the reasoning behind their opinions. Then help students make a simple chart to showcase their opinions.
Wednesday Make copies of the dinosaur patterns on page 234 in three different sizes and cut out the dinosaurs. Place three plastic hoops labeled "small," "medium," and "large" on the floor. Give each student a dinosaur and have him place it in the correct hoop. **Sorting**	Read aloud *Harry and the Bucketful of Dinosaurs* by Ian Whybrow. When Harry finds a bucketful of toy dinosaurs, the dinosaurs quickly become his favorite possessions. Then one day, Harry loses his dinosaurs!
Thursday Make copies of the dinosaur patterns on page 234 in four different colors. Cut out the dinosaurs and place them in a bag. Place corresponding color cards along the bottom of your pocket chart. Explain that no one knows what colors the dinosaurs were. Then have each student choose a dinosaur and place it above the appropriate color card. **Graphing, colors**	Reread yesterday's story. Then place the book and a bucket of plastic dinosaurs at a center for youngsters to explore.
Friday Write on a sheet of chart paper "Daisy Dinosaur Goes to School." Have students explain what they think happened when Daisy went to school. Write their words on the chart to create a story. **Writing**	Read aloud *Edwina, The Dinosaur Who Didn't Know She Was Extinct* by Mo Willems. Then have a snack of chocolate chip cookies, just like Edwina the dinosaur likes to make!

Art/Gross-Motor Skills

All Cracked Up
(See directions on page 116.)

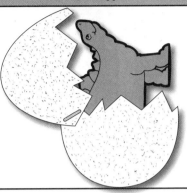

Gross Motor: Have each student imagine she is a tyrannosaurus. Instruct her to stamp around the room. When you ring a bell, prompt all the dinosaurs to roar. Then prompt the dinosaurs to resume their stamping. Repeat the process with students pretending to be both small fast dinosaurs and then large slow dinosaurs.

"Shape-a-saurus"
(See directions on page 116.)

Gross Motor: Cut out large dinosaur footprints and attach them to your floor. Tell the class that a dinosaur has been to the room and left footprints everywhere! Have the students jump over the prints, step on the prints, and dance around the prints.

Dino Headband
(See directions on page 116.)

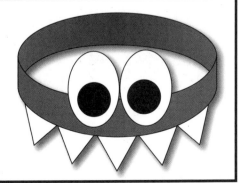

Songs and Such for the Week

If You're a Dinosaur
(tune: "If You're Happy and You Know It")

If you're a dinosaur, [show your claws].
If you're a dinosaur, [show your claws].
If you're a dinosaur,
Give a great big dino roar!
If you're a dinosaur, [show your claws].

Continue with the following: *swing your tail, stomp your feet, take a nap*

I Love Dinosaurs

Some were big and some were small.
Me? I want to learn them all.
Some ate plants and some ate meat.
Me? I think they all are neat!
Some used two legs, some used four.
Me? I love all dinosaurs!

Diggin' Up Bones
(tune: "Pawpaw Patch")

Diggin' up bones and puttin' them
   together,
Diggin' up bones and puttin' them
   together,
Diggin' up bones and puttin' them
   together
Helps us learn about dinosaurs!

Art Activities

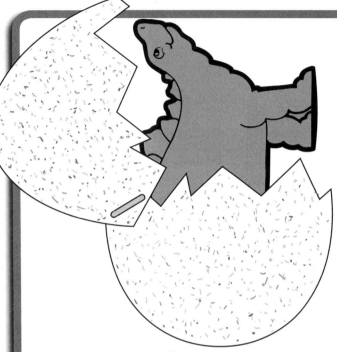

All Cracked Up

Put a few drops of food coloring in a spray bottle filled with water. Repeat using a different color for each of several bottles. Choose a bottle and spray the colored water on an egg cutout. Repeat with two more colors. When the egg is dry, puzzle-cut the egg in half and then staple the pieces as shown. Attach a dinosaur cutout (see page 234) to the back of the egg so it appears in the opening.

"Shape-a-saurus"

Attach shape cutouts to a sheet of paper to create a desired dinosaur. Then use markers to add eyes and other desired features to the project.

Dino Headband

Glue eye cutouts to the top of a headband as shown. Then glue triangle cutouts around the headband so they resemble dinosaur teeth. When the glue is dry, size the headband appropriately.

St. Patrick's Day

Centers for the Week

Literacy Center: Place in the center a supply of yellow circle cutouts (gold coins) labeled with the letter *G*. Also provide glue, a large plastic container, and gold glitter. A child uses glue to trace the *G* on a piece of gold, places the gold in the container, and sprinkles glitter over the glue. After gently shaking off the excess glitter, he places the gold aside to dry and then repeats the activity with a new piece of gold.

Sensory Table: Bury several yellow craft foam coins in your sand table. Students use sifters to locate the pieces of gold. Then they place the gold coins in a black plastic pot.

Math Center: Label shamrock cutouts (see the patterns on page 235) with numbers, letters, and a variety of other symbols. Then attach the shamrocks to a sheet of poster board. Place the poster board at a center along with a supply of craft foam coins. A child places a coin on each shamrock that shows a number.

Art Center: Place a variety of green craft items at the center along with green construction paper and glue. A youngster glues green items on a sheet of construction paper to make a collage.

Fine-Motor Area: Place laminated tagboard leprechauns (see the patterns on page 236) in the center along with colorful plastic clothespins. Attach clothespins to each leprechaun. Now each leprechaun has found his rainbow!

	Group Time	Literature
Monday	Label shamrock cutouts with numbers (pattern on page 235). Then tape each shamrock to a child's shirt. Help each youngster identify her number. Then have her find a corresponding number of small objects in the room. When she brings her objects back to the group, have students count the objects aloud. ***Making sets***	Read aloud *Jack and the Leprechaun* by Ivan Robertson. In this story, Jack the mouse travels to Ireland to celebrate St. Patrick's Day with his cousins. He ends up learning all about the holiday and even encounters a mischievous leprechaun.
Tuesday	Label gold cutouts with different shapes and place them in a black container (pot) along with a few gold cutouts labeled with shamrocks. Play a recording of music as youngsters pass the pot of gold around the circle. Stop the music and have the child with the pot close her eyes, pull out a piece of gold, and name the shape. If a piece of gold with a shamrock is drawn, all students stand up and dance a jig. ***Identifying shapes***	In advance, place a class supply of gold foil–wrapped chocolate coins in a leprechaun hat (available at party supply stores). Reread yesterday's story. Pass the hat to a student and invite him to share his favorite part of the story. When he finishes sharing, he takes a chocolate coin and passes the hat to another child. Continue until each child has a coin.
Wednesday	Program each of five leprechaun cutouts (patterns on page 236) with a different weather symbol. Have a child choose a leprechaun. Then lead students in singing the song below, inserting the type of weather. ***Identifying weather*** (tune: "London Bridge") Leprechaun, come out to play, Out to play, out to play. Leprechaun, come out to play On this [sunny] day.	Read aloud *It's St. Patrick's Day!* by Rebecca Gómez. This book uses simple verse and quaint illustrations to show a variety of St. Patrick's Day traditions.
Thursday	Make a large rainbow cutout and place it on your floor. Name a color and then invite a volunteer to find a small object of that color in the room. Encourage her to place the object on the appropriate arc on the rainbow. Continue in the same way with each youngster. ***Matching colors***	Revisit yesterday's book. Have students recall some of the ways the children in the book celebrate the holiday. Then have students add blue food coloring to glasses of lemonade to make a green St. Patrick's Day drink!
Friday	Attach green shamrock cutouts (patterns on page 235) to a length of adding machine tape. Then measure youngsters with the shamrock tape and write their height in shamrocks on a sheet of chart paper. When each youngster has been measured, have students compare the numbers. ***Measurement***	Read aloud *A Rainbow of My Own* by Don Freeman. Invite youngsters to tell you what they would do if they had a rainbow of their very own.

Art/Gross-Motor Skills

Shining Shamrocks
(See directions on page 120.)

Gross Motor: Seat youngsters in a circle. Play traditional Irish step music as you walk around the circle with a plastic leprechaun hat (available at party supply stores). When you place the hat on a child's head, she stands up and dances a jig with you. When you remove the hat, she sits back down and you place the hat on another child's head. Continue until all students have danced a jig.

Lovely Leprechauns
(See directions on page 120.)

Gross Motor: Have students hold hands. Place a rainbow and pot of gold cutout in the middle of the circle. As a class, circle the rainbow and sing the song below. Between each repetition, select a child to make a wish.

(tune: "Ring Around the Rosie")

Ring around the rainbow,
The lucky, lucky rainbow.
I found a pot of gold.
Let's make a wish!

Rainbow Art
(See directions on page 120.)

Songs and Such for the Week

St. Patrick's Day, Oh!
(tune: "Bingo")

Today's a day to wear some green,
For it's St. Patrick's Day, oh!
Look for your green clothes.
Get out your green clothes.
Put on your green clothes
For it's St. Patrick's Day, oh!

A Lucky Clover

I spy a clover patch,
As green as can be.
Most of the clover
Has leaves of three.
I spy the lucky one,
Not like the rest.
This one has *four* leaves,
I think it's the best!

A Magic Leprechaun
(tune: "If You're Happy and You Know It")

If I ever catch a magic leprechaun,
If I ever catch a magic leprechaun,
I will get a good tight hold
And ask him where he hides his gold.
I'll be lucky if I catch a leprechaun!

Art Activities

Shining Shamrocks

Place a small dollop each of yellow and of blue fingerpaint on a sheet of fingerpaint paper. Blend the colors together to paint the paper. While the paint is still wet, sprinkle green glitter and sequins on top. Once the paint dries, cut a shamrock shape from the paper.

Lovely Leprechauns

In advance, dye rotini pasta orange. Draw a face on a construction paper circle. Then glue orange yarn to the circle so it resembles hair. Glue a green hat cutout to the head and then attach a shamrock cutout to the hat. Finally, glue dyed rotini pasta on the resulting leprechaun face to make a beard.

Rainbow Art

Tape six crayons (red, orange, yellow, green, blue, and purple) together in a bunch. To create rainbow artwork, use the crayons to draw designs on oversize paper.

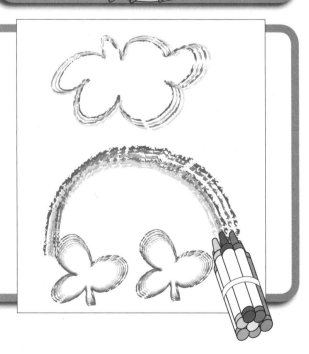

Grocery Store

Centers for the Week

Game Center: Enlarge the food cards on page 237; then make a copy. Color and cut out the cards. Then puzzle-cut each card and place the puzzles at the center. A child puts the puzzles together to show six healthy foods to buy at the grocery store.

Literacy Center: Label the cups of a clean, sterilized egg carton with 12 different uppercase letters. Then write each matching lowercase letter on an individual plastic egg. A student looks at the letters and places each egg in the matching cup.

Math Center: Label each of three pieces of paper "Freezer," "Cupboard," or "Refrigerator." If desired, add picture clues to each label. Place the papers at a center along with grocery store circulars. A child cuts a picture from the circular and places it on the paper to show where she would store the food item.

Fine-Motor Area: Set out a supply of colorful ring cereal and shoelaces. Encourage youngsters to thread the same color of cereal on different shoelaces. For an added challenge, encourage youngsters to make a pattern with two different cereal colors.

Dramatic Play: For this grocery store center, supply a broom, a mop, empty food boxes, aprons, a cash register, and play money. Students act out the different jobs of grocery store workers.

	Group Time	Literature

Monday

Give each child a cup of cereal and a paper with two circles (bowls). Name a number between zero and five and have youngsters place the same number of cereal pieces on a bowl. Repeat this step for the second bowl. Then instruct youngsters to point to the bowl with more pieces and the one with fewer pieces. ***Comparing sets***

Read aloud *To Market, To Market* by Anne Miranda. Students are sure to enjoy how this simple trip to the market turns into quite a mess!

Tuesday

Lead students in singing the song shown as they pass a paper grocery bag around the circle. At the end of the song, have the child holding the bag name a type of fruit. Repeat the activity several times, prompting students to identify meats, vegetables, and dairy products. **Categorizing**

(tune: "The Farmer in the Dell")

I'm shopping for some [fruit].
I'm shopping for some [fruit].
Good food will help me grow.
I'm shopping for some [fruit].

Revisit yesterday's story. Call attention to the bold red text on the pages. Then invite youngsters, in turn, to point to the part of the illustration on a page that matches the red text or give an explanation of how the text matches the illustration as a whole.

Wednesday

Place a variety of food cutouts in a basket. Have a student choose and identify a food. Have students discuss whether they like to eat this food. Then discuss whether eating this food is a healthy choice. ***Oral language, making decisions***

Read aloud *I Shop With My Daddy* by Grace Maccarone. Daddy takes his daughter on a shopping trip and guides her to place healthy items in the cart.

Thursday

Have a student name a food that begins with /ă/, giving the student hints if needed. Then ask a different volunteer to name a food that begins with /b/. Continue naming foods in this manner all the way to /z/! ***Phonological awareness***

Reread yesterday's story. Have youngsters share their own shopping experiences with the class.

Friday

Title a sheet of chart paper "Grocery List." Have students tell you items to write on the list, prompting them to make wise choices and include a variety of different foods to make balanced meals. ***Oral language***

Read aloud *Healthy Snacks* by Mari C. Schuh. Discuss with youngsters different healthy snacks they have tasted. Invite volunteers to share whether they liked or disliked each snack.

Art/Gross-Motor Skills

Shopping Cart
(See directions on page 124.)

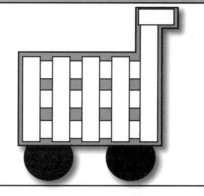

Gross Motor: Have youngsters push imaginary shopping carts around the room, encouraging them to stop at pretend locations, such as the dairy case or the canned goods aisle, to place specific items in their carts.

Funny Faces
(See directions on page 124.)

Gross Motor: Show a picture of a healthy or an unhealthy snack. If the food is a healthy snack, have youngsters make big muscles to show that they are strong. If the picture shows an unhealthy snack, have students melt to the floor in lethargy.

Pepper Prints
(See directions on page 124.)

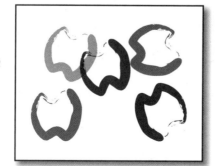

Songs and Such for the Week

To the Grocery Store
(tune: "The Mulberry Bush")

We're going to the grocery store,
The grocery store, the grocery store.
We're going to the grocery store,
So early in the morning.
We want to buy [some cereal],
[Some cereal, some cereal].
We want to buy [some cereal],
So early in the morning.

Continue with other food items.

It's Time to Buy Food

It's time to buy food.
I need bread, milk, and more.
Now where will I go?
To the grocery store!
I push a big cart
Right down every aisle.
I see what I want,
So I get it and smile.
I buy more and more,
'Til the cart's piled high!
I pay for my food
And then say goodbye!

Making a List
(tune: "Santa Claus Is Comin' to Town")

You must make a list
For food and drinks too.
Write out a list and take it with you
When shopping at the grocery store.

Art Activities

Shopping Cart

Glue strips of paper to a sheet of construction paper to make the basket and handle of a shopping cart as shown. Then cut around the perimeter of the cart. Glue two circle cutouts (wheels) at the bottom to complete the cart.

Funny Faces

Cut pictures from grocery store circulars and then attach the pictures to a paper plate so they resemble facial features. Then continue to cut out more food-related items to make hair for this funny face.

Pepper Prints

Cut yellow, red, and green peppers in half. Place the halves next to coordinating containers of tempera paint. A child presses a pepper half in the matching paint and then makes a print on a sheet of paper. He continues in the same way with other peppers and colors of paint.

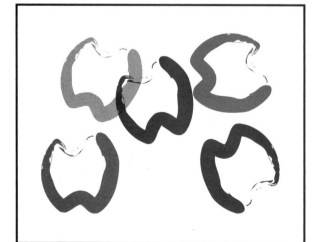

Nursery Rhymes

Centers for the Week

Literacy Center: Choose a short nursery rhyme and write it on each of two sets of sentence strips. Place one set of strips in your pocket chart, leaving a blank row beneath each line. Cut apart the words in the second set of strips. Youngsters place each word below the matching word in the chart.

Math Center: Prepare ten simple cat cutouts. Place them at the center along with ten jumbled pairs of mittens. A child chooses a mitten and finds the matching mitten. Then he places the mittens on a cat.

Discovery Center: Create Humpty Dumpty's Repair Shop by placing items in the center that can be taken apart and put back together, such as puzzles, building toys, and manipulatives. Student pairs work together to take items apart and then "repair" them by putting them back together again.

Gross-Motor Area: Attach short, medium, and tall candle cutouts to blocks in corresponding sizes so they resemble candlesticks. Place the blocks in the center. A child stands the small candlestick in an open area. Then she jumps over the candlestick, just as Jack did! She repeats the process with the medium and tall candlesticks.

Game Center: Little Boy Blue isn't under this haystack—but other objects might be! Place a haystack cutout at a center along with several picture cards. Two youngsters visit the center. One youngster studies the cards and then covers her eyes. The remaining youngster places a card under the haystack. Then his partner uncovers her eyes and guesses which picture card is missing.

	Group Time	Literature
Monday	Read the rhyme "Old King Cole" to the class. Explain that when the king is "calling for" his pipe, his bowl, and his fiddlers, it means that he is demanding these things. Go around the circle and invite students to share what they would call for if they were kings or queens. ***Oral language***	Read aloud *The Itsy Bitsy Spider* by Iza Trapani. This familiar rhyme gets a new twist by following the little spider as it climbs up other items as well as the waterspout.
Tuesday	Read aloud the rhyme "Little Bo Peep." Then place colorful sheep cutouts on the floor. Have students hide their eyes as you remove one or more sheep. Then encourage youngsters to open their eyes and name the color(s) of the sheep that are lost. ***Visual memory***	Have each child make a spider stick puppet. Then reread yesterday's story and have students move their puppets to match the spider's actions.
Wednesday	Read aloud the rhyme "Little Boy Blue." Point out that he falls asleep *under* the haystack. Then place a felt haystack cutout on your flannelboard. Place a cutout of a boy, readied for flannelboard use, under the haystack. Call out other positional words and ask volunteers to position Little Boy Blue to match. ***Positional words***	Read aloud *Big Fat Hen* by Keith Baker. This book presents the traditional rhyme "One, Two, Buckle My Shoe" with *eye-catching* illustrations.
Thursday	Prepare circle cutouts labeled with different emotions and attach them to your board. Describe part of a nursery rhyme. For example, you might say, "A spider sat down next to Miss Muffet" or "Humpty Dumpty fell off a wall." Then give a child a special pointer and have her use it to point to the cutout that shows that character's emotion. ***Identifying emotions***	Read aloud yesterday's story, pausing throughout the story to have youngsters count the sets of items on each page.
Friday	After students are familiar with several nursery rhymes, play What's My Name? Give students a character description from a nursery rhyme and have them name the character. For example, you might say, "I live in a big brown shoe. I have lots of children. Who am I?" ***Comprehension, recall***	Read aloud *Mary Had a Little Lamb* by Iza Trapani. Then have each youngster fingerpaint a lamb cutout brown to show how messy and muddy the lamb is at the end of the story.

Jack's Candlestick
(See directions on page 128.)

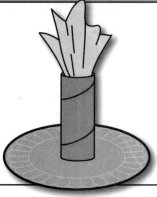

Gross Motor: Read aloud the rhyme "Mary, Mary, Quite Contrary." Choose a child to be Mary and have the remaining youngsters curl up into balls, pretending to be seeds. As Mary "waters" the seeds with an empty watering can, instruct the little ones to pretend to grow into tall flowers.

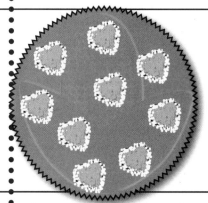

The Queen's Tarts
(See directions on page 128.)

Gross Motor: Have students hold the edge of a parachute or bedsheet. Then lead them in singing "Ring Around the Rosie" as they walk in a circle. When you reach the line "We all fall down," have youngsters sit, bringing the parachute over their heads and then behind them.

Dish and Spoon
(See directions on page 128.)

Humpty Dumpty
(tune: "I'm a Little Teapot")

I'm an egg and Humpty is my name.
Climbing up high is my favorite game.
When I try to sit on a brick wall,
I just wobble; then I fall!

Who's in Nursery Rhymes?

Who sits in the corner?
　Little Jack Horner.
Who loses her sheep?
　Little Bo Peep.
Who goes to the cupboard?
　Old Mother Hubbard.
Who can't find their mittens?
　The three little kittens.
Who makes some tarts?
　The Queen of Hearts.

Where Are the Sheep?
(tune: "If You're Happy and You Know It")

Little Bo can't find her missing sheep.
　(Baa, baa!)
Little Bo can't find her missing sheep.
　(Baa, baa!)
She has looked high and low.
Things look sad for Little Bo.
Will you please help her find her
　missing sheep? (Baa, baa!)

Art Activities

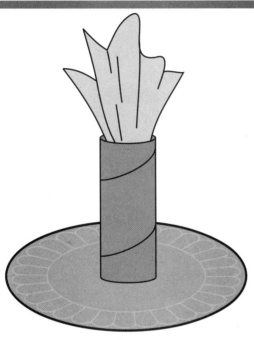

Jack's Candlestick

Paint a small cardboard tube and a small paper plate in desired colors. Once the paint is dry, tape the tube to the center of the plate in an upright position. Glue orange or yellow tissue paper to the top of the tube so it resembles a flame. Then practice jumping over the candlestick!

The Queen's Tarts

Cut out a circle using decorative-edged scissors so it resembles a tart. Place a mixture of glue and red paint in a shallow container. Press a heart-shaped sponge in the mixture and then make prints on the tart. Before the mixture dries, sprinkle red glitter over the prints.

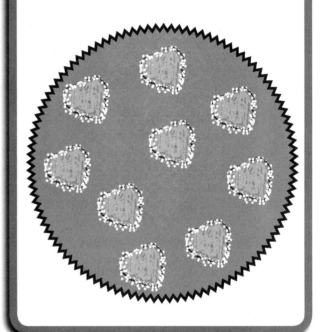

Dish and Spoon

Draw a face on a paper plate. Then attach arm cutouts to the plate. Use fabric scraps and craft materials to embellish the plate as desired. With a permanent marker, draw a face on a plastic spoon. Attach arm cutouts to the spoon. Attach the spoon and plate to each other so it appears as if they are holding hands.

Baby Animals

Centers for the Week

Literacy Center: Provide a picture of a dog and a picture of a puppy. Also provide pictures of objects with names that begin with the /d/ and /p/ sounds. A student chooses a picture of an object and says the object's name. He places the object picture on the picture of the animal that has the same beginning sound.

Literacy Center: For each child, program a sheet of paper with the words "If my mom is a _____, then I must be a _____." Provide a variety of baby animal cutouts. A child glues an animal cutout to her paper and adds scenery as desired. She names the type of animal and the term used for its offspring as you write her words in the appropriate blanks.

Math Center: Make 20 duckling cutouts using the pattern on page 238. Also make one enlarged mother duck cutout. Place the ducks at the center along with number cards from 1 to 20. A child chooses a card and names the number. Then she places the corresponding number of ducks in a row behind the mother duck.

Sensory Table: Fill your sensory table with nest-building materials, such as feathers, hay, twigs, leaves, cotton batting, and yarn. Also provide a supply of plastic eggs along with large yellow pom-poms decorated with beaks and eyes so they resemble chicks.

Play Dough Center: Provide several large laminated animal cutouts. Also provide corresponding animal cookie cutters and several different colors of play dough. Students press the cookie cutters into the play dough, remove the baby animal cutouts, and then place them on the appropriate mother.

	Group Time	Literature
Monday	Attach enlarged copies of the animal patterns from page 238 to a chart labeled as shown. Place smaller copies of the animal patterns in a bag. Have a volunteer pick an animal from the bag and attach it to the chart opposite its mother. Have students chant, "Mommy [duck], mommy [duck], what's your baby called?" Respond by saying, "My baby is called a [duckling]." *Oral language, vocabulary*	Read aloud *Baby Animals Learn* by Pamela Chanko. In this book, simple text and real-life photographs show the reader how a variety of baby animals learn to walk, climb, swim, play, groom, and more.
Tuesday	Have students pretend to be asleep. Say, "Wake up little [puppies]! It's time to play!" Have youngsters romp about the room as if they were puppies. Then say, "Go to sleep little [puppies]! It's time for a nap!" and have them lay back down. Continue in the same manner, substituting different animal names in the commands. *Role-playing, following directions*	Reread yesterday's storytime selection. As you read, have students imitate each animal's actions.
Wednesday	Write riddles, similar to the one shown, on chart paper. Tell students to listen carefully as you read a riddle aloud. Have students name the baby animal that completes the rhyme; then write the animal's name in the blank space. Continue in the same way with each remaining riddle. *Listening for information, logical thinking, rhyming* I hop on big feet And ride in mommy's pouch. I rhyme with snowy. I am a joey.	Read aloud *Owl Babies* by Martin Waddell. This is the story of three baby owls who awaken one night to discover that their mother is gone. The three owls wait anxiously throughout the night until their mother finally returns.
Thursday	Display a variety of animal cutouts (see page 238 for patterns) or animal toys. Have a volunteer choose an animal. Have the remaining students chant the first verse of the rhyme shown, substituting the animal's name. Then have the volunteer respond by making the animal's sound as she chants the second verse. *Oral language* Little [piglet], little [piglet], What do you say? I say, "[oink, oink]" Throughout the day!	Reread yesterday's story; then write on a sheet of chart paper "Mother owl went out to…" Ask each student to imagine what the mother owl was doing while she was gone; then record student responses on the paper.
Friday	Display several animal toys. Review each baby animal's name. Then have students close their eyes. Remove one of the animals and signal youngsters to open their eyes. Tell them that one of the baby animals has wandered away. Then help a volunteer name the missing animal. *Visual memory*	Read aloud *The New Baby Calf* by Edith Newlin Chase. Have students repeat the sentence "And the new baby calf liked that!" at the appropriate times. Then have youngsters recall how the mother cow cared for her calf and compare it with how their mothers care for them.

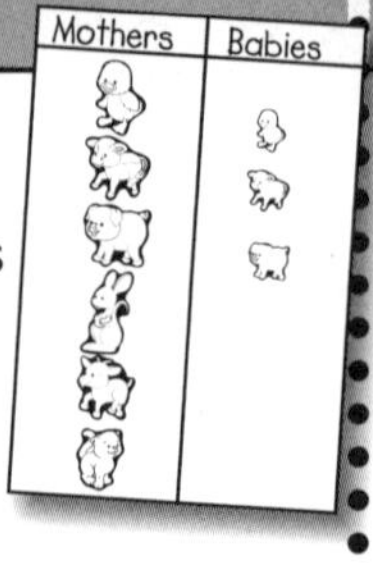

Art/Gross-Motor Skills

Cute Chicks
(See directions on page 132.)

Gross Motor: Have youngsters sit in a circle. Then give one of the youngsters a ball of yarn. Prompt her to say, "Kitten, kitten, here comes your yarn!" Then encourage her to roll the yarn to a classmate. Play continues in the same way until each child has had an opportunity to roll the yarn.

Puppy Headbands
(See directions on page 132.)

Gross Motor: For each team, place a box with brown paper strips on the floor so it resembles a chicken nest. Have each team line up at a starting line several feet from its nest. Give each child a large yellow pom-pom (chick). In turn, each team member carries his chick on a large spoon and puts it in the nest. Play continues until all the chicks are in the nest.

Playful Kitten
(See directions on page 132.)

Songs and Such for the Week

Babies, Babies
(tune: "My Bonnie Lies Over the Ocean")

A dog has a small cuddly puppy.
A bear has a wee cuddly cub.
A cat has a sweet cuddly kitten.
A duck has a duckling to love.
Babies, babies.
These mothers have babies that grow,
    that grow.
Babies, babies.
These moms love their babies, you
    know!

Baby Birds

A mother bird builds a nest
High in a tree.
There she lays her little eggs—
One, two, three!
One fine day the eggs all crack
And little beaks poke out.
The baby birds hatch from the eggs
And flap their wings about!

Animal Babies
(tune: "Rock-a-Bye, Baby")

Some animal babies, right from the
    start,
Have helpful mothers that play a part.
They help their babies eat, groom, and
    play
Until they are grown-ups in every way.

Art Activities

Cute Chicks

Glue light brown crinkle strips in each section of a clean, sanitized half-dozen egg carton. Next, glue to a yellow pom-pom an orange construction paper beak and hole-punch eyes. Then glue the resulting chick in one of the egg cups. Repeat the process to make a chick for each remaining cup.

Puppy Headbands

Use a bingo dauber to make spots on two dog ear cutouts and a construction paper headband. Attach the ears to the headband and then size it appropriately.

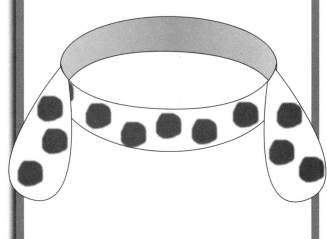

Playful Kitten

Paint a picture of a kitten on a sheet of construction paper (or color a kitten cutout and glue it to the paper). When the paint is dry, glue colorful yarn around the kitten as if it's been playing.

Weather

Centers for the Week

Literacy Center: Partially fill a resealable plastic bag with brown fingerpaint or chocolate pudding (mud). Seal the bag and secure the top of the bag with tape. Little ones use their fingers to trace letters in the mud.

Sensory Table: Punch small, medium, and large holes in different containers. Place the containers in your water table along with watering cans, colanders, and empty baby powder bottles. Students use the containers to make drizzles, showers, and downpours in the water table.

Dramatic Play: Stock this center with rain gear, such as raincoats, umbrellas, boots, ponchos, and rain hats. Laminate blue construction paper puddles and tape them to the floor for pretend splashing. Hang blue streamers or raindrops from the ceiling and play a recording of rain sounds. Encourage youngsters to have fun in the rain.

Math Center: Cut out ten colorful construction paper umbrellas (see page 239). Then number the umbrellas 1–10 and place them at the center along with blue construction paper raindrops. A student reads the number on an umbrella and places the corresponding number of raindrops on the umbrella.

Game Center: Cut pictures of hot- and cold-weather clothing from magazines and catalogs and ready each picture for flannelboard use. Divide the flannelboard in half with a strip of felt. Then label one half with a snowflake and the word *cold* and the remaining half with a sun and the word *hot.* A student sorts the clothing onto the flannelboard.

	Group Time	Literature

Monday

Place four cards showing different types of weather in the bottom of your pocket chart. Give each student a card with his name on it. Invite each child to place his card above his favorite type of weather. As a group, discuss the results. *Graphing*

Read aloud *In the Rain With Baby Duck* by Amy Hest. Mr. and Mrs. Duck can't understand why Baby Duck doesn't like the rain, but Grandpa knows just what to do to make Baby Duck sing a new tune!

Tuesday

Give each student a length of blue yarn. Help her shape her yarn into a circle on the floor to form a puddle. Say several words, some of which begin with /p/. Youngsters jump into their puddles when they hear a word that begins with /p/ and stand still if the word does not begin with /p/. *Beginning sounds*

Reread yesterday's story. Point out Baby Duck's colorful umbrella. Have students decorate umbrella cutouts (see page 239). To finish, encourage them to dip their fingertips in blue paint and dab raindrops atop their umbrellas.

Wednesday

Show youngsters a large thermometer; then draw and color a thermometer on the board to match the current temperature. Have youngsters predict what will happen if you place the thermometer in warm water. Place the thermometer in a bowl of warm water and have students observe. Then record the change on the board. Repeat the process with cold water. *Making observations*

Read aloud *The Wind Blew* by Pat Hutchins. The wind is a mischievous character in this rhyming tale. It takes things from people and mixes them up before tossing them back again.

Thursday

To make a raindrop, fill a thin blue sock with cotton batting and tie the end. On a length of blue bulletin board paper, draw five numbered puddle shapes. A volunteer thinks of a motion to do for a rain dance. Then she tosses the raindrop into a puddle. She and her classmates perform the motion the corresponding number of times. Repeat until all youngsters have had a turn. *Recognizing numbers, following directions*

Revisit yesterday's book. Help youngsters discover which objects are easy for the wind to blow and which are difficult. Place an envelope, a shirt, a balloon, and a handkerchief in front of a fan. Turn on the fan and have youngsters observe which items blow away quickly. When finished, pop and safely dispose of the balloon.

Friday

Invite little ones to help you crumple up sheets of white tissue paper to make pretend snowballs. Have students help count the snowballs as you place them on top of a parachute (or bedsheet). Then invite students to move the parachute up and down to make the snow fly. *Gross motor, counting*

Read *Rain* by Manya Stojic. Make a rainmaker for each child by placing rice in a small plastic water bottle and then securing the lid with tape. Then reread the book and have youngsters shake their rainmakers whenever they hear the word *rain*.

Art/Gross-Motor Skills

Rainy Rainbows
(See directions on page 136.)

Gross Motor: For this windy game, place tissue paper leaf cutouts on the seats of three chairs. Line up groups of students facing the chairs. On your signal, the first child in each line runs to the chair opposite her and blows the leaves with one puff, trying to blow as many leaves as she can off the chair. After her turn, she runs back to her line and the next child goes. If all the leaves are blown from the chair, replace them. The game continues until everyone has had a turn.

Storm Clouds
(See directions on page 136.)

Gross Motor: Place a class supply of plastic hoops (or yarn circles) on the floor. Invite each child to choose a hoop and pretend it is a big mud puddle. Encourage youngsters to follow your directions about how to move around and in their puddles. Have them hop, skip, and tiptoe around their puddles and jump over and in their puddles with one foot or two.

Wind Painting
(See directions on page 136.)

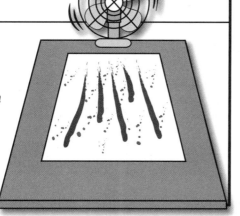

Songs and Such for the Week

If the Weather's Cold Today
(tune: "If You're Happy and You Know It")

If the weather's cold today,
Could we have snow?
If the weather's cold today,
Could we have snow?
If the weather's cold today
And a storm is on the way,
If the weather's cold today,
Could we have snow?

I Like Rainy Weather

I like rainy weather!
I really don't care
If little wet raindrops
Soak my clothes and my hair.

I like lots of raindrops
Falling on me.
Yes, I think that rain is
As nice as can be!

Weather, Weather
(tune: "Daisy, Daisy")

Weather, weather,
What will the weather be?
Check the sky and
Then tell me what you see.

Do you see bright sunshine beaming?
Or are there raindrops streaming?
Now tell me do,
Oh, what do you
Think the weather will be today?

Art Activities

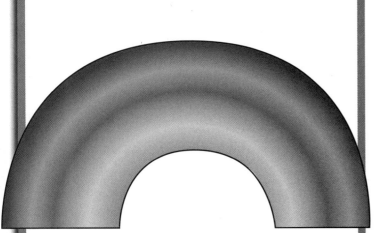

Storm Clouds

Place a spoonful each of white and black fingerpaint on a large sheet of fingerpaint paper. As you listen to a recording of rain or a thunderstorm, blend the two paints together. Once the paint has dried, cut out a thundercloud shape.

Rainy Rainbows

Cut a rainbow shape from a heavy-duty white paper towel. Use water-based markers to draw wide rainbow stripes on the paper towel, leaving a space between each stripe. With newspapers underneath, paint over the rainbow with water to watch the colors blur and blend.

Wind Painting

Tape an oversize sheet of paper to a table. Place a small electric fan at the end of the table and angle it so it blows directly down the length of the paper. Drip diluted paint onto the paper so that the fan blows it, creating unique designs. Add different colors and change the angle of the fan if desired.

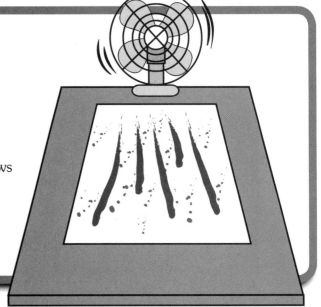

PoNds

Centers for the Week

Literacy Center: Program each of several lily pad shapes with a different uppercase letter. Program the bottoms of a corresponding number of frog toys (or cutouts) with matching lowercase letters. Place the lily pads and frogs letter-side down. In turn, students turn over a lily pad and a frog. The frog is placed on the lily pad if the letters match. If they do not, the lily pad and frog are returned to their original positions. Play continues until each frog is on its matching lily pad.

Math Center: Provide several pond shapes along with a supply of yellow duck cutouts and a large die. A student rolls the die and then places the corresponding number of ducks on a pond. She continues until each pond has a set of ducks.

Sensory Table: Cover the bottom of your water table with clean sand; then add water. Provide medium-size rocks, sticks, silk foliage, craft foam lily pads, and toy pond animals. Students arrange the materials and manipulate the toys to engage in pretend pond play.

Play Dough Center: Place laminated blue bulletin board paper on a table so it resembles a pond. Provide batches of green, brown, and yellow play dough along with short sticks (logs), medium-size rocks, and pond animal cookie cutters. Students use the materials to create pondlike scenery.

Fine-Motor Area: Cut a green paper plate so it resembles a lily pad. Add eyes to a green-painted melon baller so it resembles a frog. Provide a supply of small black pom-poms (flies). Students use the melon baller to "catch" flies and place them on the lily pad.

	Group Time	Literature
Monday	Prepare a set of cards copied from page 240. Hold up a card and have students identify the picture. Then lead the group in singing the song shown, inserting the animal's name where indicated. ***Investigating living things*** *(tune: "Are You Sleeping?")* [Ducks] live here. [Ducks] live here At the pond, at the pond. [Ducks] eat and rest here. [Ducks] eat and rest here At the pond, at the pond.	Read aloud *Look Once, Look Again: At The Pond* by David M. Schwartz. In this book, forms of pond life are depicted in partial photographs accompanied by simple clues to help the reader guess what each one is.
Tuesday	Have one volunteer pretend to be a parent duck and five more volunteers pretend to be ducklings. Lead the remaining students in singing "Five Little Ducks" as the ducklings waddle around behind the adult duck. At the end of each verse, have a duckling go back to his seat. During the final verse, have the adult duck loudly say, "Quack, quack, quack!" and have all the ducklings come waddling back. ***Participating in a song***	Revisit yesterday's book. Read aloud the clues on each page to prompt students to name the plant, animal, or insect being described. Then show students the partial photo. Finally, show the full photo to confirm youngsters' guesses.
Wednesday	Program frog cutouts with different shapes. Place the cutouts in a bag along with a few blank frogs. Students pass the bag around the circle. When they hear you say "Ribbit! Ribbit!" the child holding the bag removes a frog and identifies the shape. If he picks a blank frog, he hops around the circle and back to his seat. ***Shape identification***	Read aloud *Have You Seen My Duckling?* by Nancy Tafuri. This is the story of a mother duck who leads her brood around the pond in search of one of her missing ducklings.
Thursday	Place a class supply of numbered lily pad cutouts in a circle on the floor. During the activity, start and stop a recording of lively music. When the music plays, students hop around the circle of lily pads. When the music stops, each child quickly hops onto a lily pad and, in turn, identifies the number on his cutout. ***Number identification***	Reread yesterday's story. Have each child write her name on a duckling cutout. Then have her glue yellow craft feathers to the cutout. Attach the cutouts to a pond-themed bulletin board with the title "Have You Seen My Duckling?"
Friday	Attach a different critter card (see page 240) to each of four columns on a floor graph. Then place a supply of corresponding cards in a bag. In turn, have each student pick a card from the bag and attach it to the appropriate column on the graph. Then compare the columns. ***Graphing, comparing results***	Help each child make a pond critter headband that corresponds to an animal in the book *In the Small, Small Pond* by Denise Fleming. Have each child don his headband. Then read aloud the book and have the appropriate children stand when each animal is described.

Art/Gross-Motor Skills

Perfect Pond
(See directions on page 140.)

Gross Motor: Attach several different pond critter cutouts (see page 240) to a large paper pond. Place the pond on the floor. In turn, a student tosses a beanbag onto the pond so it lands on a critter. Then students move around the outside of the pond, imitating the sounds and movements of the critter on which the beanbag landed.

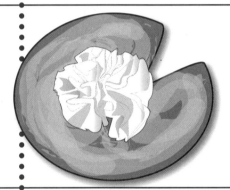

Beautiful Lily Pad
(See directions on page 140.)

Gross Motor: Attach a number of lily pad cutouts to the floor so they lead to a large pond cutout. Have students hop like frogs down the lily pad path. When each frog reaches the end of the path, she leaps onto the pond.

Terrific Turtle
(See directions on page 140.)

Songs and Such for the Week

Here Come the Ducklings
(tune: "Down by the Station")

Make way for ducklings
Early in the morning.
See the fluffy duckies
All in a row.
See the mother duckie
Lead her little babies.
"Quack, quack!" Scoot, scoot!
Off they go!

Five Little Frogs

Five little frogs in the pond so blue.
The first frog said, "I'm really hot! Are you?"
The second frog said, "Let's go swimming for a while."
The third frog said, "That makes me smile!"
The fourth frog said, "I'm ready for a swim!"
The fifth frog said, "Don't be the last one in!"
So they jumped in the cool pond one by one.
Then they hopped onto a log and sat in the sun.

Down at the Pond
(tune: "Down by the Bay")

Down at the pond where the water lilies grow,
There are lots of animals swimming to and fro.
They dive and splash; of water they're fond.
You can see the [ducks] play happily all day
Down at the pond.

Continue with the names of other pond animals.

Art Activities

Perfect Pond

To make a pond, glue twigs and sand to a clean, sterilized foam tray. After the glue is dry, wrap the tray with blue plastic wrap and secure the plastic wrap with tape. Next, attach a tab to the bottom of a frog cutout so it is self-standing. Then tape the frog to a lily pad cutout. Glue the lily pad to the plastic wrap.

Beautiful Lily Pad

Fingerpaint a sheet of paper green. After the paint is dry, cut a lily pad shape from the paper. To make a water lily, stack four large squares of white tissue paper on top of each other. Fanfold the tissue paper; then bend a piece of white pipe cleaner around the center and twist the ends together. Carefully separate each layer of tissue paper so it resembles a flower. Then attach the resulting water lily to the lily pad.

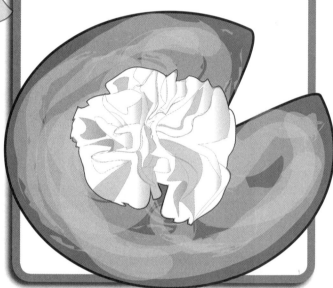

Terrific Turtle

To make a turtle shell, glue different shades of green tissue paper to the outside of a disposable bowl. Next, glue head, tail, and feet cutouts to the shell. Use a black marker to add details as desired.

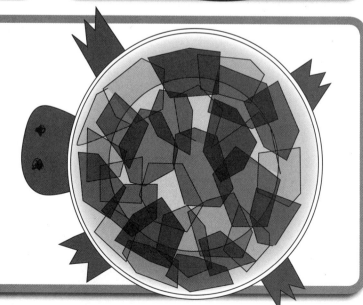

Taking Care of the Earth

Centers for the Week

Math Center: Reuse bottle caps at this center! Place sponges in containers and soak each sponge with paint. Place the containers at the center along with paper strips and bottle caps. A child presses bottle caps into the sponges and then makes prints on a strip of paper to make a pattern.

Game Center: Puzzle-cut the front panels of cereal boxes. Place each resulting puzzle in a resealable plastic bag. A student selects a bag and puts the pieces together.

Dramatic Play: Place at the center a supply of child-safe recyclable objects, along with large containers labeled with categories to match the objects. A student pretends he works at a recycling center. He sorts the objects into the appropriate containers.

Art Center: Cut clean trash items into small pieces. You may consider using cardboard tubes, candy bags, and food boxes. Place the pieces at the center along with paper and glue. A child glues the pieces to her paper to make a work of art.

Literacy Center: Reuse milk jug lids for this center! Program jug lids with letters and numbers. Label separate containers with the words *letters* and *numbers*. A youngster sorts each lid into the corresponding container.

Group Time	Literature

Monday

Give each student a small paper bag and allow him to decorate it as desired. Then take the students on a walk around the school. Have them collect any safe litter they find. (Instruct little ones to alert you to any unsafe litter.) Upon returning to the room, have the students dump their litter into a garbage can. Have students discuss the importance of throwing trash away. **Oral language**

Read aloud *The Earth and I* by Frank Asch. A little boy and the earth share a special friendship. They talk, play, and sing together, but more importantly, they help each other.

Tuesday

Present several pieces of clean trash, such as a peanut butter jar or a cardboard tube. Have students tell you ways the item could be reused. For example, a peanut butter jar could hold buttons or pom-poms. **Creative thinking**

Revisit yesterday's story. Then draw a happy face and a sad face at the top of a T chart. Have youngsters name things that make the earth happy or sad. Write their suggestions below the appropriate face on the T chart.

Wednesday

Place on the floor a large piece of blue bulletin board paper (lake). Put several fish cutouts on the lake. Give each student a piece of clean trash—such as paper, a water bottle, and aluminum foil—and have her throw it in the lake. Invite students to discuss how they think the trash affects the fish. Then instruct the students to remove the trash from the lake and put it in the proper place. **Critical thinking**

Read aloud *Each Living Thing* by Joanne Ryder. In this book, the reader is urged to protect each and every living thing—from spiders on their webs to turtles in the sea.

Thursday

Put in a bag a large amount of blue tissue paper squares and a small amount of green tissue paper squares. Place a large white circle on the board to be the earth. Each student chooses a square and attaches it to the earth. When the earth is covered, explain to students that the blue paper represents water and the green represents land. Ask the students if there is more land or water on the earth. **Comparing**

Revisit yesterday's story. Place a length of bulletin board paper on the floor. As youngsters draw animals on their paper to make a mural, remind them that we should care for the earth's animals.

Friday

Color and cut out enlarged copies of the picture cards on page 241. Share the pictures in a random order with the students. Discuss what happens in each picture. Then have the students assist you in taping the pictures to your board in the correct order. **Sequencing**

Gather number cards from 1 to 12. Read aloud *Earth Day Birthday* by Pattie Schnetzler. Throughout the reading, have volunteers place the number cards one at a time in your pocket chart to reflect the number of animals on each page.

Art/Gross-Motor Skills

Land and Water
(See directions on page 144.)

Gross Motor: Have the students stand around a sheet and hold its edges. Then place a beach ball on the sheet. Explain that the beach ball is the earth and it is their job to take care of it and make sure it doesn't fall. Then have students carefully raise and lower the sheet, taking care to keep the ball from falling.

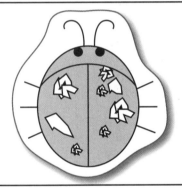

Litterbug
(See directions on page 144.)

Gross Motor: Scatter clean trash around the room. Then play a recording of lively music and have students dance about the room, picking up trash and placing it in the trash can.

Keep the Earth Clean
(See directions on page 144.)

Songs and Such for the Week

What Can We Do?
(tune: "A Tisket, a Tasket")

It's Earth Day, it's Earth Day.
What can we do on Earth Day
To make the world a better place?
Let's [pick up trash] on Earth Day.

Continue with the following: *plant a tree, recycle, walk outside, save water*

Plant a Tree

Today it is Earth Day.
I'm planting a tree
To make the world better
For you and for me.
With a shovel I'll dig
A deep hole in the ground,
Then put the tree in the hole
And put soil all around.

Recycling Song
(tune: "The More We Get Together")

The more we all recycle,
Recycle, recycle,
Oh, the more we all recycle,
The better Earth will be.
Aluminum and paper,
Glass, cardboard, and plastic.
These all can be recycled
By you and by me.

Land and Water

Lay a coffee filter flat on a protected tabletop. Use an eyedropper to put a few drops of green-tinted water on the filter. Then drip blue-tinted water over the rest of the filter. When the filter is dry, glue it to a sheet of black paper so it resembles the earth. Then attach star stickers around the earth.

Litterbug

Tear into small pieces old newspapers, magazines, and empty food boxes. Glue the resulting pieces of litter to a large bug cutout. If desired, attach this project to a board with the title "Go Away, Litterbugs!"

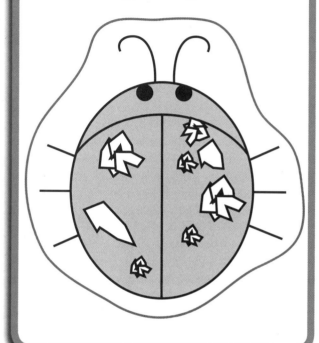

Keep the Earth Clean

On a sheet of white construction paper, draw an outdoor scene with trees, animals, grass, and water. Slide your drawing into a sheet protector. Glue assorted pieces of clean paper litter to the sheet protector. After the project is dry, show everyone how much nicer the earth looks when it is clean by sliding your drawing from the sheet protector to reveal the clean picture.

Pets

Centers for the Week

Dramatic Play: For this veterinarian's office center, provide a variety of stuffed animals, a medical kit with props, white dress shirts for lab coats, a clipboard with a sign-in sheet, a telephone, and notepads and writing tools for making appointments and writing prescriptions.

Math Center: Provide five plastic dog dishes or disposable bowls. Label each dish with a different number from 1 through 5. Also provide 15 craft foam dog bones. A student identifies the number on each bowl; then she counts out the corresponding number of dog bones and places them in the bowl.

Fine-Motor Area: Provide a cup of fish-shaped crackers and a fishbowl cutout. A student uses tweezers to pick up the fish from the cup and place them on the fishbowl.

Art Center: Obtain a pawprint stamp. A student dips the stamp in paint or presses it on an ink pad and then makes a print on a sheet of paper. He continues stamping the paper until a desired effect is achieved.

Literacy Center: Draw on two separate sheets of paper aquariums without any fish. Label each aquarium with a different letter; then laminate the aquariums and place them near the water table. Use a permanent marker to label individual craft foam fish with letters so that each matches one of the aquariums; then float the fish in your water table. A student uses a fishnet to scoop up a fish and then places the fish on the corresponding aquarium.

Group Time	Literature

Monday

Seat children in a circle. Invite a student to secretly think of a pet. Then have her go to the center of the circle and pretend to be that animal. Have the remaining students guess what animal she is pretending to be. *Dramatic play*

Read aloud *Have You Seen My Cat?* by Eric Carle. In this story, a little boy searches around the world for his lost cat. He encounters many different types of cats along the way, but none of them are his. After a long journey, he finds his cat—along with a special surprise!

Tuesday

Place several cat cutouts in different positions in the room, such as over the clock, under a chair, and beside the sink. Then lead students in singing the song shown, using a corresponding positional word in each verse. *Positional words*

(tune: "Oh Where, Oh Where Has My Little Dog Gone?")
Oh where, oh where has my little cat gone?   I see it; it is [over the clock].
Oh where, oh where can it be?   I'm glad you found it with me!

Have students make this class book to go with Monday's story. Write "Have you seen my cat?" on construction paper. Have each child draw an animal on a sheet of paper labeled "That's not my cat." Stack the papers behind the first page. Then write "This is my cat!" on a sheet of paper and attach a picture of a cat. Add this final page to the back of the stack and bind the pages together.

Wednesday

Program each dog bone–shaped cutout in a set with a sentence starter such as "If I were a dog…" and "A dog likes to…" Place the dog bones in an empty dog-treat box. Invite several students to take turns picking a bone from the box and finishing the sentence on the bone. *Oral language*

If I were a dog...

Read aloud *Harry the Dirty Dog* by Gene Zion. This is the story of a little white dog with black spots who hates to take a bath, so he runs away. When he returns home, his family doesn't recognize him because he is so dirty that he looks like a little black dog with white spots!

Thursday

To play this game, invite a student to pretend to be a cat. Have him close his eyes while you hide a fish-shaped cutout in the room. Then have him open his eyes and search the room to find the fish. As he gets closer to the fish, have his classmates meow loudly. As he gets farther away, have them meow softly. *Following directions, participating in a game*

Revisit yesterday's story. Then have students color black spots on one side of a white tagboard dog cutout. Have them color the remaining side of the cutout black, leaving white spots. Encourage students to use their cutouts to retell the story.

Friday

Attach each of four different-colored birdcage cutouts to a different wall. Give each child a bird cutout (see page 242) that matches one of the cages. Prompt students to "fly" the birds around the room while chanting, "Little birds, little birds, fly away!" Then chant, "[Red] birds, [red] birds, fly to your cage!" Continue until all the birds have flown to their matching birdcages. *Color sorting*

Read aloud *I Want a Pet* by Lauren Child; then show students pictures of domestic and wild animals. Encourage youngsters to name the animals that would make good pets and the animals that would not; then have them explain why.

Art/Gross-Motor Skills

Feather Art
(See directions on page 148.)

Gross Motor: Have students dance to some lively music. Then stop the music and call out the name of a pet along with an animal action, such as "digging dog" or "flapping canary." Have youngsters pretend to be the animal and perform the action. Start and stop the music several times, naming a different animal and action each time.

Dogs With Tags
(See directions on page 148.)

Gross Motor: Attach several large fish cutouts to a large pond cutout and place the pond on the floor in an open area. Also attach worm cutouts to a class supply of beanbags. On your signal, have each child try to toss his beanbag onto a hungry fish.

Stained-Glass Fish
(See directions on page 148.)

Songs and Such for the Week

If I Had a Dog
(tune: "If You're Happy and You Know It")

If I had a dog, I'd care for it each day.
I would teach my dog to sit and speak and stay.
I would give it food to grow
And clean water, don't you know.
If I had a dog, I'd care for it each day.

If I had a dog, I'd care for it each day.
I would make sure that it had a place to play.
I would treat my doggie right,
And I'd love it day and night.
If I had a dog, I'd care for it each day.

All Kinds of Pets

Snakes, lizards, turtles too.
Some people like reptiles. How about you?
Cockatoos, parrots, canaries too.
Some people like birds. How about you?
Dogs, hamsters, kittens too.
Some people like mammals. How about you?
Angelfish, guppies, goldfish too.
Some people like fish. How about you?

Somebody's Pet
(tune: "How Much Is That Doggie in the Window?")

Oh, some pets have lots of pretty feathers,
And some pets have lots of long fur.
Oh, some pets just love to chirp and twitter,
And other pets just like to purr!

Art Activities

Feather Art

Spotlight fun feathered pets with a bird-inspired art project! Provide a variety of craft feathers, feather dusters, and white paper. Dip a feather into a container of tinted water and then gently brush the feather across the paper. Continue in the same manner using different feathers and feather dusters until a desired effect is achieved.

Dogs With Tags

To make a dog puppet, cut out two construction paper ears and attach them to either side of a paper plate. Next, draw facial features on the plate. Then glue or tape a jumbo craft stick to the back of the plate. To make a dog tag, cut a bone shape from construction paper and personalize it with a name. Then decorate it as desired and glue it to the craft stick below the paper plate.

Stained-Glass Fish

Cut a fin-shaped opening in the center of a large construction paper fish cutout. Attach pieces of tissue paper to the sticky side of a piece of Con-Tact covering. Place the fish over the covering so the tissue paper shows through the opening. Tape the covering in place and then draw facial details on the fish.

Ladybugs

Centers for the Week

Play Dough Center: Set out a supply of red and black play dough. A student makes a large red ball (body) and a small black ball (head) and puts them together. Then she places small amounts of black play dough on the ladybug's body to make the spots.

Math Center: Cut out several red construction paper copies of the ladybug pattern on page 243. Program each one with eyes and a different number of spots. Then attach each ladybug to a small cup. Place the cup and a supply of counters (aphids) at the center. A student counts the spots on the ladybug and "feeds" her the correct number of aphids.

Literacy Center: Make a large name card for each child and place it at the center along with a red ink pad and a fine-tip permanent marker. A child finds her name card and traces the letters with her finger. Then she identifies as many of the letters as possible. Finally, she makes red fingerprints on the letters and uses the marker to add ladybug details to each print.

Sensory Table: Place a supply of crinkled green paper shreds (grass) in a tub along with very small red pom-poms (ladybugs). A child searches through the grass, finds the ladybugs, and places them in a container.

Gross-Motor Area: Wrap brown paper around a bucket and decorate it to look like a log. Then sit the bucket several feet from a tape line and place a container of large red pom-poms (ladybugs) near the tape line. A child selects ladybugs and attempts to toss them into the log.

	Group Time	Literature
Monday	Place a large spotless ladybug cutout on your floor. Then give each child a black spot cutout. (If you have an odd number of students, make a spot for yourself.) Explain that ladybugs have the same number of spots on both wings. Brainstorm ways to put the spots on the ladybug so each wing has the same amount. Test the ideas to see which ones work. ***Critical thinking, sharing equally***	Read aloud *Little Buggy* by Kevin O'Malley. Little Buggy wants to learn to fly today. Even though he falls several times, he picks himself up and tries again.
Tuesday	Place red, yellow, and orange ladybug cutouts in a bag. Lay on the floor three large leaf cutouts, each labeled with a color word to match a ladybug. In turn, a student chooses a ladybug and places it on the correct leaf. ***Sorting***	Revisit yesterday's story. Invite students to share things they have learned to do even though it was difficult. Record these on chart paper.
Wednesday	Write descriptive words on individual cards. Some of these words should describe ladybugs and some should not. Place the cards in a basket. A student chooses a word. Read the word aloud. Then have students decide if the word could be used to describe ladybugs. ***Descriptive language***	Read aloud *The Grouchy Ladybug* by Eric Carle. A very rude ladybug learns an important lesson that makes it a much nicer ladybug.
Thursday	Write the word *ladybug* on a large ladybug cutout. Review the /l/ sound at the beginning of *ladybug* and the letter *L*. Invite students to think of as many words as possible that begin with the same sound as *ladybug*. Record these words on the ladybug cutout. ***Beginning sounds***	Write the times on the hour from 5:00 AM to 6:00 PM on separate index cards and attach the cards to a wall. Cut out a copy of the picture cards on page 243. Reread the story, having youngsters attach each picture card next to the corresponding time.
Friday	Program ladybug cutouts (see page 243 for a pattern) with different numbers of spots. Label the columns on a floor graph with numbers that correspond to the numbers of spots. Give each student a ladybug. He counts the number of spots on his ladybug and places it in the correct column of the graph. ***Graphing***	Read aloud *Are You a Ladybug?* by Judy Allen and Tudor Humphries. Gather a set of name cards. Choose a card and ask the youngster, "Do you eat aphids?" When the youngster responds "No," have all students chant, "Then you are not a ladybug!" Repeat the process with different youngsters and questions.

little

Brilliant Beetles

(See directions on page 152.)

Gross Motor: Place green circle cutouts (aphids) around your classroom. Have students crawl around the room looking for aphids. Encourage youngsters to place each aphid found into a basket. When all the aphids are found, have students count the number of aphids.

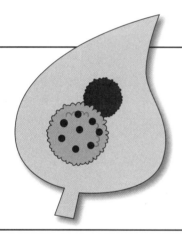

Ladybug on a Leaf

(See directions on page 152.)

Gross Motor: Put ten ladybug cutouts at various locations around the school. Then lead the students around the school, prompting them to look up high; down low; and above, behind, and below objects. Continue the hunt until all ten ladybugs have been found.

Potato Prints

(See directions on page 152.)

A Ladybug's an Insect

(tune: "Have You Ever Seen a Lassie?")

Oh, a ladybug's an insect,
An insect, an insect.
Oh, a ladybug's an insect,
With six little legs.
Her legs wiggle this way.
Her legs wiggle that way.
Oh, a ladybug's an insect,
With six little legs.

Ladybug, Ladybug

Ladybug, ladybug,
Red with spots.
I love watching you
Lots and lots.
Crawling, climbing,
And flying all around;
Never making
A tiny sound.

Crawl, Climb, Fly

(tune: "Row, Row, Row Your Boat")

Little ladybug
Crawls along the ground.
It crawls on its little legs.
See it crawl around.

Little ladybug
Climbs right up a stick.
It climbs with its little legs.
It climbs oh so quick.

Little ladybug
Spreads its wings to fly.
It flies with its little wings
High up in the sky!

 # Art Activities

Brilliant Beetles

Paint the outside of a paper bowl with red tempera paint. Then make black fingerprint spots on the bowl. When the paint is dry, punch two holes in the side of the bowl and twist a pipe cleaner through the holes to make antennae. Attach eye cutouts below the antennae. Then draw a smile below the eyes.

Ladybug on a Leaf

Glue a large red pom-pom to a green construction paper leaf. Then glue a black pom-pom next to the red one so they resemble a ladybug's head and body. Finally, glue hole-punched dots to the red pom-pom.

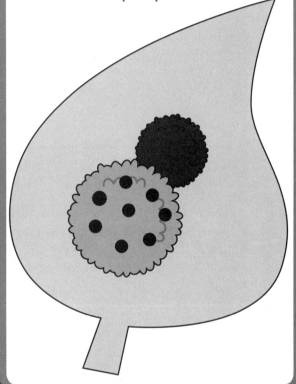

Potato Prints

In advance, cut a small potato in half. Draw an outside scene on a sheet of paper. Dip a potato half in a shallow pan of red paint and press the potato on the paper to make ladybug prints. When the paint is dry, add details to the ladybugs with a permanent black marker.

Feelings

Centers for the Week

Dramatic Play: Provide several pictures of children making different facial expressions, along with a few unbreakable mirrors. A student looks at each picture and then watches himself in the mirror as he imitates each facial expression.

Fine-Motor Area: Make a large happy face cutout and a second cutout with a sad face. Punch holes along each of the mouth outlines and attach a string for lacing. A student laces the mouth outline and then unlaces it, making it ready for the next child.

Play Dough Center: Provide play dough and several laminated circles in different flesh tones. A student molds the play dough to create a facial expression on a circle.

Literacy Center: Program a supply of paper with the sentence starter "I feel happy when…" Students dictate or write words to complete the sentence and then illustrate the page. Throughout the feelings unit, replace the papers with similar sentence starters that use different emotions.

Math Center: Use a permanent marker to draw happy, scared, mad, and sad faces on milk caps. Make four large paper circles with matching expressions to use as sorting mats. A student sorts the milk caps onto the mats.

	Group Time	Literature
Monday	Display a picture chart that shows a variety of facial expressions that correspond to different emotions. Name an emotion and have a volunteer find the picture on the chart that shows the correct expression. Then have students name things that could make them feel that way. ***Recognizing emotions***	Read aloud *Go Away, Big Green Monster!* by Ed Emberley. Descriptive text, a host of bright colors and die-cut pages help the Big Green Monster begin to grow. But then, in the second half of the story, the monster slowly disappears!
Tuesday	Gather several photographs or magazine pictures of children and adults expressing different feelings. Display one of the pictures. A student identifies the emotion the person is feeling. Then she uses the picture to explain why she thinks the person feels that way. ***Identifying emotions***	Reread yesterday's story, prompting students to chant the line, "Go away, big green monster!" Then give each student a sheet of paper programmed with the words "Go away, _____ _____ monster!" Have each child dictate descriptive words for you to record and then have her add an illustration to the page.
Wednesday	Prepare four construction paper faces (happy, sad, angry, and scared) and place them in a bag. During the activity, start and stop a recording of music. When the music plays, students pass the bag around the circle. When the music stops, the child holding the bag picks a face and holds it in the air. Students respond with an appropriate action such as laughing, pretending to cry, stomping their feet, or looking scared. ***Participating in a game, using facial expressions to illustrate feelings***	Read aloud *Franklin's Bad Day* by Paulette Bourgeois. This is the story of a little turtle whose good friend moves away. Feeling mad and sad, Franklin talks to his father, and together they find a way to make Franklin feel better.
Thursday	Program a happy face cutout with a speech bubble that says "I feel happy when…" Make similar cutouts for other emotions. Read aloud the speech bubble and invite students to finish the sentence. Then continue in the same way with the remaining cutouts. ***Critical thinking*** I feel happy when…	Revisit yesterday's story. Then have youngsters pretend to be Franklin and act out parts of his bad day. Have students brainstorm what they do to help themselves get rid of sadness. Record their responses on a large turtle-shaped cutout.
Friday	Lead youngsters to talk about appropriate choices they can make in situations when they become angry, such as using their words, walking away, or getting help from an adult. Then have students role-play situations such as a child taking their toy or calling them names. ***Problem solving, role-playing***	Read aloud *Leo the Late Bloomer* by Robert Kraus. Have students recall things that Leo wasn't able to do that made him feel sad and made his dad feel worried. Then invite students to share things that little brothers and sisters can't do but will be able to do when they reach preschool age.

Art/Gross-Motor Skills

Two-in-One Puppet
(See directions on page 156.)

Gross Motor: Label each of four containers with a happy, a sad, an angry, or a scared face. In turn, have each student toss a beanbag into a container. After each child has had a turn, lead youngsters in counting aloud the number of beanbags in each container. Then have students act out the emotion from the container that has the most beanbags.

Monster Mania
(See directions on page 156.)

Gross Motor: In advance, hide a monster cutout in the classroom. Then lead youngsters in the chant shown as you take them on a monster hunt. Repeat the second verse substituting new movements until you reach the hiding place. Reveal the monster with great fanfare.

We're going on a monster hunt,
But we're not scared! But we're not scared!
Let's [stomp] to find the monster
'Cause we're not scared! 'Cause we're not scared!

Feeling the Music
(See directions on page 156.)

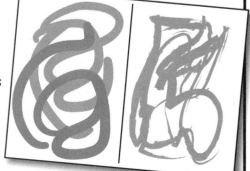

Songs and Such for the Week

When I'm Scared
(tune: "The Itsy-Bitsy Spider")

When I'm scared at night
Of creatures I can't see;
If I imagine monsters
Watching over me,
I just tell those critters,
"Shoo! Do what I say!"
And those not-so-scary monsters
Just vanish clear away!

My Feelings Can Change

My feelings can change
From happy to sad.
Sometimes I'm excited,
And sometimes I'm mad.
Sometimes I feel good.
Sometimes I feel bad.
But the times I like best
Are the times I feel glad!

How Do You Feel?
(tune: "Do Your Ears Hang Low?")

Do you feel very happy?
Do you feel a little sad?
Could you show a great big smile
Or cry a little while?
Do you want to show you're mad
Or scared or very glad?
How do you feel?

Art Activities

Two-in-One Puppet

Use markers or crayons to draw a happy face on the back of one paper plate and a sad face on the back of a second paper plate. Attach a jumbo craft stick to the front of one plate; then staple the edges of the two plates together. Glue yarn pieces or crinkle shreds to each side of the resulting puppet so they resemble hair. Add embellishments to the puppet as desired.

Monster Mania

Have each child stuff a lunch bag with newspaper strips and tie the top of the bag closed with a piece of string. Then encourage her to paint the bag. After the paint is dry, have her decorate the bag using a variety of collage materials. Then help her glue a tagboard copy of the monster feet on page 244 to the bottom of the bag. Have each child hold her monster and describe something that she finds scary.

Feeling the Music

For each child, fold a sheet of construction paper in half; then unfold the paper. Provide shallow containers of tempera paint and paintbrushes. Play a recording of melancholy music while the child paints on one half of her paper. Then play a recording of upbeat music while she paints on the remaining paper half. When the paint is dry, have the student compare the two halves of her painting.

Vegetable Garden

Centers for the Week

Dramatic Play: For this vegetable stand, provide several baskets with a variety of real or plastic vegetables, a scale, a cash register, play money, and grocery bags. Students use the props to engage in pretend play.

Discovery Center: Provide a variety of fresh vegetables—such as carrots, ears of corn, green beans, onions, radishes, white potatoes, and sweet potatoes—along with vegetable-related books, a scale, a tape measure, and string to use as a nonstandard measuring tool. Students investigate, weigh, measure, and compare the vegetables.

Sensory Table: Fill your sensory table with potting soil. Provide a variety of real or plastic vegetables, craft foam seed cutouts, gardening gloves, baskets, and toy gardening tools, such as plastic shovels, rakes, and watering cans. Students pretend to plant seeds and then harvest their vegetables.

Literacy Center: Program a supply of paper with "_____ are yummy in my tummy!" and "_____ are not yummy in my tummy!" A student dictates or writes on the corresponding line the name of a vegetable she likes to eat and the name of a vegetable she doesn't like to eat. Then she draws a matching picture.

Math Center: Draw rows on a large sheet of brown paper so it resembles a vegetable garden. For each row, provide a different set of vegetable cutouts, each set in graduated sizes. A student places each set of vegetables in size order on a different garden row.

Group Time	Literature
Monday Have each child color a vegetable card cut from a copy of page 245. In turn, have each child show her card and then identify the vegetable and its color. Then have her name something else that is the same color. For example, she might say, "The peas are green, and grass is too!" If a youngster has difficulty thinking of something, have her look for an object of the same color in the room. **Color identification**	Read aloud *Growing Vegetable Soup* by Lois Ehlert. This is the story of a father and child who share in the joy of planting and caring for a vegetable garden. Then, when the vegetables are ready to harvest, they use them to make the best soup ever!
Tuesday In advance, ask each child's parent(s) to send a can of vegetables to school with her. Have a student show the label on her vegetable can and then identify the vegetable. Then have her place the can on the floor. Continue in the same manner, having students sort the vegetable cans into groups by type. **Print awareness, sorting**	Revisit yesterday's story, showing students the recipe for vegetable soup provided with the book. Then use the cans of vegetables brought in by students to make a pot of vegetable soup. Tasty!
Wednesday After discussing that seeds need soil, sunlight, and water to grow, turn off the lights and have each child curl up on the floor pretending to be a vegetable seed in the ground. Then turn on the lights (sun) and walk around the garden with a watering can pretending to water each seed. Each seed pretends to grow bigger and bigger and then tells what kind of vegetable he is pretending to be. **Dramatic play, creative thinking**	Read aloud *The Ugly Vegetables* by Grace Lin. This is the story of a little girl and her mother who plant a garden very different from the gardens of all the neighbors. The garden is filled with Chinese vegetables, and it makes very tasty soup!
Thursday Label each column on a floor graph with a different vegetable picture card (see page 245). Make additional copies of the cards. In turn, have each student choose a card that corresponds to his favorite vegetable and then place it in the appropriate column. Discuss the results of the graph. **Graphing, oral language**	Revisit yesterday's story; then have students help plant lima beans and flower seeds in separate containers of soil. Have youngsters care for the seeds over the next few weeks, observing and discussing similarities and differences in the plants as they grow.
Friday Place several different vegetables on a brown paper garden. Choose one student to pretend to be a raccoon. Have the remaining students close their eyes. Have the raccoon quietly remove one vegetable and place it out of sight. Have youngsters open their eyes and try to guess which vegetable is missing. **Visual memory, participating in a game**	Read aloud *Up, Down, and Around* by Katherine Ayres. Have youngsters stand up, crouch down, and twirl around to reflect how the vegetables grow in this engaging picture book.

Art/Gross-Motor Skills

Colorful Carrot
(See directions on page 160.)

Gross Motor: Put a little twist on the traditional game of Duck, Duck, Goose by substituting a variety of vegetable names. You might say, "Corn, corn, carrot," "Onion, onion, peas," or "Broccoli, broccoli, cabbage"!

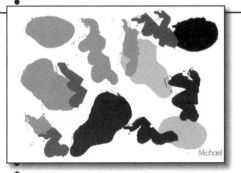

Veggie Art
(See directions on page 160.)

Gross Motor: Lead youngsters in singing the song shown. Then have them pantomime digging a hole and planting a seed. Repeat the song and motions with other vegetables.

(tune: "The Farmer in the Dell")

What seed should we plant?
What seed should we plant?
Let's plant a [carrot] seed.
Yes, that's what we'll plant!

Terrific Turnip
(See directions on page 160.)

Songs and Such for the Week

Crunchy Carrots
(tune: "I'm a Little Teapot")

I'm a little carrot.
Crunch, crunch, crunch!
Here in this garden
You'll find a bunch.
When I get all scrumptious, sweet, and ripe,
Bunnies come to take a bite!

In the Vegetable Garden
(tune: "Pawpaw Patch")

Where, oh, where can we pick tomatoes?
Where, oh, where can we pick tomatoes?
Where, oh, where can we pick tomatoes?
Way down yonder in the vegetable garden.

Hat, Shovel, Gloves, and Boots
(tune: "Head and Shoulders")

Hat, shovel, gloves, and boots,
Gloves and boots.
Hat, shovel, gloves, and boots,
Gloves and boots.
Harvesting my veggies and my fruits.
Hat, shovel, gloves, and boots,
Gloves and boots.

Art Activities

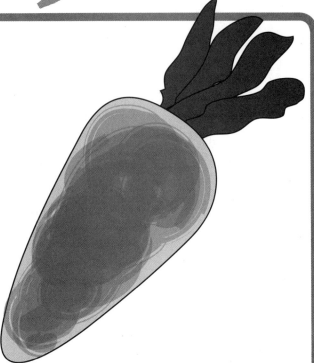

Colorful Carrot

Draw a large carrot outline on a sheet of fingerpaint paper. Place a dollop of yellow fingerpaint and a dollop of red fingerpaint on the paper inside the outline; then fingerpaint the carrot. When the paint is dry, cut out the carrot shape. Then attach torn green construction paper strips to the carrot so they resemble leaves.

Veggie Art

Cut in half fresh vegetables such as potatoes, turnips, and sweet potatoes. Also provide whole carrots and asparagus. Prepare several shallow containers of different-colored paint. Dip a vegetable in paint and then press it on a sheet of paper or paint with the vegetable. Repeat the process with the remaining vegetables.

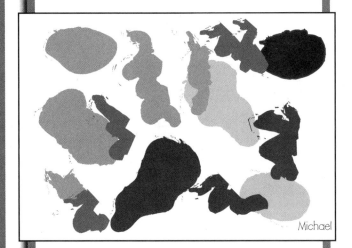

Michael

Terrific Turnip

Stuff a paper lunch bag with newspaper strips; then gather the opening of the bag and tie it closed with a piece of string. Press each corner of the bag in to round off the bottom. Paint the stuffed portion of the bag white; then use a sponge to pat a small amount of purple paint near the bottom of the turnip. Then paint the gathered portion of the bag green.

Caterpillars and Butterflies

Centers for the Week

Fine-Motor Area: A student cuts construction paper scraps into a variety of shapes and puts them in a resealable plastic bag. He seals the bag and then gathers the bag in the middle. After he twists a pipe cleaner around the gathered section, he bends the pipe cleaner so it resembles antennae.

Literacy Center: Provide 26 butterfly cutouts, each labeled with a different letter. Place a length of tape on the floor. A youngster places the butterflies on the tape line in alphabetical order, using an alphabet strip as a guide if needed.

Math Center: Place at the center a supply of jumbo craft sticks, pom-poms, and glue. Make sample caterpillars by gluing pom-poms to craft sticks in simple patterns. A student glues pom-poms to a craft stick to copy a caterpillar's pattern.

Play Dough Center: Place an oversize laminated leaf cutout at the center. Provide several different colors of play dough and butterfly-shaped cookie cutters. A student rolls play dough into caterpillar shapes and presses cookie cutters into flattened play dough to make butterflies. Then he places his creations on the leaf.

Dramatic Play: In this entomology center, provide white dress shirts for lab coats; plastic butterflies and caterpillars; plastic tweezers; magnifying glasses; bug boxes; notepads and writing tools; and insect-related books, magazines, and pictures. A student pretends to be an entomologist studying caterpillars and butterflies.

Group Time	Literature

Monday

Give each child a piece of pipe cleaner (caterpillar) and a paper leaf with a hole in it. Give positional directions, such as "Make your caterpillar crawl through the leaf." For an added challenge, give two positional directions, such as "Make your caterpillar crawl *under* the leaf and then *between* your feet!" ***Positional words, following directions***

Read aloud *The Very Hungry Caterpillar* by Eric Carle. In this story, a ravenous caterpillar eats its way through a huge amount of food and then encases itself in a chrysalis, from which it emerges as a beautiful butterfly!

Tuesday

Prepare a green circle so it resembles a caterpillar's head and place it on the floor. Give each child a die-cut letter C. Lead students in reciting the chant shown. Then have a child place his letter next to the caterpillar's head and say /k/. Have each child repeat the process. ***Letter sounds***

Caterpillar, caterpillar starts with C.
Can you make its sound with me?
/k/, /k/, /k/, /k/, caterpillar!

Reread yesterday's story; then have students name other foods the caterpillar might eat. Have each student draw and cut out a food and then attach it to a mural with a caterpillar cutout that resembles the very hungry caterpillar.

Wednesday

Prepare a class supply of different-colored butterflies. During the activity, start and stop a recording of soothing music. When the music plays, students gently glide their butterflies through the air. When the music stops, each child lands his butterfly on an object in the room that matches the color of the butterfly. ***Color matching***

Read aloud *I'm a Caterpillar* by Jean Marzollo. This book is about a little caterpillar going through the stages of metamorphosis. The author and illustrator beautifully capture the transformation through simple descriptions.

Thursday

Place a large butterfly cutout and a large caterpillar cutout on the floor. Collect a class supply of items that begin with /b/ and /k/ and store the items in a pillowcase. A student picks an item from the pillowcase and says its name. If the name begins with /b/, he places it on the butterfly. If it begins with the /k/ sound, he places it on the caterpillar. ***Beginning sounds, sorting***

Revisit yesterday's story. Review with students the metamorphosis cycle on the last page of the book. Then give each child a paper plate that has been divided into fourths. Have youngsters glue pasta shapes to the plate to make a representation of the cycle.

Friday

After discussing butterfly metamorphosis with youngsters, encourage each student to curl up in a little ball so he resembles an egg. Then have him pretend to hatch into a caterpillar and munch on leaves. Next, encourage him to mimic a chrysalis hanging from a leaf. Finally, invite him to pick up colorful scarves and "fly" around the room to show he is a butterfly. ***Role-playing, investigating living things***

Read aloud *Waiting for Wings* by Lois Ehlert. Then have youngsters use a straw to drink a cup of fruit juice just like the butterflies in the book use their proboscis to drink nectar.

Caterpillar Circles

(See directions on page 164.)

Gross Motor: Make four flower cutouts in different colors and mount them on a wall. A group of students line up several feet from each flower. The first child in each team is given a butterfly cutout that matches his team's flower. He "flies" his butterfly to the flower, touches the butterfly to the flower, and then flies the butterfly back to his team, handing it off to the next student.

Butterfly Drizzles

(See directions on page 164.)

Gross Motor: Review the /k/ sound in *caterpillar* and the /b/ sound in *butterfly* before playing this game. Then call out a word. If the word begins with the /k/ sound, students wiggle around on the floor as if they were caterpillars. If the word begins with the /b/ sound, they flap their arms as if they were butterflies.

Caterpillar and Butterfly

(See directions on page 164.)

My Butterfly

(tune: "My Bonnie Lies Over the Ocean")

My butterfly flies by the flower.
My butterfly flies by the tree.
My butterfly flies by the bushes.
I wish it would fly back to me.
Fly back, fly back,
I wish it would fly back to me, to me.
Fly back, fly back,
I wish it would fly back to me.

Creeping

Creeping, creeping, creeping, crawl.
I can be fuzzy or not at all.
Creeping, creeping, creeping, crawl.
Sometimes I can be a ball.
Creeping, creeping, creeping, crawl
Inch by inch along the wall.

The Little Caterpillar

(tune: "The Itsy-Bitsy Spider")

The little caterpillar
Curled up under a leaf.
It formed a chrysalis
And then it fell asleep.
It grew and it changed and the days flew right on by.
When it popped out of the chrysalis,
It was a butterfly!

Art Activities

Butterfly Drizzles

Tint several containers of glue different colors. To make a butterfly, dip the end of a spoon into the glue and then drizzle the glue onto a construction paper butterfly cutout. Repeat the process with the remaining colors until a desired effect is achieved. Let the project dry thoroughly; then attach pipe cleaner pieces to the butterfly to make antennae.

Caterpillar Circles

Dip an end of a cardboard tube into a container of paint and then press it on a sheet of paper several times to make a caterpillar. Use markers or crayons to add facial details and antennae to the caterpillar. Then glue green crinkle paper below the caterpillar so it looks as though the caterpillar is crawling through the grass.

Caterpillar and Butterfly

On a folded sheet of construction paper, draw a caterpillar shape similar to the one shown. Draw a face on the caterpillar. Then cut out the caterpillar, leaving a section of the fold intact. Next, unfold the caterpillar to reveal a butterfly shape. Glue pieces of torn tissue paper to the resulting butterfly.

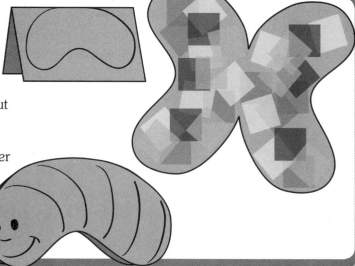

Flowers

Centers for the Week

Math Center: For each of several large tagboard cards, place pattern blocks on the card so they resemble a flower. Trace around the blocks. Then place the cards and pattern blocks at a center, and have each student cover the flowers with the corresponding blocks.

Sensory Table: Place moist sand in your sand table and provide access to empty seed packets, plastic gardening tools, a watering can, and silk flowers. Students use these materials to create a beautiful flower garden.

Literacy Center: Fill a plastic window box with soil. Make flower stick puppets, each labeled with an uppercase or lowercase letter so each letter has a match. A child finds flowers with corresponding letters and then places them side by side in the window box. He continues in the same way with the remaining flowers.

Discovery Center: Gently uproot a few small plants. Shake the dirt off the roots and place the plants at the center along with paper, crayons, and magnifying glasses. Youngsters use the magnifying glasses to explore the parts of a plant and then use the paper and crayons to draw what they see.

Art Center: Post pictures of famous artwork featuring flowers. Provide paint, paper, and brushes. Each student uses the supplies to create his own floral masterpiece.

	Group Time	Literature
Monday	Seat youngsters in a circle. Have individuals pass a flower cutout around the circle, counting as they go. When a student says, "Ten," have all the students pretend to grow like a flower and say, "Beautiful blooms!" Then have little ones sit down and start the game again. Play for several rounds. ***Oral language***	Read aloud *Chrysanthemum* by Kevin Henkes. Chrysanthemum, a little mouse, thinks her name is beautiful. Then she goes to school and learns that her classmates have a different opinion.
Tuesday	Draw on a sheet of chart paper a flower with a stem, leaves, and roots. Help youngsters label the parts of the plant. Then show youngsters an actual flowering plant and encourage them to name its different parts as they did with the drawing. ***Investigating living things***	Revisit yesterday's story. Help students use the book's illustrations to retell the story. Display two name cards. Have youngsters identify the names. Then help students count the number of letters in each name and compare the results.
Wednesday	Copy the chant "Five Little Flowers" from page 167 onto sentence strips, replacing some of the words with pictures to make a rebus chant. Have students help you read the chant. Then place a picture card over one of the rebus pictures. Have students help you read the new, silly version of the chant! ***Print awareness***	Read aloud *The Tiny Seed* by Eric Carle. This book tells the story of how a tiny seed becomes a humongous flower!
Thursday	Attach a small bunch of artificial flowers to a dowel to make a pointer. Display colorful flower cutouts around your classroom. Invite a child to find a flower and use the pointer to gesture to it. Then have him name the color of the flower he found. ***Identifying colors***	Revisit yesterday's story. Then attach a supersize stem and leaves to a wall along with the yellow center of the flower. Encourage each child to use watercolors to paint a white petal cutout. Attach the petals to the flower center.
Friday	Label each of several large cards with a different number. Collect a variety of artificial flowers and place them in a container. Have youngsters help place the correct number of flowers on each card. ***Number identification, counting***	Read aloud *What Does Bunny See?* by Linda Sue Park. During a rereading of the story, have youngsters find something in the room that matches the color of each flower Bunny sees.

Art/Gross-Motor Skills

Beautiful Blooms

(See directions on page 168.)

Gross Motor: Gather youngsters in a tight circle and have them pretend to be seeds in a pot. As you "water" them, have students slowly stand and pretend to sprout leaves and flowers. As the flowers release seeds into the air, have students dance and twirl about the room.

Marvelous Marigolds

(See directions on page 168.)

Gross Motor: Play a recording of music and have little ones pretend to be wildflowers swaying in the breeze. To the beat of the music, have them sway left and then right, back and then forth. Have youngsters alter their movements to reflect a light breeze and then a strong gust of wind.

Handsome Flowers

(See directions on page 168.)

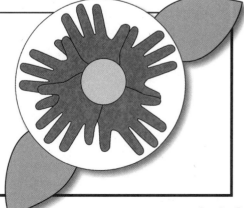

Songs and Such for the Week

Little Flowers
(tune: "Ten Little Indians")

One little, two little, three little flowers,
Four little, five little, six little flowers,
Seven little, eight little, nine little flowers,
Ten little flowers in the sun.

Five Little Flowers

Five little flowers growing in a row,
The first one said, "I'm purple you know."
The second one said, "I'm pink as pink can be."
The third one said, "I'm blue like the sea."
The fourth one said, "I'm a very red fellow."
The fifth one said, "My color is yellow."
Then out came the sun, big and bright,
And five little flowers smiled in delight.

I'm a Little Flower
(tune: "I'm a Little Teapot")

I'm a little flower,
Pretty and pink.
My stem and leaves
Are nice, I think.
When the sun shines bright
And the raindrops fall,
I will grow so big and tall.

Art Activities

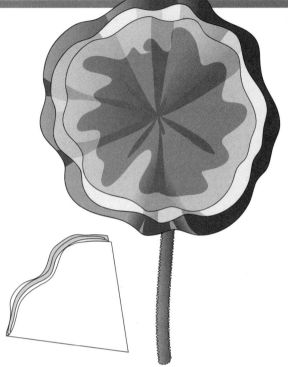

Beautiful Blooms

Fold three coffee filters as shown. Then dip the edges of each filter in tinted water, unfold it, and set it aside. When the filters are dry, stack them and then fold them in half. Gather the filters at the center along the folded edge and wrap a green pipe cleaner stem around the gathered portion. Separate the filters to make a lovely flower.

Marvelous Marigolds

Attach a flowerpot cutout to a sheet of paper. Then slightly swirl yellow, orange, and red paint in a shallow pan. Dip a dish scrubber in the paint and then make prints above the pot. Finally, glue leaf cutouts to the project.

Handsome Flowers

Glue a circular flower center to a sheet of paper. To make petals, make handprints around the flower center with fingers facing outward. If desired, cut out the flower and attach leaf cutouts to the back as shown.

Bees

Centers for the Week

Game Center: Cut out two hives and draw 20 dots on each one. Place the hives at the center along with a die and a container of Honeycomb cereal (with extra cups of cereal for snacking). A student places a cereal piece on each dot. A player rolls the die and removes that number of cereal pieces from his hive. Play continues until both hives are empty.

Math Center: Cut out several copies of the stripeless bee pattern on page 246. Program each bee with a chosen number of stripes. Place the bees and a set of corresponding number cards at the center. A student matches each number card to the correct bee.

Play Dough Center: Set out a supply of yellow and black play dough along with pipe cleaner pieces for the antennae and transparency film cut into the shape of wings. A student uses the supplies to make bees.

Dramatic Play: Put a yellow sheet over a table to make a beehive and place a supply of silk flowers around the outside of the hive. A student pretends to collect the pollen from the flowers and bring it back to the hive to make honey.

Literacy Center: Program a sheet of poster board with various letters, including several *B*s. Place the poster board at the center along with several bee cutouts (see page 246). A child places a bee on each *B*.

	Group Time	Literature
Monday	Give each child a numbered striped bee cutout (see page 246). Have the student with bee number one stand in the front of the room with her bee. Continue in the same way with each student until all the bees are displayed in numerical order. Then play a lively recording of music and have the line of bees dance around the room. ***Identifying numbers, number order***	Read aloud *The Very Greedy Bee* by Steve Smallman. All the bees in the hive work hard making honey except one very greedy bee that spends all day drinking nectar.
Tuesday	Gather objects (or pictures of objects) with names that begin with /b/ and /h/. Place on the floor a large bee cutout and a large hive cutout. Show youngsters an object and have them say its name. Help students identify the name's beginning sound and then place it on the appropriate cutout. ***Beginning sounds***	Revisit yesterday's story. On slips of paper, write some phrases that describe friends and some phrases that do not. Read each phrase aloud to the class and have youngsters decide whether it describes a good friend.
Wednesday	Gather a supply of student name cards. Then have youngsters sit around a large bee cutout. Show youngsters one of the cards and have students identify the name. Have students determine whether there are any *B*s in the name. If there are, have the named youngster place her name card on the bee. If not, have her place her name card beside the bee. ***Letter recognition***	Read aloud *Happy Bees!* by Arthur Yorinks. Bees have a reputation for being hard workers. In this story, learn what bees like to do for fun. Invite students to share things that they like to do for fun.
Thursday	Make a supply of striped bee cutouts using the pattern on page 246. Then place the bees on a bedsheet. Have students hold the edges of the sheet and then toss the bees into the air. Prompt students to say, "Bees, bees, come back to the hive!" Then have youngsters pick up the bees and place them back on the sheet. ***Following directions***	Reread yesterday's book. Then review the rhyming words from the story. Give each student a striped bee cutout (see page 246) and have him place it in his lap. Announce two words. If the words rhyme, he raises his bee into the air.
Friday	Place plastic hoops on the floor to represent the cells in a honeycomb. Tell students that they are hardworking honeybees but, for now, only two bees can work in each cell. Place two bees in each cell. Then have the remaining youngsters count the bees to determine that they have been placed correctly. Repeat the process, making sets of three and four bees. ***Making equal sets***	Read aloud *The Honey Bee and the Robber* by Eric Carle. Have youngsters share both positive and negative feelings about bees.

Art/Gross-Motor Skills

Me As a Bee
(See directions on page 172.)

Gross Motor: Have each child paint black and yellow stripes on a cardboard tube so it resembles a bee. Add wings and antennae to the bee. Then cut the tube from end to end and have a child slip it over his wrist as if it were a cuff bracelet. Play a recording of fast-paced music and have youngsters "fly" their bees around the room.

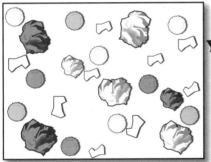

Yellow and Black
(See directions on page 172.)

Gross Motor: Attach laminated flower cutouts to the floor to make a path. Then place yellow beanbags (pollen) on the flowers. A child pretends to be a bee and "flies" from flower to flower holding a basket. He collects the pollen from each flower and places it in his basket.

Hexagon Honeycomb
(See directions on page 172.)

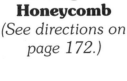

Songs and Such for the Week

Over in the Garden
(tune: "Over in the Meadow")

Over in the garden,
In the flowers near the trees,
Flew a mother bumblebee
And her baby bees three.
"Buzz," said the mother.
"We buzz," said the three.
So they buzzed and they buzzed
In the flowers near the trees.

Working Hard

Little bees are always working hard,
Flying to the flowers in my yard.
They gather nectar and make honey,
Which makes my toast taste oh so
    yummy.

Big Bumblebee
(tune: "Three Blind Mice")

Big bumblebee, big bumblebee,
Yellow and black, yellow and black!
I see you flying around my head.
Once you stung my cousin Ned.
Then your friend stung my Uncle Fred.
So please, fly away; please, fly away!

Art Activities

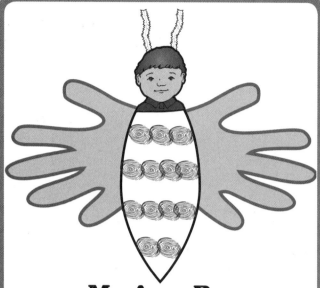

Me As a Bee

Have each child dip his thumb in black tempera paint and make thumbprints across a bee cutout to make stripes. Attach a close-up of the child to the bee's head. Then tape pipe cleaner antennae behind the head. Help him trace and cut out handprints from waxed paper and attach them to the body to make wings.

Yellow and Black

Celebrate bees with a yellow and black collage. Gather a variety of yellow and black paper and craft items. Then glue desired items to a sheet of white construction paper to make a lovely bee-colored masterpiece.

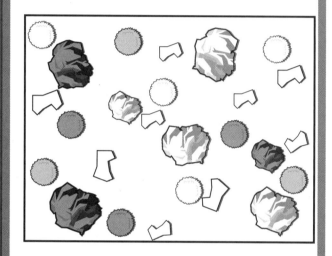

Hexagon Honeycomb

Trim a sponge into a hexagon shape. Then press the sponge into a shallow pan of yellow paint and make prints on a sheet of paper to resemble a honeycomb. If desired, glue yellow construction paper copies of the striped bee pattern on page 246 to the artwork.

Ocean

Centers for the Week

Sensory Table: Moisten the sand in your sand table and provide access to plastic containers and sand toys. Students build sand castles using the provided materials.

Math Center: Make wave cutouts along the tops of several sheets of blue construction paper. Then program each sheet with a different number and place the sheets at the center along with a supply of small ocean animal cutouts. A student puts the appropriate number of ocean animals on each paper.

Discovery Center: Put a variety of seashells at the center, along with magnifying glasses and small plastic pails. Students use the magnifying glasses to study the shells and then sort the shells into pails.

Dramatic Play: For this beach-themed dramatic play, provide a towel, plastic beach toys, sunglasses, beach balls, and ocean-themed books. Youngsters use the items for oodles of pretend play fun.

Art Center: Place at the center a class supply of starfish cutouts and a mixture of purple tempera paint and glue in a shallow pan. Also provide sponges and glitter. Each student sponge-paints a starfish cutout and then sprinkles glitter on the paint.

Group Time	Literature

Monday

Seat students in a circle. Place ocean animal cutouts in a small paper bag and pass the bag around the circle. Each student, in turn, takes a picture from the bag and says, "When I went swimming in the deep blue sea, I saw a(n) _____ looking at me!" *Oral language*

Read aloud *Ten Little Fish* by Audrey Wood. This adorable story invites students to practice counting brilliantly colored fish backward and then forward. Youngsters will adore the unique illustrations in this storybook.

Tuesday

Write "I went to the beach with my friend" on an oversize sand castle cutout. Then attach the castle to a wall. Invite students to continue the story as you write their words on the castle. *Writing*

Reread yesterday's story; then give each student a fish cutout. Each student colors her fish using her favorite color. Use the cutouts to make a graph that shows youngsters' favorite colors.

Wednesday

Tell students that you need help packing items for a trip to the beach. Display items that you would and would not take and a suitcase. Have each student choose an item. If the item is something that would be appropriate for a beach trip, she places it in your suitcase. If it is not, she places it beside your suitcase. *Classifying*

Read aloud *The Whales' Song* by Dyan Sheldon. In this book, a child listens to her grandmother's tales about hearing whales sing after giving them a special gift, such as a pretty stone or a seashell. Striking oil paintings accompany the text.

Thursday

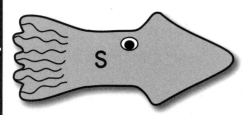

Place on a bedsheet (net) simple squid cutouts, each programmed with a letter. Students hold the edges of the net and lift it in the air to toss the squids. Each student finds a squid and then names the letter. *Letter identification*

Revisit yesterday's story. Then give each child a large whale cutout and ask him to draw on it a picture of a gift he would give to the whales so he could hear their song. Allow students to share their drawings. Then bind the drawings together to make a class book.

Friday

Display several common classroom objects and have youngsters predict whether each one will sink or float. Write their predictions on a simple two-column chart. One at a time, place the objects in a pan of water. If the students' prediction for the object is correct, place a star beside the object's name on the list. *Making predictions*

Read aloud *Hello Ocean* by Pam Munoz Ryan. Discuss the experiences the little girl has at the beach, focusing on the different scents the youngster encounters. Invite students to discuss different scents they have smelled.

Art/Gross-Motor Skills

All Puffed Up!
(See directions on page 176.)

Gross Motor: Have students imagine they are fish swimming in the ocean. Play a recording of music that has varying tempos. Students "swim" about the room, reflecting the tempo of the music.

Going Swimming
(See directions on page 176.)

Gross Motor: Give each student a blue crepe paper streamer (wave). Have students stand in a circle and move their waves in a variety of ways, such as wiggling them from side to side, up and down, near the ground, and way up high. You may even have youngsters move their waves outside and then inside the circle.

Fishy Feet
(See directions on page 176.)

Songs and Such for the Week

Show Your Teeth
(tune: "If You're Happy and You Know It")

If you're a [shark] in the ocean, [show your teeth (chomp, chomp)].
If you're a [shark] in the ocean, [show your teeth (chomp, chomp)].
You'd be happy as can be in the ocean, wild and free.
If you're a [shark] in the ocean, [show your teeth (chomp, chomp)].

Continue with the following;
whale, spout some water (whoosh, whoosh); dolphin, jump with glee (splash, splash); crab, snap your claws (snap, snap); fish, flap your fins (flap, flap).

Five Ocean Friends

Five ocean friends near the ocean floor,
Crab went away and then there were four.
Four ocean friends living in the sea,
Lobster went away and then there were three.
Three ocean friends in the water so blue,
Jellyfish went away and then there were two.
Two ocean friends having some fun,
Sea horse went away and then there was one.
One ocean friend all alone,
Closed up in the shell that he calls home.

Rolling Waves
(tune: "The Hokey-Pokey")

The waves roll in,
And the waves roll out.
The waves roll in,
And they move the sand about.
Waves can be so big
Or can be so very small.
The ocean is fun for all!

All Puffed Up!

To make this porcupine fish, use markers to draw eyes and a mouth on a polystyrene ball. Then use craft glue to attach fin and tail cutouts to the ball. (You may need to use tacks to hold the cutouts in place until the glue dries.) Next, randomly stick pieces of spaghetti into the ball to make spines.

Going Swimming

Staple a short wave cutout to a tall wave cutout, leaving the bottom open as shown. Then attach a few fish stickers or foam cutouts to the waves. Next, add details to a person cutout so the cutout resembles a person at the beach. Attach a wooden craft stick to the back of the person to make a puppet. Insert the puppet between the waves.

Fishy Feet

Place a bare foot in a shallow pan of tempera paint. Then step on a sheet of blue construction paper. After the footprint is dry, draw details so the footprint resembles a fish. Use markers and paper to make other items found in the ocean, such as shells, seaweed, and rocks. Then attach the items to the project.

Zoo

Centers for the Week

Math Center: Make two copies of the picture cards on page 247. Use a marker to color the animals on one set of cards black. Spread the cards out facedown. In turn, students turn over two cards at a time to try to find matching pairs of animals and silhouettes.

Literacy Center: Attach zoo animal cards to a sheet of poster board (see page 247 for cards). Cover an empty cubic box with paper. Label each side of the cube with the beginning letter of a different one of the zoo animals. A student rolls the cube; then he identifies the letter and its sound. He places a pom-pom on the animal with the corresponding beginning sound. He repeats the process until all the animals are covered.

Block Center: Provide zoo animals, people figurines, rocks, twigs, paper, markers, and small containers for feeding the animals. A student uses the items to create a zoo and make signs for the various animals.

Play Dough Center: Trace zoo animal cookie cutters onto a sheet of construction paper; then laminate the paper to create a nonstick surface. Provide a supply of play dough, along with the cookie cutters. A student presses a cookie cutter into flattened play dough, removes the animal from the cookie cutter, and places it atop the matching outline on the mat.

Art Center: Provide brown and yellow paper strips, a yellow paper plate, glue, and markers. A child curls strips around a marker and then glues them around the edge of the plate to make a mane. She uses permanent markers to draw facial features on the resulting lion.

	Group Time	Literature
Monday	Place large plastic zoo animals in various centers in your classroom. Take students on a pretend train ride through this makeshift zoo, collecting the animals along the way. After settling in for group time, have youngsters name each animal and describe similarities and differences between the animals. ***Oral language, making comparisons***	Read aloud *1, 2, 3 to the Zoo* by Eric Carle. This colorful train ride to the zoo provides youngsters with plenty of counting practice!
Tuesday	Provide each student with three different animal crackers along with a strip of paper labeled with the three boxes. Instruct students to put the elephant in the first box, the giraffe in the second, and the monkey in the third. Then have them remove the crackers and listen for new directions. ***Ordinal positions***	Revisit yesterday's book; then give each child a sheet of paper programmed with a number. Have her use a zoo animal rubber stamp and an ink pad to stamp the appropriate number of animals on the paper.
Wednesday	Place zoo animal cards in a bag (see cards on page 247). Write on a sheet of chart paper, "I went to the zoo and I saw a _____." To begin, ask a student to pick an animal from the bag and attach it to the blank space. Read the sentence aloud. Then encourage youngsters to add to the story, inviting a student to pick an animal from the bag each time a new character is needed. ***Contributing to a class story***	Read aloud *Polar Bear, Polar Bear, What Do You Hear?* by Bill Martin Jr. The repetitive text and colorful illustrations in this book invite youngsters to join in as you read.
Thursday	Play some lively music and have students pass a zoo animal stuffed toy around the circle. When you stop the music, have the youngster holding the animal tell one thing about it, such as, "It has spots," or "It has four legs." Continue in the same manner, encouraging each child to name something different. ***Observation skills***	Reread yesterday's story; then lead students in saying the chant, "Zookeeper, zookeeper, what do you see?" Invite students to respond to the chant, naming animals they might see at the zoo.
Friday	Mount pictures of zoo animals on separate sheets of paper. Staple a second sheet of paper to the top of the first sheet; then cut flaps in the paper. Lift a flap to reveal part of the animal; then have students try to guess what the animal is. Continue in the same manner. ***Visual discrimination***	Read *Corduroy at the Zoo* by Don Freeman. Have students guess what's behind each flap as you read the pages aloud; then invite volunteers to lift the flaps and reveal the hidden surprises!

Elegant Elephant
(See directions on page 180.)

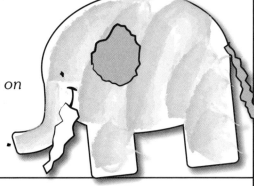

Gross Motor: Position youngsters so they have a lot of room to move. Then pretend to be the zookeeper and call out directions such as, "Zookeeper says, 'walk like an elephant,'" or 'Hop like a kangaroo.'" After you have played a few rounds, let volunteers pretend to be the zookeeper and give the directions.

Gorgeous Giraffe
(See directions on page 180.)

Gross Motor: Partially fill several plastic bottles with sand; then attach a zoo animal picture to each bottle. Set the bottles up in an open area and provide students with a ball. Have youngsters take turns rolling the ball to try to knock down the bottles. Encourage students to name the animal on each bottle they knock down. Then instruct each child to set the bottles back up for the next child's turn.

Zippy Zebra
(See directions on page 180.)

Going to the Zoo
(tune: "For He's a Jolly Good Fellow")

We're going to the zoo.
We're going to the zoo.
We're going to the zoo.
I hope that you come too.

We'll see lots of animals.
We'll see lots of animals.
We'll see lots of animals
When we are at the zoo!

At the Zoo

There are lots of animals at the zoo.
Monkeys, zebras, and kangaroos.
Elephants, polar bears, and hippos too.
There's so much to see when you visit the zoo!

Animals Talk
(tune: "Do Your Ears Hang Low?")

Do you hear the [bears]
When you see them at the zoo?
They will make this sound
If they want to talk to you.
[Grr, grr, grr, grr, grr, grr, grr, grr, grr, grr, grr, grr].
Do you hear the [bears]?

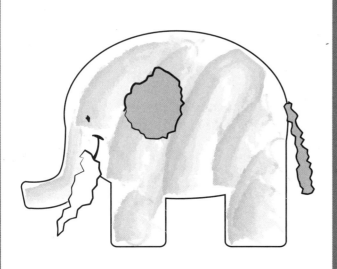

Elegant Elephant

To make an elephant, sponge-paint a sheet of white construction paper with gray tempera paint. After the paint is dry, draw a simple elephant shape (minus the tail) on the paper; then cut out the shape. Next, tear from the remaining paper an ear and a tail; then glue the pieces in place. Then tear a strip of white construction paper so it resembles a tusk and glue it near the trunk. Finally, use a marker to draw facial details.

Gorgeous Giraffe

Pour orange and brown paint into separate containers. To make a giraffe, dip your fingertips into the orange paint and then make fingerprints on a sheet of manila paper. Repeat the process with the brown paint. After the paint dries, draw a simple giraffe outline on the paper and cut it out. Glue yarn to the giraffe to make a mane and tail. Use a marker to draw details on the face.

Zippy Zebra

To make this zebra, place a horse pattern in a plastic container. Drop black paint–covered golf balls in the container and then secure the lid. Shake the container back and forth. Then remove the lid to reveal the zebra. When the paint is dry, cut out the zebra. Glue rickrack to the zebra to make a mane and tail, and use a marker to add details to the face.

Picnic

Centers for the Week

Dramatic Play: For this picnic area, provide a blanket, a picnic basket, a cooler, plastic food, a pretend grill, cooking and eating utensils, empty condiment bottles, and picnic-related books. A student uses the props to engage in pretend picnic play.

Math Center: Provide a picnic basket filled with an equal number of plastic forks, knives, and spoons, along with napkins and cardboard tube sections to use as napkin rings. A student makes sets consisting of one fork, one knife, and one spoon. Then she wraps each set in a napkin and secures it with a napkin ring.

Literacy Center: Cut out several copies of the pattern pieces on page 248 from appropriate-colored paper. Label each peanut butter shape with a different uppercase letter and each jelly shape with a corresponding lowercase letter. A student matches his peanut butter and jelly patterns and places them between two slices of bread.

Sensory Table: Place mustard, ketchup, and small pieces of pickle and watermelon in separate disposable cups. Cover each cup with aluminum foil; then poke holes in the foil. A student sniffs each cup and tries to identify the smell. As an alternative, make pairs of scent cups for matching.

Play Dough Center: Cover a table with a vinyl tablecloth. Provide several colors of play dough along with a frying pan, a spatula, empty condiment containers, and plastic tableware. A student molds the play dough into picnic-related food and pretends to cook and eat it.

Group Time	Literature
Monday Prepare a three-column graph. Label each column with the name of a different picnic location, such as the zoo, the park, and the beach. In turn, each student attaches a personalized basket cutout to the graph to show his preferred picnic location. Then youngsters compare the results. ***Graphing, counting*** 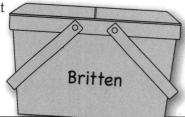 Britten	Read aloud *The Most Perfect Spot* by Diane Goode. This is the story of a little boy named Jack who thought he had the perfect place to take Mama on a picnic. But with a number of humorous mishaps, Jack's perfect picnic does not go quite as he had planned!
Tuesday Place near a picnic basket several picnic-related items and several unrelated items. In turn, students pick an item, name it, and then place it in the basket if it is picnic-related. If it is not picnic-related, they place the item to the side. ***Categorizing, sorting***	Revisit yesterday's story. Have students use the book's illustrations to retell the story. Then, following the book's format, have each child add a surprise element to a class picnic story.
Wednesday Give each student a napkin and a cup with ten Ritz Bits minicrackers, along with ten small black pom-poms (ants). Have each child count out a predetermined number of crackers and place them on her napkin. Then say, "Oh no! Here come the ants!" Have each student count out a corresponding number of ants, and then place each ant next to a cracker. Repeat the activity several times. Then invite youngsters to eat the crackers. ***One-to-one correspondence***	Read aloud *The Best Picnic Ever* by Clare Jarrett. In this story, a little boy named Jack meets up with some very unusual playmates while waiting for his mother to prepare their picnic!
Thursday Have students create a picnic list. Begin by saying, "I will bring…" and then name an item. Have the first child in the circle repeat the phrase, including the item you named, and then name an item of his own. In turn, each child in the circle repeats the phrase, naming all the previous items and then adding a word of his own. Provide help as needed to prompt students' memories. ***Auditory memory, oral language***	Reread yesterday's story and then have students compare Jack's picnic experience in this story with another Jack's picnic experience in Monday's story, *The Most Perfect Spot.*
Friday Secretly place an item, such as a pair of sunglasses, in a picnic basket. Give students a clue to help them determine what the item is. For example, you might say, "You wear these on your head." Provide additional clues until youngsters identify the item. Repeat the activity with other items as time allows. ***Critical thinking***	Read aloud *It's the Bear!* by Jez Alborough. Have one child (the bear) cover his eyes while another child hides in a box (a picnic basket). The bear taps on the basket, and the child inside says, "I want my mom!" just as Eddie does in the story. The bear listens and tries to guess who is in the basket.

Art/Gross-Motor Skills

Picnic Placemats
(See directions on page 184.)

Gross Motor: Play a recording of music and have students join hands and walk in a circle. Stop the music periodically throughout the activity. When the music stops, students drop hands and dance around like they have ants in their pants! When the music restarts, youngsters hold hands and walk in a circle again.

Adorable Ants
(See directions on page 184.)

Gross Motor: Place a picnic basket in the center of a blanket. Have students stand around the edge of the blanket; then give each child a large black pom-pom (ant). In turn, each child tries to toss his ant into the basket. After everyone has had a turn, count aloud the number of ants that made it into the basket. Repeat the activity as time allows.

Delicious Watermelon
(See directions on page 184.)

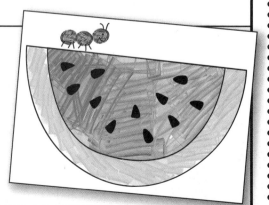

Songs and Such for the Week

Down by the Picnic
(tune: "Down by the Station")

Down by the picnic,
Right around my lunchtime,
See the little ants all
Marching in a row.
See them take my apple
And then take my sandwich.
Tug, tug, pull, pull.
Off they go!

Picnic Mood

I packed a picnic basket
With fruit and cheese and meat,
Sandwiches and salads—
Such tasty things to eat!
I'll spread the picnic blanket
And set out picnic food.
Oh, won't you come and join me?
I'm in a picnic mood!

In My Basket
(tune: "Twinkle, Twinkle, Little Star")

In my basket you will see
A picnic lunch for you and me.
Apples, carrots, cupcakes too.
Sandwiches for me and you.
In my basket you will see
A picnic lunch for you and me.

Art Activities

Picnic Placemats

Cut four 1" x 12" red craft foam strips. Fold a 9" x 12" sheet of white craft foam in half horizontally. Starting at the fold, cut several slits, stopping each slit about one inch from the edge. Weave a red foam strip through the slits. Weave the remaining strips, reversing the pattern with each strip added. Trim any excess foam from the strips and glue the ends in place. Finally, glue a place setting of disposable tableware to the placemat.

Adorable Ants

To make an ant, stuff a small black, brown, or red sock with fiberfill stuffing. Use three rubber bands to segment the ant's body and then fold the sock cuff over as shown. Finally, use craft glue to attach six felt legs, two felt antennae, and two construction paper eyes.

Delicious Watermelon

Tint separate containers of light corn syrup with red and green food coloring. Paint a watermelon pattern with the prepared corn syrup. Then press seed cutouts onto the red portion of the watermelon. Next, make three black fingerprints above the watermelon. Then use a marker to draw antennae and legs on the fingerprints so they resemble ants.

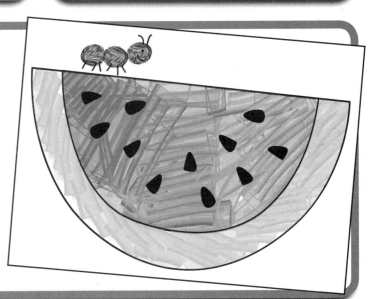

Ice Cream

Centers for the Week

Dramatic Play: Provide ice cream parlor–themed items, such as clean, empty ice cream containers and ice cream topping bottles, plastic ice cream sundae glasses, ice cream scoops, tagboard cones and foam balls (ice cream), placemats, napkins, aprons, a cash register, and play money.

Play Dough Center: Provide white (vanilla ice cream), pink (strawberry ice cream), and brown (chocolate ice cream) play dough along with a spring-loaded ice cream scoop, plastic bowls, plastic spoons, and tagboard ice cream cones. Students scoop the play dough ice cream into the bowls and cones.

Writing Center: Place at the center construction paper scraps, markers, and glue, as well as copies of page 249. A youngster decorates the ice cream on the reproducible as desired and then dictates a description of his ice cream as you write his words in the space provided.

Math Center: Make construction paper cones and different-colored scoops of ice cream. Then place the cutouts at the center along with several patterning cards. A child chooses a pattern card and then places scoops above a cone to match the pattern.

Literacy Center: Provide a supersize banana split bowl cutout and place it on the floor in the center, along with 26 ice cream scoop cutouts (see patterns on page 250), each labeled with a different letter. Also provide an alphabet strip. A student places the scoops of ice cream in the bowl in alphabetical order, using the strip as a guide.

Group Time	Literature

Monday

Obtain a container of Neapolitan ice cream. Label the columns on a large graph "vanilla," "chocolate," and "strawberry." Provide a supply of white, pink, and brown ice cream scoop cutouts (see patterns on page 250). Give students a sample of each flavor of ice cream. In turn, have each student attach to the graph a cutout that represents his favorite flavor. **Graphing**

Read aloud *From Milk to Ice Cream* by Stacy Taus-Bolstad. This book takes youngsters through a simple step-by-step process of how milk is factory-made into ice cream with easy-to-understand text and real-life photographs.

Tuesday

Seat students in a circle. Give each child a three-dimensional tagboard cone. Begin by placing a ball (ice cream) in a child's cone. Have the child pass the ice cream from his cone to the cone of the child sitting next to him. Continue in the same way until the ice cream has been passed around the entire circle. **Eye-hand coordination, fine-motor skills**

Revisit yesterday's book. Ask students to recall the steps of how ice cream is made through the sequence of photographs.

Wednesday

Gather a supply of pom-poms and a clean, empty ice cream container. Ask students to estimate how many pom-poms (scoops of ice cream) will fit into the container. Record student responses. Lead the class in counting aloud as you place pom-poms in the container. Then compare the number of pom-poms that fit in the container to student estimates. **Estimating, counting**

Read aloud *Curious George Goes to an Ice Cream Shop* by H. A. Rey. George makes the shopkeeper very angry when he messes up a big order. But the story ends happily when George attracts a lot of customers into the store by making a huge ice cream sundae in the front window!

Thursday

Place three ice cream cones upside down on a tray. Have students observe while you place a red pom-pom (cherry) under one of the cones. Then rearrange the cones and have a volunteer guess which cone the cherry is under. Continue in the same manner as time allows. **Observation skills**

Reread yesterday's story. Then pass a big bowl around the circle along with an ice cream scoop. In turn, have each student pretend to put a scoop of her favorite ice cream and topping in the bowl.

Friday

Give each student a small resealable bag containing milk, sugar, and vanilla inside a large resealable bag containing salt and ice cubes (see recipe below). Tape each sealed bag. Have students shake the bags until the mixture turns to ice cream. Then pass out spoons and enjoy! **Following directions, cause and effect**

½ cup whole milk
1 tablespoon sugar
¼ teaspoon vanilla
2 cups ice cubes
½ cup salt

Read aloud *Milk to Ice Cream* by Inez Snyder. Review how Mark and his dad make homemade ice cream; then have youngsters follow the recipe in Friday's group activity. Yummy!

Yummy Sundae!
(See directions on page 188.)

Gross Motor: Gather students in a circle. Place a plastic punch bowl (ice cream dish) on the floor. In turn, each student tosses a wad of fiberfill or tissue paper (scoops of ice cream) into the bowl. Youngsters continue in the same manner until the ice cream dish is full!

Creamy Cone
(See directions on page 188.)

Gross Motor: Divide your group into equal teams. Place a clean, empty ice cream container at one end of an open area for each team. Give each team an ice cream scoop and a bowl of pom-poms. In turn, each student scoops up a pom-pom, runs to the container, drops the pom-pom in, and then runs back and passes the scoop to the next child. Play continues until all the pom-poms are in the containers.

Thick Shake
(See directions on page 188.)

Do You Like Ice Cream?
(tune: "Do Your Ears Hang Low?")

Do you like ice cream
In a bowl or in a cone?
Do you like it with some chocolate,
With some nuts, or all alone?
Do you like it with some sprinkles
Or some syrup poured on top?
Do you like ice cream?

The More We Eat Ice Cream
(tune: "The More We Get Together")

The more we eat ice cream,
Eat ice cream, eat ice cream;
The more we eat ice cream,
The happier we'll be!
'Cause ice cream is yummy
And cold in my tummy.
The more we eat ice cream,
The happier we'll be!

Yummy Treat

Ice cream tastes delicious!
Ice cream tastes so sweet!
In a bowl or in a cone,
It's a yummy treat!

Art Activities

Thick Shake

Tint separate containers of glue different colors so the glue resembles different ice cream flavors. To make a thick shake, paint the inside of a large clear plastic cup with a desired color of glue. Next, glue a flexible drinking straw to the inside of the cup. Then fill the cup with wads of tissue paper in a coordinating color. Glue a wad of white fiberfill to the top of the project so it resembles whipped cream; then glue a red pom-pom (cherry) to the whipped cream.

Creamy Cone

Make a brown construction paper crayon rubbing of a piece of plastic canvas. Cut a cone shape from the paper and glue it to a sheet of construction paper. Mix equal amounts of shaving cream and glue; then place dollops of the mixture above the cone so it resembles ice cream. If desired, decorate the cone with colorful paper dots or pom-poms.

Yummy Sundae!

To make an ice cream sundae, glue a wad of fiberfill to a disposable bowl. Squeeze brown or red tempera paint over the fiberfill so it resembles chocolate or strawberry topping. Shake candy sprinkles onto the wet paint. Dip a red pom-pom in glue and place it on top of the project so it resembles a cherry. Then dip the end of a plastic spoon in glue and place it in the bowl.

Camping

Centers for the Week

Sensory Table: Add a variety of medium-size rocks and plastic fish to your water table. Also provide small fish nets and plastic pails. A student uses a fish net to scoop up the fish and put them in a pail.

Literacy Center: Glue brown-painted tubes (logs) to a cardboard base. Then glue orange and yellow tissue paper to the logs so the paper and logs resemble a campfire. Provide picture cards (or objects) that show items that begin with /f/ as well as items that do not. A child chooses a picture card. If the item pictured begins with /f/, he places it on the fire. If it does not, he places it in a separate pile.

Math Center: For each of several pairs of fish, label one fish with a number and the other with a corresponding dot set. A child uses a spatula to place a numbered fish in a frying pan. He finds the fish with the corresponding dot set and places it next to the fish in the pan. He removes the fish and repeats the process with each remaining pair.

Art Center: Provide construction paper and several containers of paint. Also provide rubber worms tied to craft stick fishing poles. A student dips a worm in paint and then manipulates the craft stick to wiggle the worm on a sheet of paper.

Dramatic Play: Provide camping-themed items, such as a small tent, sleeping bags, backpacks, rain ponchos, canteens, flashlights, a compass, binoculars, a cooler, toy food, cookware, plastic plates, utensils, a makeshift campfire, stuffed forest animals, and fishing poles.

	Group Time	Literature
Monday	Lead a discussion about camping. Ask camping-related questions, such as the following: "What types of things do you need to go camping?" "What kinds of things do you do when you go camping?" "What do you eat?" "How is it different from being at home?" Invite students who have gone camping to share their experiences with the class. ***Oral language, critical thinking***	Read aloud *Bailey Goes Camping* by Kevin Henkes. This is the story of a bunny named Bailey who was too little to go camping. But with the help of Mama and Papa, Bailey went camping right in his own home.
Tuesday	Prepare four copies of each card on page 251 for a game of Concentration. Spread the cards facedown on the floor. Have students take turns flipping over pairs of cards. Remove matches as they are found. Continue the game until all the cards have been matched. ***Visual memory, taking turns***	Revisit yesterday's story. Then give students an indoor camping adventure just like Bailey's. Have youngsters sit around a makeshift campfire pretending to roast marshmallows (cotton balls glued to craft sticks) as you lead them in singing several songs.
Wednesday	Display several camping-related items and then place them in a backpack. Zipper the backpack, leaving an opening large enough for a child's hand to fit inside. In turn, invite students to reach into the backpack, feel an object, and then identify what the item is. ***Tactile discrimination***	Read aloud *Maisy Goes Camping* by Lucy Cousins. In this giggle-inducing story, Maisy and her friends find out that pitching a tent is not so easy and that squeezing too many campers into one tent is even harder!
Thursday	Program fish cutouts with different shapes and attach a jumbo paper clip to each cutout. Scatter the fish on your floor. Attach a magnet to a craft stick fishing pole. Lead students in reciting the chant; then name a shape. Have a child use the fishing pole to "catch" the appropriate fish and then place the fish on a plastic dish. ***Shape recognition*** We're going on a camping trip to catch some tasty fish! Please find the fish whose shape I call and put it on the dish!	Reread yesterday's story; then have students, in turn, climb into a pretend classroom tent. After everyone has squeezed in, have each child, in turn, spill out of the tent! Then have youngsters think of solutions to this camping dilemma.
Friday	Place several camping-related items near a sleeping bag. Have a student get in the sleeping bag and pretend to be asleep. Have another child remove one of the items and place it out of sight. Then have the class chant, "Wake up, little camper!" The sleeping child wakes up and guesses which item is missing. ***Visual memory***	Read aloud *A Camping Spree With Mr. Magee* by Chris Van Dusen. Then have youngsters dip bear-shaped crackers into marshmallow fluff for a tasty treat.

Art/Gross-Motor Skills

Milk-Carton Campsite
(See directions on page 192.)

Gross Motor: Place a makeshift campfire in the middle of your circle-time area. Gather youngsters in a circle around the campfire and have them join hands. Encourage them to sing familiar songs as they walk in a circle around the campfire. (Be sure to reverse the direction several times throughout each song).

Nature Frames
(See directions on page 192.)

Gross Motor: This activity is best done outside or in a gym. Lay on the floor two jump ropes parallel to one another and a short distance apart (babbling brook). Youngsters try to jump over the brook without getting their feet wet. After each child has had a turn, move the ropes to widen the brook. Continue in the same manner as time allows.

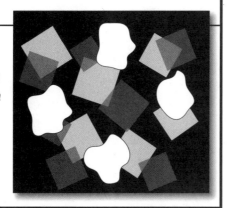

Super S'mores
(See directions on page 192.)

Songs and Such for the Week

Sleepy Time Tent
Climb in your tent
When you're ready to sleep.
Zip up the flap,
And don't make a peep.
Crawl in your sleeping bag;
Snuggle up tight.
Close your eyes slowly
And whisper, "Goodnight."

Round the Campfire
(tune: "The Mulberry Bush")

Here we go roasting marshmallows,
Marshmallows, marshmallows.
Here we go roasting marshmallows;
They're [tasty] and they're warm!

Continue with the following:
gooey, yummy, sticky, puffy

Camping Trip
Pack your gear.
Come on, let's go!
We'll go hiking,
High and low!
We'll pitch a tent
And catch some fish;
Then fry them up
For a tasty dish!

Art Activities

Milk-Carton Campsite

Cut a slit down the middle and then across the bottom of a clean milk carton. Fold the resulting flaps back so they resemble the flaps on a tent. Paint the tent a desired color; then glue the tent to a cardboard base. Decorate the project with green crinkle shreds (grass), rocks, and twigs so it resembles a campsite.

Nature Frames

Glue twigs and small silk flowers and leaves to a tagboard frame. After the glue is dry, attach a piece of twine to the back of the frame for hanging. Then tape a desired photo to the back of the frame so the picture is displayed through the opening.

Super S'mores

To make this s'more collage, gather light-brown tissue paper squares (graham crackers) and dark-brown tissue paper squares (chocolate). Then glue the pieces to a sheet of black construction paper until a desired effect is achieved. Next, place dollops of shaving cream mixed with glue on the paper so it resembles melted marshmallows. Allow the artwork to dry.

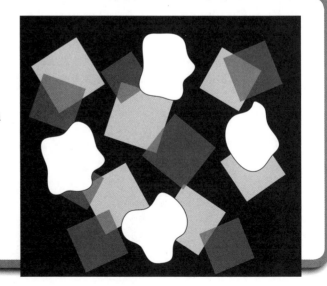

Construction

Centers for the Week

Block Center: Provide a plastic toolbox with a variety of children's tools. Also provide work aprons, hard hats, and safety goggles. Students use the tools and props to engage in construction play as they build structures with the blocks.

Fine-Motor Area: Provide polystyrene foam blocks, clay, golf tees, craft sticks, plastic screws, plastic screwdrivers, and rubber mallets. Students use the tools and materials of their choice to build sculptures.

Math Center: Trace a variety of shapes onto several sheets of construction paper so each tracing resembles a house or a building. Provide a supply of matching construction paper shapes. A student places matching shapes on each outline to complete the building.

Sensory Table: Fill your sensory table with soil. Add some medium-size rocks and sticks, along with a supply of toy construction vehicles and small wooden blocks. Students use the vehicles and the blocks to engage in pretend construction play.

Art Center: Provide four equal squares of cardboard to each child. A student brushes diluted glue on the back of a scrap of wallpaper. Then she attaches it to a piece of cardboard. On the opposite side of the cardboard, she draws windows and doors. She repeats the process for each piece of cardboard. Then she tapes the pieces together (wallpaper facing in) so they resemble the walls of a house.

Group Time	Literature

Monday

Color and cut out a copy of the cards on page 252; then place them in a toolbox. Choose a volunteer to stand by the toolbox. Lead students in chanting, "Construction worker, construction worker, what do you say? What is in your toolbox today?" The student removes a card from the toolbox and identifies the tool on the card. *Vocabulary*

Read aloud *One Big Building* by Michael Dahl. In this counting book, the simple text and illustrations take a building from one simple plan to a beautiful 12-story structure!

Tuesday

Gather pairs of matching blocks; then give each child a block. A student walks around the inside of the circle until she finds the child with the matching block. The two children put their blocks on the floor to begin a structure. Play continues in the same way, with each pair of youngsters adding to the structure. When the activity is done, each child removes a block and puts it away. *Recognizing shapes*

Revisit yesterday's story. Have students look carefully at each page to find the number hidden in each picture.

Wednesday

Place construction tools and kitchen tools in a bag. Place two plastic hoops on the floor. Label one hoop *kitchen* and the remaining hoop *construction*. In turn, volunteers remove an item from the bag, identify it as a construction tool or a kitchen tool, and then place it in the corresponding hoop. *Categorizing*

Read aloud *Get to Work Trucks!* by Don Carter. In this book, big machines are hard at work—lifting, dumping, digging, and filling—under the watchful eye of an unexpected onlooker!

Thursday

Collect three toy hard hats and a strong magnet. Tape a metal hardware item, such as a large bolt or a hinge, to the inside of one hat. Place the hats in a row on the floor, showing students the location of the hat containing the item; then mix the hats. Ask a volunteer to guess which hat contains the item; then have her use the magnet to check her guess. *Visual tracking*

Reread yesterday's story. Have students decorate a turtle cutout so it resembles the turtle that watches the truck drivers on each page. Then attach a hardhat cutout to the turtle. Safety first!

Friday

Place a small cardboard box (house) on a tray. Display a piece of each of the following items: fabric, paper, cardboard, and wood. Ask students to predict which material would make the best roof in a rainstorm. Record student predictions. Place one of the items on the house, and have a child use a watering can to water the house. Remove the item to see if any water is inside the house. Repeat the process with each remaining item. *Critical thinking*

Read aloud *Raise the Roof!* by Anastasia Suen. Then have students recall things that need to be done to build the house, referring to the pictures as necessary.

Art/Gross-Motor Skills

Blueprint Designs
(See directions on page 196.)

Gross Motor: Give each student a small wooden block and a tool, such as a plastic hammer, wrench, screwdriver, wooden dowel, piece of plastic pipe, or ruler. Play a recording of lively music and have students march around the room tapping their tools on their blocks. Stop the music occasionally to have each youngster trade his makeshift instrument with a classmate's.

Beautiful Buildings
(See directions on page 196.)

Gross Motor: Have students pantomime working with a variety of tools, such as using a hammer to pound nails, using a saw, using a wrench to tighten a bolt, and turning a screwdriver. Then say, "Lunchtime!" and encourage students to pretend to eat a sandwich.

Mallet Painting
(See directions on page 196.)

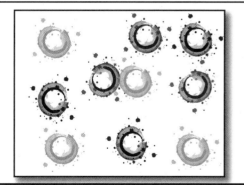

Songs and Such for the Week

On the Job
(tune: "Row, Row, Row Your Boat")

Saw, saw, saw the wood,
Working hard all day.
Pound, pound, pound the nails;
Then put your tools away!

The Toolbox Song
(tune: "She'll Be Comin' Round the Mountain")

I'll be filling up my toolbox; yes, I will!
I'll be filling up my toolbox; yes, I will!
With my hammers and my pliers
And my Phillips screwdrivers,
I'll be filling up my toolbox; yes, I will!

Five Construction Workers

[Five] construction workers at the
    hardware store,
They had some tools but they needed
    more.
Along came [Marcus] with some money
    to pay.
He bought a [hammer] and he drove
    away.

Continue counting down, substituting the number, the child's name, and the tool.

Art Activities

Blueprint Designs

Cut the edges from a foam vegetable tray so the tray lies flat. Draw a house on the tray by pressing a dull pencil into the foam. Next, load a small paint roller with blue paint and then roll it over the design. Press the painted design onto a sheet of white paper; then remove the tray from the paper to reveal a print of the house.

Beautiful Buildings

Paint the outside of a cardboard box a desired color. When the paint is dry, decorate the house with items such as wooden shapes, toothpicks, craft sticks, fabric scraps, and wallpaper samples.

Mallet Painting

For this outside art project, secure a supersize sheet of paper to a sidewalk. Then don a paint smock. Dip a rubber mallet into a shallow pan of washable tempera paint and then hammer the mallet on the paper. Repeat the process with several different colors of paint.

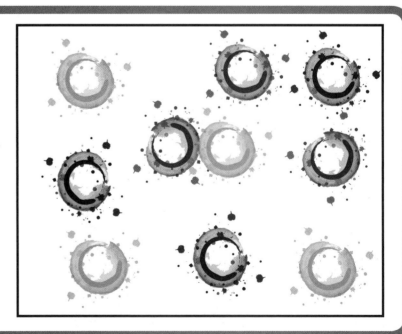

Teddy Bears

Centers for the Week

Math Center: Cut out six brown construction paper copies of the bear pattern on page 253. In the center of each bear, attach a different pattern block cutout. Place the bears and a supply of pattern blocks at the center. A student stacks matching pattern blocks on each bear.

Discovery Center: Place a few stuffed bears, teddy bear counters, and a balance scale at the center. A student places a stuffed bear on one side of the balance. Then she adds teddy bear counters to the remaining side until the weights are balanced.

Play Dough Center: Set out a supply of brown play dough along with bear-shaped cookie cutters in several sizes. A student makes play dough bear cutouts to create a teddy bear family.

Gross-Motor Area: Attach a large bear cutout to the front of a tub and place the tub at the center along with a supply of beanbags (fish). A student "feeds" the bear by tossing the fish into the tub.

Block Center: A student brings his teddy bear from home to the center. At the center, he uses a variety of blocks to build a house for his teddy bear.

Group Time	Literature

Monday

Have the students sit in a circle with teddy bears they brought from home. Place on the floor three plastic hoops labeled "small," "medium," and "large." In turn, have each student examine the size of his bear compared to the other bears and place it in the appropriate hoop. There will be plenty of opportunities for size-related discussion. **Sorting**

Read aloud *A Pocket for Corduroy* by Don Freeman. Corduroy gets lost while looking for a pocket at the laundromat. Lisa is very worried because she can't find Corduroy. After an adventure with a dryer and a box of soap flakes, Lisa finds Corduroy and gives him his very own pocket.

Tuesday

Fold a sheet of paper in half and then unfold it for each child. Give each child a paper and four bear-shaped cookies. Have her place the cookies on one half of the paper. Slowly say a two-word sentence. The student moves a bear to the opposite side of the paper for each word in the sentence. Repeat this activity with three- and four-word sentences. **Print awareness, counting**

Revisit yesterday's story. Give each child a paper labeled with the sentence "I put _____ in my pocket." Have him glue a pocket cutout to the paper so the top is open. Next, have him draw on an index card an item that he would put in a pocket. Then have him slide the card in the pocket and help him finish the sentence.

Wednesday

Cut out a class supply of colorful bear patterns (see pattern on page 253). Label the columns on a floor graph to match the bears' colors. Give each student a bear and have him place the bear in the correct column on the graph. **Graphing**

Read aloud *My Friend Bear* by Jez Alborough. Eddie and Bear are lonely until they meet each other and realize they have a lot in common. Then Eddie and Bear aren't lonely anymore because they are friends.

Thursday

Before the students arrive, place items around the room with names that begin with /b/. Show students a teddy bear and a large bag labeled with letter B. Explain that Teddy needs help finding things that belong to him. Help youngsters walk around the room, find the items that begin with the /b/ sound, and place them in the bear's bag. **Letter-sound association**

Revisit yesterday's story. Display a supersize bear cutout on a wall. Then ask youngsters to name things that friends can do together while you write their ideas on the bear.

Friday

In advance, hide a teddy bear somewhere in your school and put clues in different locations around the school. Tell the students that your teddy bear is hiding, but he left clues to help find him. Read the first clue, leading students to the next clue. Continue in the same way until the teddy bear is found. **Listening, critical thinking**

Read aloud *Dear Bear* by Joanna Harrison. After reading the story, share a snack of bear-shaped crackers and juice with the class.

Art/Gross-Motor Skills

Fuzzy Wuzzy Bear
(See directions on page 200.)

Gross Motor: Have a teddy bear parade! Have the students line up with teddy bears they brought from home. While playing a recording of lively music, lead the class and their bears in a march around the room.

Circle Teddy
(See directions on page 200.)

Gross Motor: To play Teddy Says, have a bear puppet or teddy bear tell the students to do things that real bears would do, such as stomp, growl, snarl, sniff, and scratch. The students listen carefully and follow the bear's directions.

Teddy Bear's Picnic
(See directions on page 200.)

Songs and Such for the Week

I'm a Little Teddy Bear
(tune: "I'm a Little Teapot")

I'm a little teddy bear,
Cute and sweet.
I'm soft and brown right
Down to my feet.
I have large black eyes
And a bright bow.
Hug me tight!
I love you so.

My Best Friend

My best friend isn't a rabbit
With ears so pointy and floppy.
My best friend isn't a frog
That likes to go hoppity, hoppity.
My best friend cannot bark or meow,
But I don't really care.
'Cause my best friend
In the whole wide world
Is my lovable teddy bear.

My Teddy Bear
(tune: "Mary Had a Little Lamb")

[Child's name] has a teddy bear,
Teddy bear, teddy bear.
[Child's name] has a teddy bear.
Give teddy a big hug.

Art Activities

Fuzzy Wuzzy Bear

Cut out a construction paper copy of the bear pattern on page 253. Dip a toothbrush into a shallow pan of brown tempera paint and brush the paint over the bear to give it a soft, furlike effect.

Circle Teddy

Fingerpaint the back side of a paper plate brown. When the paint is dry, attach two brown circles (ears) to the top of the plate. Glue a black circle in each white circle and glue the white circles on your plate to make eyes. Next, glue a black pom-pom near the bottom of the plate to make a nose.

Teddy Bear's Picnic

Attach a fabric scrap to a sheet of green construction paper so it resembles a picnic blanket. Cut out pictures of food from a grocery store circular and glue the cutouts to the blanket. Next, color and cut out a copy of the bear pattern on page 253. Glue the bear next to the blanket.

Circus

Centers for the Week

Block Center: Place a supply of animal manipulatives in your block center. A child uses the blocks to build a circus and then has the animals "perform."

Sensory Table: Place packing peanuts in your sensory table. Place small paper bags and scoops near the table. Students scoop the peanuts into the bags as if preparing peanuts for customers (or elephants) for the big show!

Gross-Motor Area: Place long strips of tape (tightropes) on the floor and set out small balls and umbrellas. Each student, in turn, takes heel-to-toe steps as he walks across a tightrope while holding a ball or an umbrella.

Literacy Center: Provide a class supply of clown cutouts (see page 254 for a pattern), each labeled with a desired letter. Also provide scissors, glue, and magazines. A student chooses a clown and identifies the letter. Then she cuts samples of the letter from the magazines and glues each sample to the clown's costume.

Math Center: Make balloon cutouts in a variety of sizes and attach a length of yarn to each one. A student arranges the balloons in a row from smallest to largest.

	Group Time	Literature
Monday	Have students pretend to be seals in a circus show! Seat students in a circle. Then roll a ball to a child. Name a word. If the word begins with /s/, encourage the child to slap her flippers together and make seal noises. Then have her roll the ball back to you. Play several rounds of the activity. ***Letter-sound association***	Read aloud *Circus Shapes* by Stuart J. Murphy. The colors and drawings of circles, triangles, squares, and rectangles within familiar circus sights are perfect to introduce and review shapes.
Tuesday	Gather a variety of instruments clowns might use for entertaining a crowd, such as cymbals, cowbells, and horns. Then give each instrument to a child and help youngsters make simple sound patterns. ***Patterning***	Make a shape cutout for each shape mentioned in yesterday's story. Reread the story. As each shape is mentioned, have a child find the coordinating shape and place it in your pocket chart.
Wednesday	Clowns show many emotions! Program each side of a cube with a different facial expression. Have a youngster roll the cube and identify the emotion represented. Then invite students to imitate the facial expression. ***Self-awareness***	Read aloud *Star of the Circus* by Michael and Mary Beth Sampson. The repetitive text in this tale invites youngsters to join in while each circus animal tries to prove that it is the star of the circus.
Thursday	Post circus animal cutouts. Then give clues that describe one of the animals posted. When a student successfully names the animal, begin a new round with a different set of clues. ***Listening skills***	Review the characters in yesterday's story. Then assign different parts to children to act out during a retelling of the story.
Friday	Make an enlarged copy of the clown pattern on page 254. Cut out the pattern and display the cutout on a wall. Give each child a circle shape (ball) labeled with a letter. In turn, a child identifies the letter and then tapes the ball above the clown as if the clown is juggling. ***Letter identification***	Read aloud *Olivia Saves the Circus* by Ian Falconer. Then lead youngsters in a picture walk of the book to identify the real and imaginative parts of Olivia's story.

Art/Gross-Motor Skills

In the Big Top
(See directions on page 204.)

Gross Motor: Assign each student a circus role, such as a ringmaster, a lion, an elephant, or a tightrope walker. Then lead youngsters in a parade around the room, in character, as if they were entering the big top for the big show! For more exercising fun, have the children trade roles and then lead a second circus parade!

Cotton Candy Craft
(See directions on page 204.)

Gross Motor: Give each child a beanbag. Invite youngsters to balance the beanbag on various parts of their bodies, just as a seal balances a ball on its nose. Challenge youngsters to bark and clap like a seal throughout the balancing game.

Cute Clown
(See directions on page 204.)

Songs and Such for the Week

The Traveling Circus
(tune: "The Itsy-Bitsy Spider")

There is a great big tent
In the middle of the town.
I watched it go up;
Then I watched it all come down.
While under that tent,
We had a lot of fun.
It makes me kind of sad
That the circus is all done.

Big Top Treats

Circus treats are yummy to eat.
Some are crunchy; some are sweet.
Candy, popcorn, ice cream too—
Lots of choices for me and you!

Circus Clowns
(tune: "The Wheels on the Bus")

Circus clowns can make us laugh,
Make us laugh, make us laugh.
Circus clowns can make us laugh,
All day long.

Continue with the following lines:
They smile and then say ha, ha, ha!
They ride in cars that beep, beep, beep; They have big shoes that bump, bump, bump; They ride on bikes that squeak, squeak, squeak.

Art Activities

Cute Clown

Draw a clown face on a paper plate. Then glue yarn hair to the clown. Embellish a hat cutout and glue it to the clown as well. If desired, glue a doily to the backside of the project, as shown, so it resembles a collar.

Cotton Candy Craft

Glue a white cone shape to a sheet of construction paper. Then glue pink cotton balls above the cone so they resemble cotton candy.

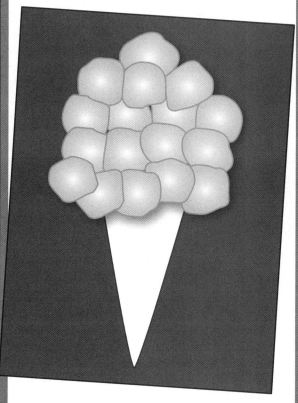

In the Big Top

Color a circus tent cutout similar to the one shown. Cut a slit in the tent to form flaps and open them. Then glue the tent to a sheet of construction paper and draw an animal or a circus performer in the tent.

Outer Space

Centers for the Week

Block Center: Laminate a supersize moon cutout and place it in your block center. Display photos of the space shuttle and space stations. Provide toy people manipulatives. A youngster uses blocks to build structures on the moon.

Sensory Table: Place rocks of different sizes and weights near the sand table. A youngster learns how craters are formed by dropping rocks into the sand and then observing the indentations left behind.

Math Center: Set out number cards from 1 to 10 along with a simple rocket ship cutout. A student arranges the numbers to count down from 10 to 1. Then he points to each number as he counts backward again and pretends to make the shuttle blast into space.

Literacy Center: Post on chart paper a copy of the familiar song "Twinkle, Twinkle, Little Star." Provide a glittery star wand. A youngster points to each word with the wand while singing the tune. Then he makes his own glittery star cutout at a nearby table.

Play Dough Center: Provide colorful play dough and Mr. Potato Head facial features. Students mold the play dough to make an alien being. Then they insert as many facial features as desired.

	Group Time	Literature
Monday	Make a personalized star cutout for each child. Then show a star to the class and lead students in singing the song below. ***Identifying names*** *(tune: "Twinkle, Twinkle, Little Star")* Welcome, welcome, preschool star. We're so glad you're who you are. It's good to see you today. Stand up tall and we will say, "Welcome, welcome, preschool star. We're so glad you're who you are."	Read aloud *I Took the Moon for a Walk* by Carolyn Curtis. In this storybook filled with gorgeous illustrations, an imaginative boy takes the moon for a walk.
Tuesday	Glue a sun cutout and a moon cutout to opposite sides of a craft stick. Show the moon and have youngsters pretend to be asleep. Then show the sun and prompt youngsters to wake. Encourage a youngster to share something they do during the daytime hours. Then turn the stick back to the moon once again. ***Concept of time***	Reread yesterday's story. Then have each child paint a paper plate so it resembles the moon. Have him draw a face on the moon. Then have him add arm cutouts and leg cutouts with red construction paper shoes so his moon resembles the moon in the book.
Wednesday	Make a rocket ship stick puppet. Then have students pass the prepared rocket ship around in a circle, counting down from ten as they go. When students reach one, have the individual holding the rocket ship jump up and shout, "Blast off!" ***Counting backward***	Read aloud *Star Climbing* by Lou Fancher. When the young narrator of the story cannot sleep, the child goes star climbing! Preschoolers are sure to enjoy this imaginative introduction to stars and constellations.
Thursday	Make a moon snack for later in the day! Have students help pour a box of corn cereal onto a baking sheet. Then pour melted white candy bark over the cereal. Shake the sheet slightly so the bark will spread uniformly. Have students notice how the treat looks like the bumpy surface of the moon. When the snack has solidified, break it into pieces. ***Observation***	Reread yesterday's story. Guide youngsters to recognize each of the six constellations (the Lion, the Great Bear, the Fish, the Dragon, the Winged Horse, and the Swan) in the book.
Friday	Attach a yellow circle (sun) to a sheet of chart paper. Cut a supply of yellow construction paper strips (sun rays). Show youngsters a letter card. If students name the letter correctly, have a youngster attach a ray to the sun. Continue in the same way with several letter cards. ***Letter identification***	Read aloud *I Want to Be an Astronaut* by Byron Barton. Then discuss with students why they would or would not like to be an astronaut.

Beautiful Sun
(See directions on page 208.)

Gross Motor: Have each student pretend to get dressed for an adventure in space. Have him put on a spacesuit, pull up space boots, and then put on a space helmet. Then lead your little astronauts on a space walk.

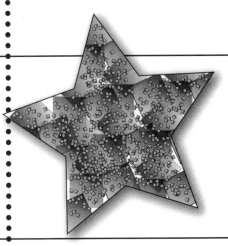

Shiny Stars
(See directions on page 208.)

Gross Motor: Have students jump as high as they can and try to hang in the air—gravity is sure to pull them down! After several jumps, discuss the weakness of gravity on the moon. Then have youngsters use exaggerated slow motions to demonstrate what it might look like if they were jumping on the moon.

Fiery Liftoff
(See directions on page 208.)

Blast Off!
(tune: "The More We Get Together")

Are you ready for the rocket to blast off,
   to blast off?
Are you ready for the rocket to blast off
   today?
Ten, nine, eight, seven, six, five, four,
   three, two, and then one.
Blast off! Up goes the rocket
Into outer space.

Mr. Moon and Ms. Sun

Mr. Moon and Ms. Sun
Live up in the sky.
But Mr. Moon and Ms. Sun
Must be kind of shy.
Although they both are friendly,
When one comes out to play,
The other seems to disappear,
As if to hide away.

The Milky Way
(tune: "Row, Row, Row Your Boat")

Stars, moons, planets too,
Up in outer space.
All are in our galaxy,
Each in its own place.

Shiny Stars

Brush glue over a white star cutout. Then glue iridescent cellophane squares to the star. Brush another layer of glue over the cellophane and then sprinkle a light dusting of iridescent glitter over the glue. When the glue is dry, suspend the stars from the ceiling.

Fiery Liftoff

Cut out a simple rocket ship pattern similar to the one shown. Then tear strips of red, yellow, and orange paper and attach the strips to the bottom of the rocket.

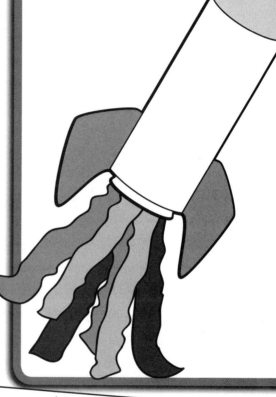

Beautiful Sun

Paint a yellow circle in the center of a sheet of paper so the circle resembles the sun. Then drip diluted yellow, orange, and red paint around the edge of the sun. Blow the paint outward with a straw to make sun rays.

Bugs and More!

Centers for the Week

Play Dough Center: Place a plastic tablecloth, a picnic basket, and black play dough in your play dough center. Have youngsters roll play dough to make ants for the picnic.

Math Center: Label each of several rock cutouts with a different number. Then make a supply of slug cutouts (see the pattern on page 255). Place the rocks and slugs at the center. A child places the correct number of slugs under each rock.

Art Center: Fold and then unfold a sheet of construction paper for each child. Place the papers at the center along with paint, eyedroppers, and markers. A child drips paint onto the middle of the paper with an eyedropper. Then he folds the paper and smooths the surface. After he unfolds the paper, he draws legs and antennae on the resulting blotch to make a bug.

Literacy Center: Provide for each child a card labeled with the first letter of his name written in pencil. Also provide bingo daubers and fine-tip permanent markers. A youngster makes dots on his letter with a bingo dauber. Then he uses markers to add bug details to each dot.

Sensory Table: Place fake spiderwebs in your empty sand table and then nestle a supply of plastic bugs in the web. Place several containers nearby. A child removes the bugs from the web and then sorts them into the containers.

Group Time	Literature

Monday

Draw on a sheet of paper a bug and a simple flight path. Make student copies of the prepared sheet and invite each youngster to cut along the bug's path. For more practice, prepare a different path for each day of the week, making the path more complicated each day. *Fine-motor skills*

Read aloud *The Very Quiet Cricket* by Eric Carle. In this book, a little cricket struggles to make a sound as he ventures out into the world and encounters a variety of tiny creatures.

Tuesday

Give each youngster a bug cutout (see the pattern on page 255) programmed with a number from 1 to 5. Then sing the song below, encouraging youngsters with number 1 bugs to jump up. Repeat the process with each remaining number. *Number identification*

> *(tune: "Bingo")*
> There is a number on your bug;
> Please listen for that number.
> Jump up, number [1]; jump up, number [1];
> Jump up, number [1]! Let's look at number [1]!

Revisit yesterday's story. Encourage youngsters to use sounds and motions to mimic each creature's friendly greeting to the cricket.

Wednesday

Draw a leaf on the board and then draw several simple bugs on the leaf. Gather a set of letter cards. Explain that the bugs are eating the leaf. Then show students a letter card. If they identify the letter correctly, erase a bug. Continue in the same way until all the bugs have been removed. *Letter identification*

Read aloud *Because a Little Bug Went Ka-Choo!* by Rosetta Stone. This little bug's sneeze invites lots of discussion about cause-and-effect relationships!

Thursday

Cut out several copies of the bug pattern on page 255 and then label the bugs with colorful shapes. Place the bugs on the floor and give a child a flyswatter. The child swats a bug and then names the shape on it and its color. For example, he could say, "That is a red triangle bug!" *Shape identification*

Reread yesterday's story; then give each child a copy of the bug pattern on page 255. Have him cut out the bug and glue it to one side of a sheet of paper. Then have him dictate what might happen if his bug sneezed as you write his words on the other side of the paper.

Friday

Make a supersize leaf cutout from green bulletin board paper and place it on the floor. Tell students that they will pretend to be bugs. Then have them predict how many bugs will fit on the leaf. Have students stand on the leaf, stepping on one at a time as they count aloud. Stop when the leaf is full and then have students recount the bugs. Encourage youngsters to evaluate their predictions. *Estimation*

Read aloud *Hey, Little Ant* by Phillip and Hanna Hoose. Lead youngsters to discuss what life is like from an ant's point of view. Then ask, "What would you do if you were the kid with the raised-up shoe?"

Art/Gross-Motor Skills

Bug Bracelets
(See directions on page 212.)

Gross Motor: Have students march in a line as you lead them in singing the first verse of "The Ants Go Marching." As you continue the song, divide youngsters into groups, such as twos and threes, to match the corresponding verses.

Clip Bugs
(See directions on page 212.)

Gross Motor: Lead youngsters on a nature walk outside to look for bugs in their natural habitats. When a bug is spotted, invite a youngster to describe how the bug travels. Encourage students to act out the bug's movement for a desired amount of time. Then regroup to look for more bugs.

Busy Bug Headbands
(See directions on page 212.)

Songs and Such for the Week

Bugs!
(tune: "Shoo Fly")

Some bugs are very big.
Some bugs are very small.
Some crawl along the ground,
And some can fly around and round!

Industrious Bugs

Bugs are very interesting;
Watch and see them go.
The bees make honey.
The fireflies do glow.
The crickets will sing to you
In the dark of the night.
But mosquitoes?
I'm pretty sure that all they do is bite!

What Kind of Bug Are You?
(tune: "Do Your Ears Hang Low?")

Do you have bright spots?
Do you bite or do you sting?
Do you have a lot of stripes?
Do you peep or do you sing?
Do you fly up in the sky or crawl in the
    morning dew?
What kind of bug are you?

Art Activities

Bug Bracelets

Make colorful fingerprints on a strip of construction paper. Use a fine-tip permanent marker to add details to the bugs. Then staple the strip to make a bracelet.

Clip Bugs

Thread three pipe cleaner pieces of equal lengths through a spring-style clothespin as shown. Then adjust the pipe cleaners so they resemble legs. Glue a simple bug cutout to the top of the clothespin. Then glue pom-pom eyes to the bug. When the glue is dry, clip your bug to an object in the classroom. What fun buggy decorations!

Busy Bug Headbands

Draw spots on a construction paper strip. Then staple the strip to make a headband. Bend six paper strips (legs) as shown and then glue them to the headband. Then tape pipe cleaner pieces to the headband to make antennae.

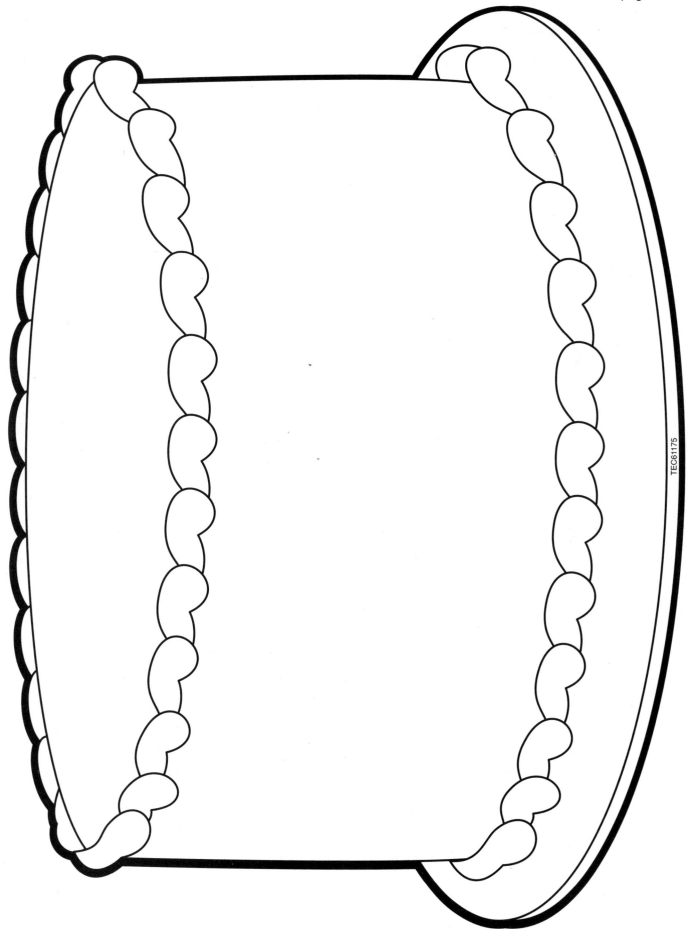

TEC61175

Pig Pattern
Use with the "Farm Animals" unit on pages 17–20.

TEC61175

Day-by-Day Preschool Plans • ©The Mailbox® Books • TEC61175

TEC61175

TEC61175

TEC61175

TEC61175

TEC61175

TEC61175

TEC61175

TEC61175

TEC61175

TEC61175

TEC61175

TEC61175

Cat Pattern

Use with the "Pumpkins and More" unit on pages 33–36.

TEC61175

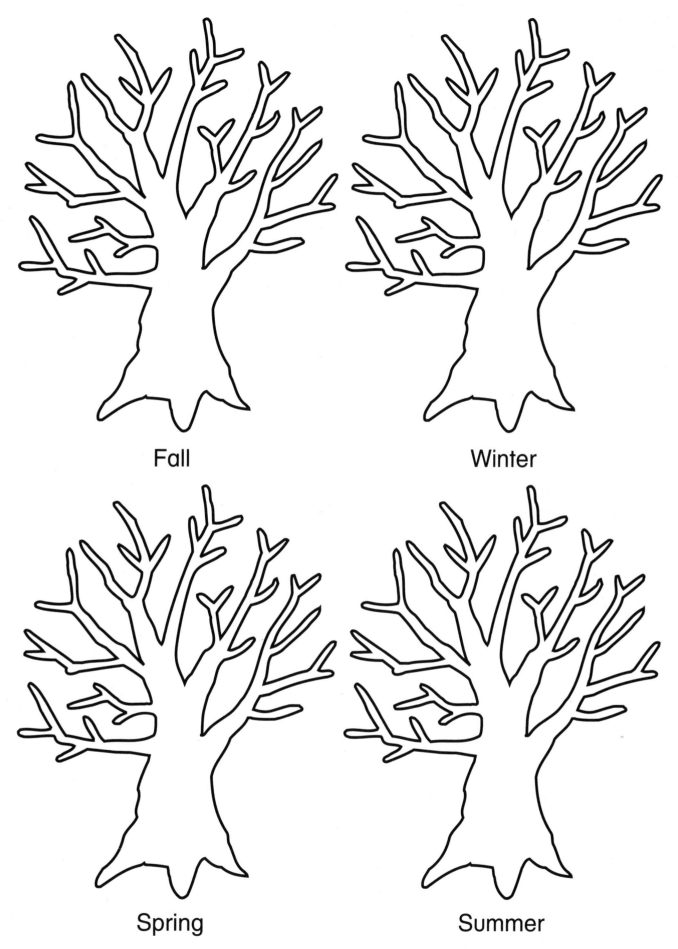

Fall

Winter

Spring

Summer

Day-by-Day Preschool Plans • ©The Mailbox® Books • TEC61175

Note to the teacher: Use with the "Seasons" unit on pages 37–40.

217

Seasonal Picture Cards

Use with the "Seasons" unit on pages 37–40.

TEC61175

TEC61175

TEC61175

TEC61175

TEC61175

TEC61175

TEC61175

TEC61175

Day-by-Day Preschool Plans • ©The Mailbox® Books • TEC61175

TEC61175

TEC61175

Family Member Patterns
Use with the "Family" unit on pages 45–48.

Day-by-Day Preschool Plans • ©The Mailbox® Books • TEC61175

Transportation Patterns

Use with the "Transportation" unit on pages 57–60.

TEC61175

TEC61175

TEC61175

TEC61175

TEC61175

TEC61175

TEC61175

TEC61175

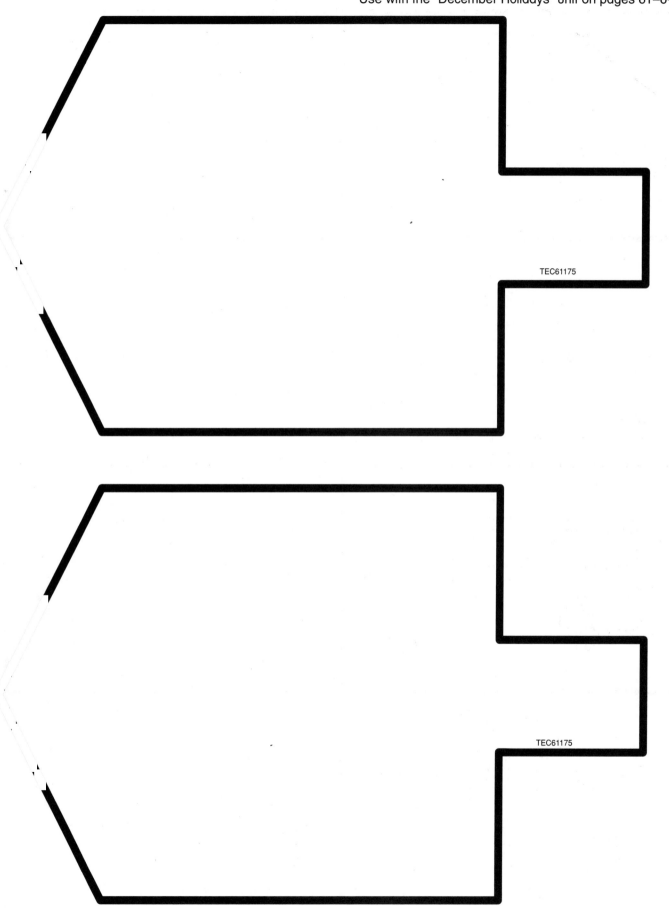

TEC61175

TEC61175

Opposite Cards

Use with the "Opposites" unit on pages 73–76.

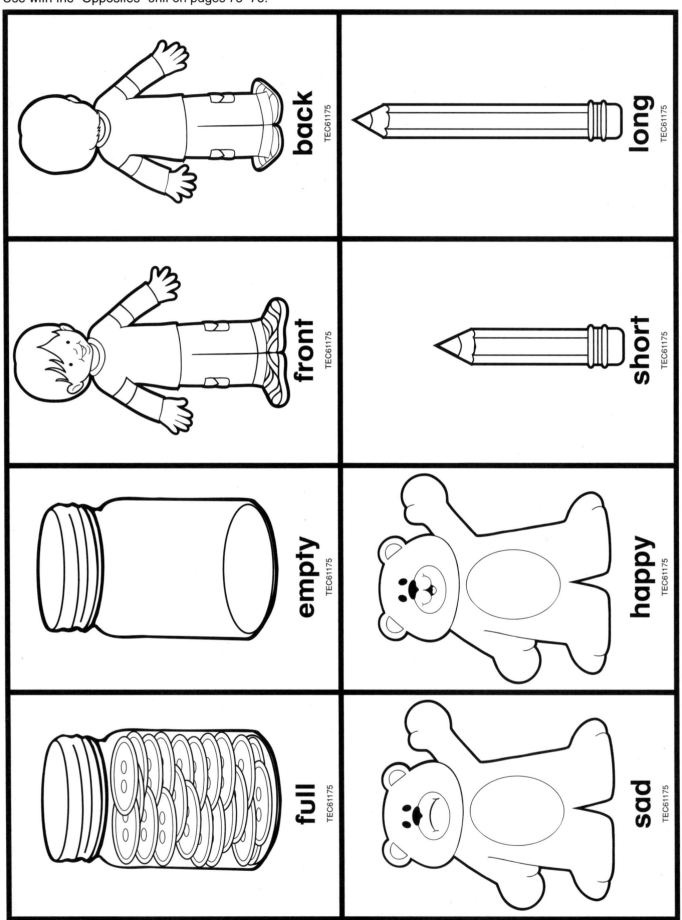

back TEC61175

long TEC61175

front TEC61175

short TEC61175

empty TEC61175

happy TEC61175

full TEC61175

sad TEC61175

Day-by-Day Preschool Plans • ©The Mailbox® Books • TEC61175

clean

TEC61175

under

TEC61175

dirty

TEC61175

over

TEC61175

night

TEC61175

small

TEC61175

day

TEC61175

big

TEC61175

Woodland Animal Cards

Use with the "Snow and Mittens" unit on pages 77–80.

TEC61175

TEC61175

TEC61175

TEC61175

TEC61175

TEC61175

TEC61175

TEC61175

Day-by-Day Preschool Plans • ©The Mailbox® Books • TEC61175

Polar Animal Patterns

Use with the "Polar Animals" unit on pages 85–88.

TEC61175

TEC61175

TEC61175

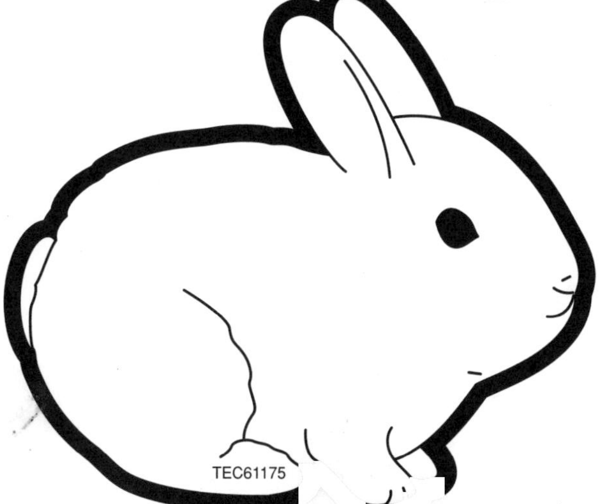

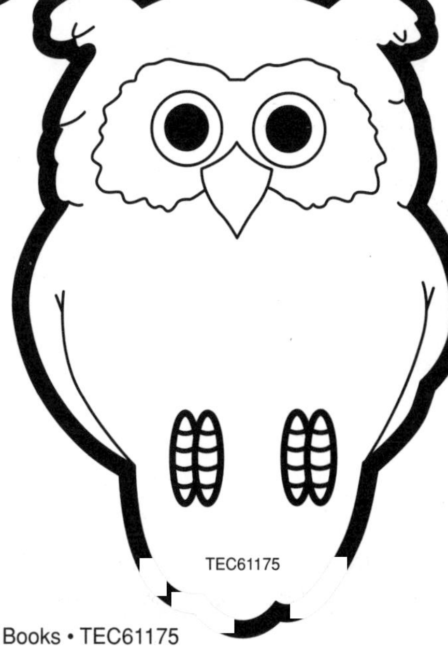

TEC61175

TEC61175

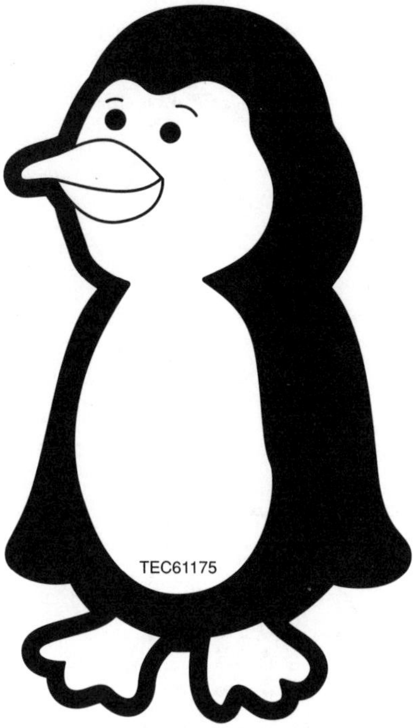

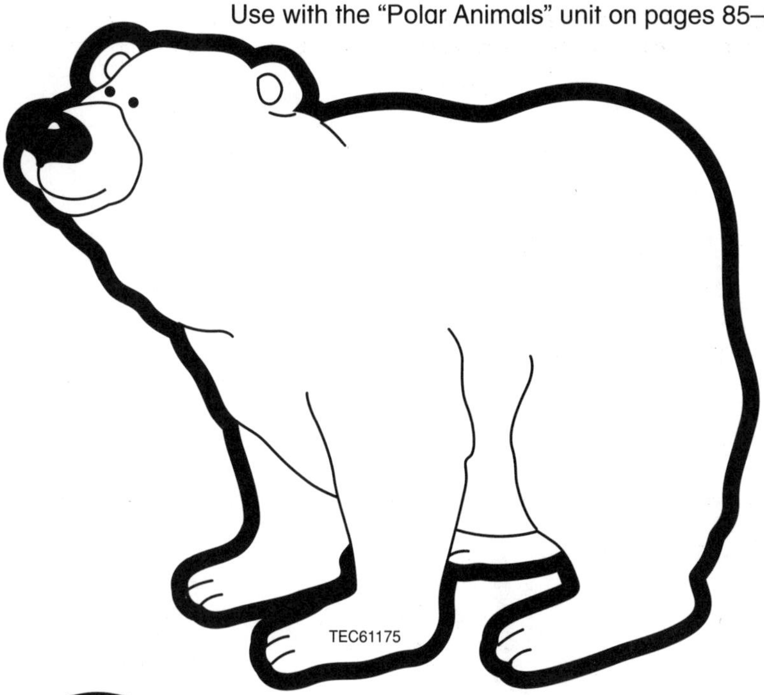

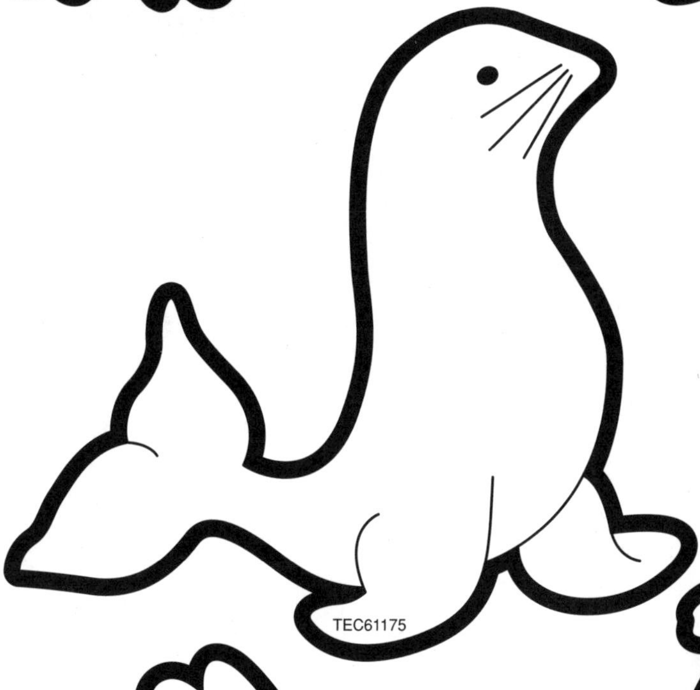

Wolf Pattern

Use with the "Fairy Tales" unit on pages 89–92.

TEC61175

TEC61175

TEC61175

TEC61175

TEC61175

TEC61175

Cupid and Arrow Patterns

Use with the "Valentine's Day" unit on pages 97–100.

TEC61175

TEC61175

Day-by-Day Preschool Plans • ©The Mailbox® Books • TEC61175

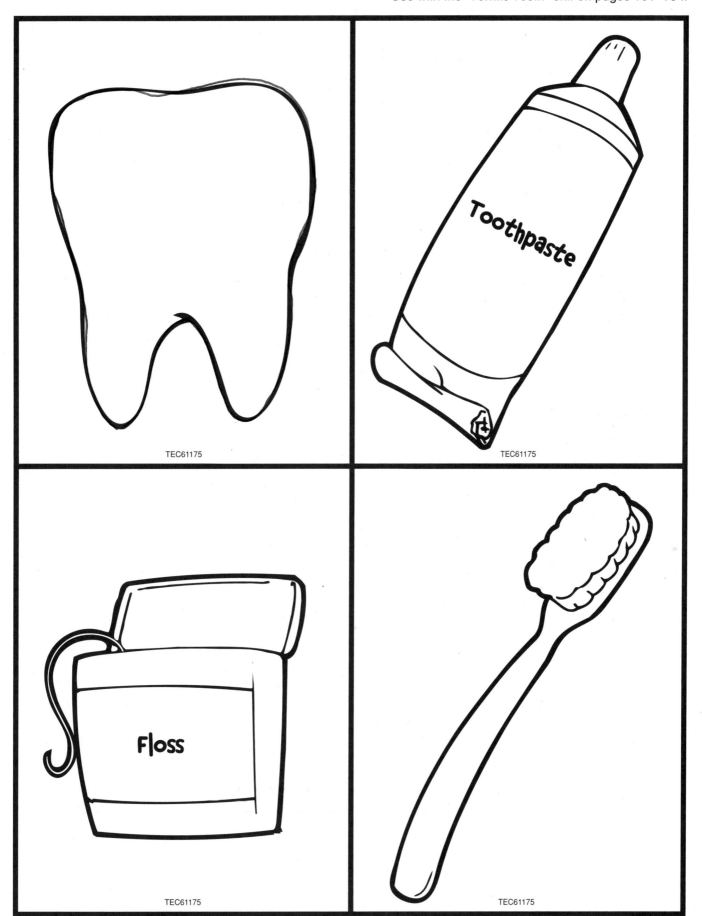

TEC61175

TEC61175

Toothpaste

Floss

TEC61175

TEC61175

Picture Cards

Use with the "Community Helpers" unit on pages 105–108.

Police Officer   TEC61175

Construction Worker   TEC61175

Firefighter   TEC61175

Dentist   TEC61175

Teacher   TEC61175

Clerk   TEC61175

Veterinarian   TEC61175

Farmer   TEC61175

Doctor   TEC61175

Postal Worker   TEC61175

Day-by-Day Preschool Plans • ©The Mailbox® Books • TEC61175

Use with the "Dr. Seuss" unit on pages 109–112 and Monday's Group Time on page 62.

TEC61175

TEC61175

TEC61175

TEC61175

TEC61175

TEC61175

TEC61175

TEC61175

TEC61175

TEC61175

Dinosaur Patterns
Use with the "Dinosaurs" unit on pages 113–116.

Day-by-Day Preschool Plans • ©The Mailbox® Books • TEC61175

Shamrock Patterns
Use with the "St. Patrick's Day"
unit on pages 117–120.

TEC61175

TEC61175

Leprechaun Patterns

Use with the "St. Patrick's Day" unit on pages 117–120.

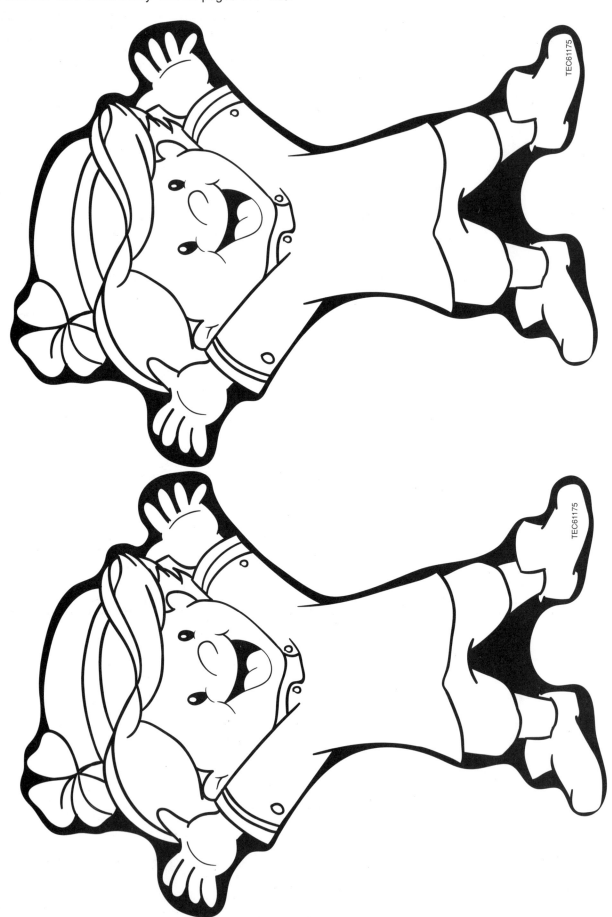

Day-by-Day Preschool Plans • ©The Mailbox® Books • TEC61175

TEC61175

TEC61175

TEC61175

TEC61175

TEC61175

TEC61175

Animal Patterns

Use with the "Baby Animals" unit on pages 129–132.

Day-by-Day Preschool Plans • ©The Mailbox® Books • TEC61175

TEC61175

Pond Critter Cards

Use with the "Ponds" unit on pages 137–140.

TEC61175

TEC61175

TEC61175

TEC61175

TEC61175

TEC61175

TEC61175

TEC61175

TEC61175

TEC61175

TEC61175

TEC61175

Bird Pattern

Use with the "Pets" unit on pages 145–148.

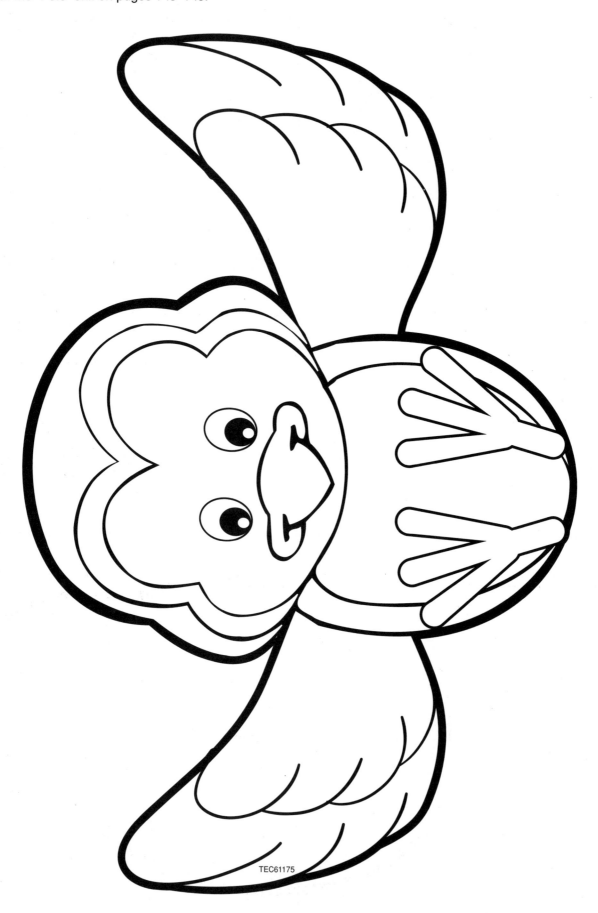

TEC61175

Day-by-Day Preschool Plans • ©The Mailbox® Books • TEC61175

TEC61175

TEC61175

TEC61175

TEC61175

TEC61175

TEC61175

TEC61175

TEC61175

TEC61175

TEC61175

TEC61175

TEC61175

TEC61175

TEC61175

Monster Feet Pattern

Use with the "Feelings" unit on pages 153–156.

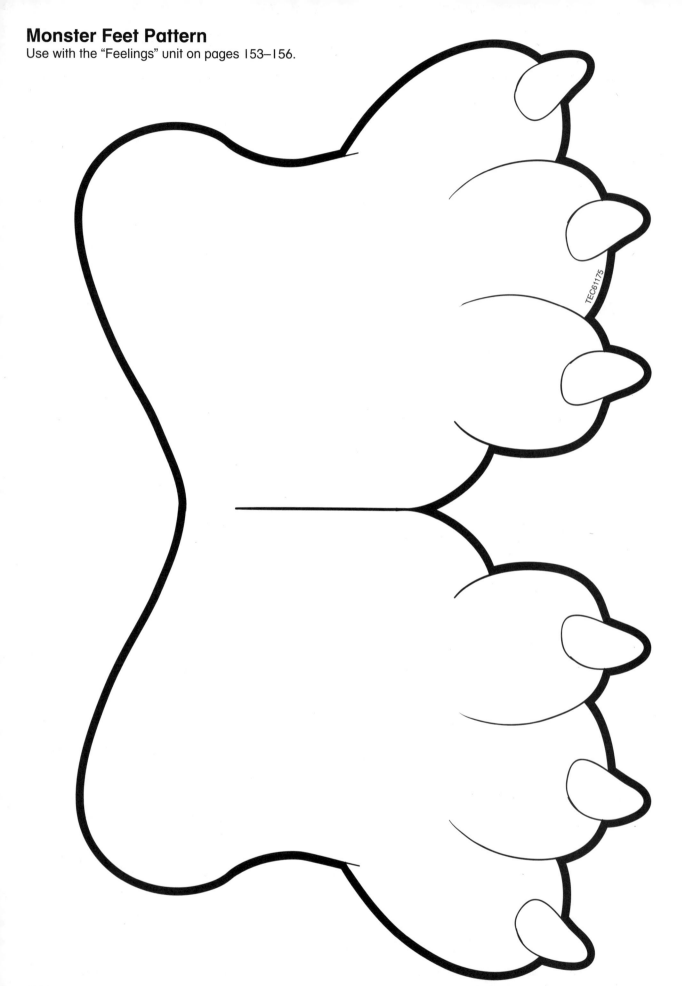

TEC61175

Day-by-Day Preschool Plans • ©The Mailbox® Books • TEC61175

TEC61175

TEC61175

TEC61175

TEC61175

TEC61175

TEC61175

TEC61175

TEC61175

Bee Patterns

Use with the "Bees" unit on pages 169–172.

TEC61175

TEC61175

Zoo Animal Cards

Use with the "Zoo" unit on pages 177–180.

TEC61175

TEC61175

TEC61175

TEC61175

TEC61175

TEC61175

Bread, Peanut Butter, and Jelly Patterns
Use with the "Picnic" unit on pages 181–184.

TEC61175

TEC61175

TEC61175

TEC61175

My ice cream _____

_____

Ice Cream Scoop Patterns

Use with the "Ice Cream" unit on pages 185–188.

TEC61175

TEC61175

TEC61175

TEC61175

TEC61175

TEC61175

Tool Picture Cards

Use with the "Construction" unit on pages 193–196.

TEC61175

TEC61175

TEC61175

TEC61175

TEC61175

TEC61175

TEC61175

Clown Pattern
Use with the "Circus" unit on pages 201–204.

TEC61175

Slug Pattern
Use with the "Bugs and More!" unit on pages 209–212.

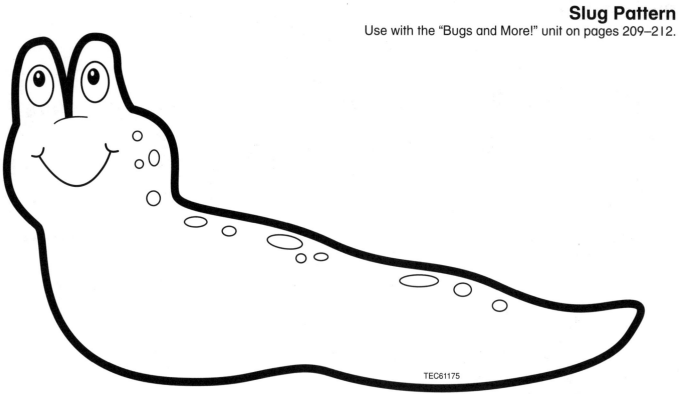

TEC61175

Bug Pattern
Use with the "Bugs and More!" unit on pages 209–212.

TEC61175

Theme
Index